JOHN THEIS

~~7462736~~

8369558

TALKING IRISH

ALSO BY STEVE DELSOHN

THE FIRE INSIDE: FIREFIGHTERS TALK ABOUT THEIR LIVES
THE EMMITT ZONE (WITH EMMITT SMITH)
BROTHER SAM: THE SHORT, SPECTACULAR LIFE OF SAM KINISON
JOHN WAYNE, MY FATHER (WITH AISSA WAYNE)
OUT OF BOUNDS (WITH JIM BROWN)
NECESSARY ROUGHNESS (WITH MIKE TROPE)
CRUISIN' WITH THE TOOZ (WITH JOHN MATUSZAK)

FOR YOUNGER READERS

MARINO! (WITH DAN MARINO)
ON THE RUN (WITH ERIC DICKERSON)
SAX! (WITH STEVE SAX)

TALKING IRISH

THE ORAL HISTORY OF NOTRE DAME FOOTBALL

STEVE DELSOHN

AVON BOOKS NEW YORK

AVON BOOKS, INC.
1350 Avenue of the Americas
New York, New York 10019

Library of Congress Cataloging in Publication Data:

Delsohn, Steve.
  Talking Irish : the oral history of Notre Dame football / Steve Delsohn.
—1st ed.
    p. cm.
  1. University of Notre Dame—Football—History. 2. Notre Dame Fighting
Irish (Football team)—History.   I. Title.
GV958.N6D45 1998   98-18859
796.332'63'0977289—dc21   CIP

First Avon Books Printing: October 1998

Printed in the U.S.A.

FIRST EDITION

QPM   10   9   8   7   6   5   4   3   2   1

For Mary Kay, Emma, Hannah and Grace

ACKNOWLEDGMENTS

THERE ARE MANY PEOPLE TO THANK. ABOVE ALL, I THANK ALL those Domers who were gracious enough to be interviewed for this book. It could not have been written without their cooperation.

I am especially indebted to David Black, my remarkable agent and friend. My editor, Patricia Lande Grader, provided unending support and honest criticism. Patricia's assistant, Laura Richardson, was simply a pleasure to work with. Thanks also to Avon's Lou Aronica, for acquiring the book and nurturing it.

I am grateful to John Heisler and Susan McGonigal from the University of Notre Dame sports information department. They were extraordinarily helpful, despite the dozens of times I dialed their numbers.

Thanks to these talented writers for their generosity and expertise: Bill Bilinski, Joe Doyle, Chris Dufresne, Tim Layden, Dan McGrath, Joe Mooshil, Terrence Moore, Chuck Nevius, Dick Schaap, Lou Somogyi, John Underwood, and especially Tim Prister. Thanks as well to Charles Lamb, an archivist at Notre Dame, for sharing his vast knowledge and for allowing me access to countless newspapers, magazines and videotapes.

Every author needs a guru and I had two. Pete Schivarelli and Jack Connor used to be Notre Dame players. Now they are Notre Dame history buffs. Their insights and referrals were crucial to me.

For their various contributions, I'd also like to say thank you to Kathleen Anthony, Michael Bennett, Jeff Blum, Sarah Boss, Tom Brown, Robert Burns, Dick Conklin, Kevin Connor, Jaime Cripe, Gary Delsohn, Niall Foley, Jim Gillis, Brian Harlan, Dr. Nicholas Johns, John Kalenda, Charles Lennon, Dan Martin, Brian Malekian, Gary Morris, Frances Morrow, Andrew Mushett, Scott Ostler, Ann Price, Steve Ponisciak, Susan Raihofer, Mike Richardson, Tom Rhoads, David Rubenstein, Dick Russell, Michael Salmon, Dr. Kenneth Saul, Joe Signiago, Diane Talbot and Tim Tessalone.

My greatest debt is to my wife, Mary Kay. She helped me every day. She was most valuable player.

C O N T E N T S

---❦---

AUTHOR'S NOTE

I GREW UP PLAYING ORGANIZED FOOTBALL IN CHICAGO. I started in sixth grade and quit when I finished high school. I loved the game so fiercely, I cried harder than I expected when I left it behind.

And so to be quite frank, it wasn't Notre Dame that first drew me to this book. It was my desire to revisit football. Then, once I decided to write about one team, I made my mind up quickly. Notre Dame is the very soul of football.

To bring this story to life, I have interviewed 144 players, 13 coaches, and seven administrators. This pool of Notre Damers spanned six decades—from the 1940s to the 1990s—and included 62 All-Americans, 32 consensus All-Americans, 47 team captains, five Heisman Trophy winners and five head coaches.

In 1996, I was privileged to attend the 50th reunion of Frank Leahy's 1946 national championship team, and the 30th reunion of Ara Parseghian's 1966 national champions. These weren't only two of Notre Dame's best teams ever, but two of the greatest in college football history.

One moonlit night in Palm Springs, I sat on a porch and drank beer with Johnny Lujack. I talked with Parseghian in South Bend, Indiana, where the view from his office window took in the sparkling Golden Dome. About 18 hours after I interviewed Lou Holtz, my wife gave birth to our daughter Grace. Holtz surprised me with a phone call later that evening. He wanted to know how mother and baby were doing.

I started researching this book two years ago. But as blasphemous as it sounds, I had never before set foot on the campus of Notre Dame. Now I know the scuttlebutt is true. Once you arrive in the land of gold and blue, leprechauns and Touchdown Jesus, you will be seduced. No other sports team, college or pro, has such a rich blend of tradition and mystique.

In 1842, on a wooded plain in northern Indiana, the University of Notre Dame du lac (Our Lady of the Lake) was founded by a young French priest named Edward Frederick Sorin. The ambitious Holy Cross brother wrote two years later: "When this school, Our Lady's school, grows a bit more, I shall raise her aloft so that without asking, all men will know why we have succeeded here. To that lovely Lady, raised high on a dome, a Golden Dome, men may look and find the answer."

It was 1882 when the Golden Dome first cast its glint across the heartland. The university took up football in 1887. The first team went 0–1, losing 8–0 to a visiting Michigan squad that agreed to teach Notre Dame the country's rugged new game.

In 1909, Notre Dame was still referred to as "the Catholics" by sportswriters when Rev. Michael J. Shea wrote the music and words to the Notre Dame Victory March. Nearly 90 years later, its chorus can still brings tears to grown men's eyes:

Cheer, cheer for old Notre Dame,
Wake up the echoes cheering her name,
Send a volley cheer on high,
Shake down the thunder from the sky,
What though the odds be great or small,
Old Notre Dame will win over all,
While her loyal sons are marching,
Onward to Victory.

By 1918, when Knute Rockne became head coach, the program already had a winning tradition. Jesse Harper, Rockne's predecessor, had gone 34–5–1 over five seasons. But while few non–Notre Damers remember Harper, Rockne is still the most famous coach who ever lived.

A balding, broken-nosed genius, Rockne did more than win a school-record 105 games. He transformed a small and obscure Catholic university into an American institution.

In 1924, the year Notre Dame won its first national championship, Rockne's backfield consisted of quarterback Harry Stuhldreher, left halfback Jim Crowley, right halfback Don Miller and fullback Elmer Layden. Though they averaged 158 pounds per man, they grew immortal when Grantland Rice of the *New York Herald-Tribune* sat down to write his story on the Notre Dame–Army game in New York City.

"Outlined against a blue-gray October sky the Four Horsemen rode again," Rice wrote in the most unforgettable newspaper lead of all time.

"In dramatic lore they are known as famine, pestilence, destruction and death. These are only aliases. Their real names are Stuhldreher, Miller, Crowley and Layden. They formed the crest of the South Bend cyclone before which another fighting Army team was swept over the precipice at the Polo Grounds this afternoon . . ."

Notre Dame had only won this game 13–7, but there was no turning back. The Irish had become the stuff of myth.

Rockne's single most fabled player was George Gipp. An extraordinary halfback and a prodigious gambler and drinker, he was named Notre Dame's first All-American in 1920. Gipp died two weeks later, at age 25, from a strep throat infection.

According to Rockne, Gipp made this stirring request from his deathbed: "I've got to go, Rock. It's all right. I'm not afraid. Sometime, Rock, when the team is up against it, when things are wrong and the breaks are beating the boys—tell them to go in there with all they've got and win just one for the Gipper. I don't know where I'll be then, Rock. But I'll know about it, and I'll be happy."

No one has ascertained if Gipp actually said these words. But in 1928, Rockne made his storied "Win one for the Gipper" speech before his outmanned Irish played unbeaten Army at Yankee Stadium. Notre Dame's soaring emotions ignited a 12–6 upset.

In 1931, millions of people grieved when they read the sky-scraping headlines: KNUTE ROCKNE DIES IN PLANE CRASH. Notre Dame spent its next ten years trying vainly to maintain its mammoth tradition. Then, in 1941, a brooding, eccentric Frank Leahy took over as coach.

Leahy made Notre Dame a powerhouse again, and it is Leahy's first decade that kicks off *Talking Irish*. Why did I begin in 1940? *Talking Irish* is an oral history, based on first-person accounts of Notre Dame football heroes. And if you go all the way back to 1930, a number of those heroes are deceased.

In 1998, Notre Dame still has college football's most

hallowed legacy. After 110 seasons, the Fighting Irish have had only nine losing records. Their 11 national championships, seven Heisman Trophy winners, 77 consensus All-Americans and .757 winning percentage are all collegiate bests.

But the heritage goes much deeper. Numbers can't capture the spirit and the grit. Here is the story of Notre Dame football—told by the men who lived it.

TALKING
IRISH

PART I

THE FORTIES

1

SHADOW OF THE ROCK
1 9 4 0 – 1 9 4 1

ON DECEMBER 7, 1940, DURING THE SEASON FINALE AT SOUTH-ern California, Notre Dame coach Elmer Layden charged onto the field to protest what he felt was a rotten call. But Layden didn't stop there. After blistering the refs, he screamed at USC coach Howard Jones.

A normally genial man, Layden had finally submitted to the abnormal pressure of coaching Notre Dame foot-ball. This pressure had increased for nine straight years—ever since March 31, 1931, the stunning day Knute Rockne died in an airplane crash.

In the hard economic times of the 1920s, Rockne had brought the school glamour and fame. He envisioned a Notre Dame Stadium, then twisted enough arms to see it get built in 1930. Rockne scheduled road games in New York City, Chicago, Los Angeles, Baltimore, and Philadel-phia, which in turn created the so-called subway alumni. These were the millions of fans who never attended the university, but had passionate feelings for its football team. During the 1920s, many of these fans were poor, Catholic, and Irish. As they battled prejudice and struggled to join the country's middle class, they were inspired by Notre Dame's football success.

Then there were the remarkable statistics. Rockne's teams lost only 12 games in 13 years, posted five unbeaten seasons and won three national titles. His lifetime winning percentage of .881 (105–12–5) is still the highest in both college and pro football.

After Rockne's shocking death at age 43—his small commercial plane went into a lethal spin over Bazaar, Kansas—Heartley (Hunk) Anderson replaced him. Anderson had starred at guard under Rockne and still ranks among Notre Dame's all-time hard guys. In one game against Army, after George Gipp got kneed by a Cadet, Anderson dropped the Cadet with one good shot to the face.

Never the smooth politician Rockne had been, Anderson swore like a trooper and lacked head coaching skills. His three-year-mark of 16–9–2, including 3–5–1 his final season, got Anderson fired on December 9, 1933.

Next came the ex-Four Horseman, Elmer Layden. As Irish head coach from 1934–1940, Layden won nearly eight of every ten games. At most other schools, this would have enhanced his legend. But not at a Notre Dame still mourning Rockne, whose three national titles had set a towering standard.

Layden didn't win any championships. So in February 1941, two months after his outburst at USC, he resigned before his imminent dismissal. Then it was Frank Leahy's turn to grapple with Rockne's ghost.

Leahy grew up, aptly, in Winner, South Dakota. After playing tackle on Rockne's last three Notre Dame teams, he returned to South Bend fresh from an 11–0 season at

Boston College. Leahy, at age 33, had only been a head coach for two seasons. Yet he was college football's hottest name.

Leahy was also a slew of contradictions. He dressed expensively in double-breasted dark suits, wide-brim hats and bow ties. But Leahy worked such late hours, he often slept on campus and wore the same rumpled clothes for days at a time. Leahy always displayed a certain bloodlust, both in his famously violent practice sessions and earlier as a promising young boxer. Yet when Leahy spoke, he sounded more platitudinous than pugilistic.

"Approximately one month ago, I received the greatest surprise of my entire life," Leahy told the Notre Dame student body in his first speech to them in spring 1941. "For it was just about four weeks ago that the authorities at the University of Notre Dame saw fit to ask me to coach at my Alma Mater. My vocabulary lacks the words to describe fittingly the monumental feeling of joy which permeated my entire body and soul."

The greatest paradox was Leahy's transformation during games. Fanatically organized and a master tactician, he was a brilliant practice-field coach. But Leahy got so emotional on Saturdays, he could be more of a sideshow than a leader. Times like these for instance:

- Long snapper Jim Schrader botched a key extra point, and Leahy grabbed him and screamed, "You'll burn in hell for this!"

- An Irish player hit an opponent so hard he knocked himself unconscious. Then, as the trainer ran up with smelling salts, Leahy sniffed them himself.

- Notre Dame and USC were tied 14–14 late in the fourth quarter. Thinking the Irish were winning,

Leahy instructed his offense to run out the clock. Notre Dame wasted a key timeout in its confusion, the game ended 14–14, and the tie cost the Irish the 1948 national championship.

Still, these incidents happened later in Leahy's career, when the strain of the job may have taken a mental toll. In 1941, according to freshman quarterback George Dickson, it was Leahy's obsession with winning that made him the perfect candidate for Notre Dame.

GEORGE DICKSON: "Leahy and I got close over the years. Probably because I went into coaching myself. Well, Leahy told me himself what happened when Notre Dame hired him.

"He met Father John Cavanaugh in Albany, New York. Cavanaugh was the school's vice president, and the Notre Dame VP is always in charge of athletics. So Cavanaugh goes over to this hotel. He signs into a room under an assumed name. Leahy also checks in under an assumed name. Leahy, remember, was still at Boston College at the time. This was his job interview.

"Now this is what the old man told me himself. He said he told Cavanaugh, 'Well, Father, Elmer Layden's been doing a pretty good job.' Cavanaugh said, 'Yes, Frank, you're right. But we want winning teams here. *All* winning, Frank.'

"So Leahy said, 'Tell me, Father. Are you prepared to meet the demands of national championship football?' Cavanaugh said, 'Yes, we are prepared. At *all* levels, Frank.'

"See, this was very different. Because after Rockne died, the school had tightened the screws on Anderson and Layden. And here they're essentially giving Leahy carte blanche. They're telling him flat-out: 'We want you to win big-time.' "

Bob McBride was also a Leahy confidante. After playing guard for Leahy's first two teams, he was captured by German troops at the Battle of Bulge. In 1949, back in South Bend, McBride became Leahy's most trusted assistant coach.

BOB McBRIDE: "Leahy arrived in February of 1941. From then until spring football officially opened, Leahy had us practicing inside. We played on this big dirt floor inside the old field house.

"We had a trainer that year named Scrap Iron Young. Any time a player got punctured or cut, Scrap ran over and gave him a tetanus shot. Because whenever that dirt floor got hard like concrete, they had a farmer come in and plow it with his horses. That put some softness back into the dirt, but there was a lot of horse manure plowed in too. Therefore, the tetanus shots."

During the early 1940s, the game was more primitive in other ways. There were only four officials to watch for cheapshot artists. The rules on clipping were sketchy and barely enforced, so players often got wiped out from behind. Players also still wore leather helmets—the kind they folded up and stuck in their back pockets. Even as helmets converted from leather to plastic (between 1941 and 1943), the plastic ones did not have built-in face masks. Those needed to be specially attached, which meant nobody bothered most of the time.

Notre Dame end Bob Dove, a two-time consensus All-American, never wanted to wear a face mask anyway. Dove didn't care if this meant shedding blood. He was old school before the term got coined.

BOB DOVE: "I just couldn't get used to that damn thing. In fact, when we played Navy in 1941, I didn't have a mask and they broke my nose. When I reached up to feel it, my nose was way over here. Under my eye.

"I kept playing of course. We all did at Notre Dame. With Leahy, you weren't hurt unless a bone stuck out."

BOB MCBRIDE: "Bob Dove was a hitter. He was exactly the kind of player Leahy wanted. That's why Leahy had so much live contact at practice. He wanted the hitters, not the hittees."

BOB DOVE: "Creighton Miller was one of our sophomore fullbacks. He made All-American as a senior. He was unstoppable in the open field.

"But Creighton wasn't on a scholarship. His family paid his way. You know what that meant to Leahy, don't you? He couldn't control Creighton Miller the way he controlled us.

"Leahy didn't like that. He was more or less of a control freak. So he and Creighton Miller weren't on the best of terms. One time we watched a game film and Creighton missed a block. Leahy kept making us watch the play again. Finally he said, 'Lads, can you spot Creighton Miller on this block? He's the one who owns the fur-lined jock strap.' "

CREIGHTON MILLER: "I didn't know much about Leahy before he got here. But he had a reputation as a tough guy. Everyone kept saying he was a boxer. That's how he was set up.

"I don't think the priests at Notre Dame understood Leahy. I don't think they knew how tough he was. When you came back to Notre Dame after the summer, Leahy would look at your hands. If they weren't covered with calluses, Leahy figured you were a candy ass."

BOB MCBRIDE: "We played Carnegie Tech in Pittsburgh that season. A year or two before this, they had started deemphasizing football. So most people were beating them pretty badly.

"We only won 16–0, but that wasn't what made Leahy so irate. We had two short yardage situations. Once we needed a yard to score a touchdown. Once we needed a yard to get a first down. Both times we got stopped by Carnegie Tech.

"We were supposed to stay in Pittsburgh that night and come back to South Bend on Sunday by train. But Leahy got us together after the ball game. He said they were changing the plans. He said we didn't deserve to stay overnight in Pittsburgh.

"So we went straight from the locker room to the railroad station. Next morning around 4:30, we arrived at a train stop in Indiana. They had busses waiting to take us to Notre Dame Stadium. We went straight inside and put on our pads, then came out and practiced at Cartier Field. We started around 6 A.M. and practiced for three hours. For two hours, we did live hitting. This was on Sunday morning after a game."

Through exploits like this, Leahy molded the prototypical Notre Dame player: a fiercely committed young Catholic who liked banging heads. In 1941, Leahy's inaugural season, the Irish went 8–0–1 and wound up ranked No. 3. It was their first undefeated record since 1930, when Rockne's final team was 10–0.

However, the glow from that year diminished quickly, when on December 7, 1941, Japanese aircraft bombed the

U.S. Naval Base at Pearl Harbor, taking 2,403 American lives.

Since most people believed that it would happen soon, our entrance into World War II wasn't shocking. But our vulnerability at Pearl Harbor was. "Our planes were destroyed *on the ground*," President Roosevelt said in angry disbelief. "On the *ground*."

2

LEAHY TAKES CHARGE
1 9 4 2 – 1 9 4 3

IN 1942, WHEN LEAHY DUMPED THE HISTORIC ROCKNE SHIFT for the rapidly emerging T formation, millions of Rockne disciples called it sacrilege. But the Chicago Bears and Stanford were scoring loads of points with the exciting new offense and Leahy felt the T was Notre Dame's future.

In the ground-based Rockne Shift, the offense had largely relied on the fullback or two halfbacks. Even when Notre Dame passed, it was frequently one of those running backs doing the throwing.

But in the more pass-oriented T formation, the quarterback ran the show. He stood directly behind the center (rather than several yards back as in the Rockne Shift). From there he could spin, fake hand-offs, and throw downfield.

All of which suited the skills of Angelo Bertelli. In 1941, as a tall skinny halfback in the Rockne Shift, Bertelli couldn't run over a speed bump. But with his powerful arm and clever faking, he led the Irish in passing.

ANGELO BERTELLI: "So in 1942, Leahy switched me to quarterback. He also went to the T, which was a monumental change for Notre Dame. Because you're getting rid of the Rockne Shift. That was an honored piece of Notre Dame folklore.

"We mastered the T somewhat before the 1942 season. But once the games began, we started screwing up. We tied Wisconsin 7–7 in our opener. Then we lost at Georgia Tech 13–6.

"Well, all these Rockne fans were ripping Leahy. He took so much heat—and he was so stressed out that we were struggling—he ended up going into the Mayo Clinic. And this became a pattern throughout Leahy's career. He didn't lose many games at Notre Dame. But Leahy suffered physically after each one."

Leahy spent three weeks in the Mayo Clinic, where he was diagnosed with spinal arthritis. But even when Notre Dame finished a disappointing 7–2–2, Leahy refused to abandon his new offense.

In 1943, with Bertelli and Creighton Miller returning for their senior years, the Irish routed their first two opponents. Then, in what was supposed to be an epic encounter, top-ranked Notre Dame thrashed second-ranked Michigan 35–12 in Ann Arbor.

Irish tackle Ed Mieszkowski recalls what happened just moments afterward.

ED MIESZKOWSKI: "Remember how the coaches used to come out to midfield and shake hands? I was standing ten yards away when Leahy met with Michigan's Fritz Crisler. Crisler told Leahy, 'That was the dirtiest football game I've ever seen. If I have anything to say about Michigan athletics, we will never play Notre Dame again.'

"Then Crisler turned around and walked away. Leahy was sort of speechless."

GEORGE DICKSON: "Let me tell you something about Michigan and scheduling and all that bullshit. It goes all the way back to Rockne and that goddamn Fielding Yost, Michigan's coach. Yost was pissed off because Rockne was so successful. So the whole time Rockne was there at Notre Dame, Michigan never played us.

"Then, when we finally got them back on our schedule, Crisler pulls that crap about Notre Dame playing dirty. Which *was* a bunch of crap. Crisler was pissed off because Leahy beat him so bad in 1943. So then Michigan starts dodging us again."

Leahy evidently thought so, too. He kept asking in print and on the banquet circuit: "Why isn't Michigan willing to play Notre Dame?" In the absence of any hard answers from Michigan, rumors swept South Bend that Crisler was anti-Catholic, and that Michigan was concerned that its Catholic fans would defect and root for Notre Dame. While this has never been proved, it did take 35 years and Crisler's retirement for the Michigan-Notre Dame rivalry to resume.

By the first week of November 1943, the 6–0 Irish were still ranked No. 1. Bertelli had already thrown ten touchdown passes and was averaging better than 20 yards per completion. Leahy's T formation, so violently criticized the year before, was exploding for 43.5 points a game.

ANGELO BERTELLI: "But then came the real test. Army was ranked No. 3 and they hadn't lost yet either. The game was at Yankee Stadium, and I was really looking forward to it. I had just thrown three touchdown passes the week before against Navy. It was probably the best game of my life.

"But I never got to play against Army. Early Sunday morning after we played Navy, I was on a train for Parris Island. There was no way around it. People from Notre Dame had even called the Marine Corps. They said, 'You let Bertelli play against Navy. Why can't he play one more week against Army?' The Marines said, 'This is the program. We want him here now.'

"It was a terrible feeling getting on that train. It was raining. It was cold. I was leaving a college campus for a boot camp. And those Marines were waiting for us, too. We were the first college group to arrive at Parris Island. Those devils ran us right into the ground."

As Bertelli learned what it took to be a Leatherneck, sophomore Johnny Lujack took over at quarterback for Notre Dame. Lujack came to South Bend from Connellsville, Pennsylvania, a gritty railroad town in the Allegheny Mountains outside Pittsburgh. As an unheralded freshman in 1942, Lujack had been lumped with the rest of the cannon fodder, the rinkydinks, the shit squad. These were the various names for freshmen and other scrubs, who got pulverized by the varsity each day at practice.

Lujack distinguished himself quickly, running and tackling so hard that Leahy knew his name the first week of practice. Still, veteran players were skeptical one year later, when Lujack abruptly stepped in at starting quarterback.

ED MIESZKOWSKI: "Lujack was *eighteen* his sophomore year. And here we are looking at Army. So sure we had reservations about Lujack. You're going from Bertelli to a kid who's barely played. It's like trading in a Cadillac for a Volkswagen.

"The rest is history, right? Lujack passed for two touchdowns. He ran for another TD. We destroyed a good Army team, 26–0."

JOHNNY LUJACK: "We were 8–0 when we played Iowa Pre-Flight. They were a service team with a bunch of professionals on it. We were No. 1 and they were No. 2. So this game was for the national championship.

"Leahy was honestly worried we might lose. So he wanted to find a way to fire us up. So he put us all on a bus and took us to the Notre Dame cemetery. He wanted to say a team prayer over Rockne's grave.

"I guess I prayed a little faster than the other guys, because I finished first. Then I stood up and moseyed around the other gravesites. I was eighteen years old. I had heard all these Notre Dame stories about 'Win one for the Gipper' and all that. I thought Gipp was probably buried there. Or maybe some other legends of Notre Dame. I kept waiting to hear voices: 'Throw the ball more to Jack Zilly tomorrow.'

"Now, I don't know what happened at that cemetery. I never heard any voices. But we beat Iowa Pre-Flight 14–13, and their extra point hit the upright."

On November 27 in the season finale, 9–0 Notre Dame faced Great Lakes Naval Station. The Irish led 14–12 with 28 seconds left, but their perfect season was ruined by a shocking 46–yard touchdown pass.

Final score: Great Lakes 19, Notre Dame 14.

ANGELO BERTELLI: "We were listening in a hut at Parris Island. There were five or six Notre Damers sitting around this Philco radio. We thought Notre Dame won. Then

Great Lakes scores and we're crying. We're actually crying.

"Then a guy walks up to me as I leave the hut. He hands me a telegram. It says I just won the Heisman Trophy. I didn't know whether to laugh or keep on crying."

Despite its crushing defeat, Notre Dame had gone 9–1 with victories over Michigan, Navy and Army. This was more than enough for the Associated Press, which overwhelmingly voted the Irish No. 1.

Leahy, in only his third year on the job, had already won his first national championship. Not incidentally to the Irish faithful, it was also Notre Dame's first national title since Rockne's death.

3

THE WAR-TORN YEARS
1 9 4 4 — 1 9 4 5

NOBODY EVER QUESTIONED PAT FILLEY'S TOUGHNESS. A CON-
sensus All-American at guard—though only 5 feet 8
inches and 175 pounds—Filley played college football
through seven broken noses and two ravaged legs.

In December 1943, Filley had followed Bertelli to Parris
Island. He received a medical discharge six months later,
when government doctors reexamined his legs. A South
Bend doctor operated that June, scraping out all the carti-
lage from both his knees.

Filley, whom teammates had reelected captain, could
barely walk by the final week of August. But in the season
opener September 30, he played five minutes. Two weeks
later he started.

Filley started every game through week seven. Then,
playing in Yankee Stadium against Army, Filley got hit
in the legs and his year ended. He spent the month of
December wearing two casts.

Filley's courageous comeback is still what he's best

known for. And yet throughout the 1944 season, he believed that he was somehow unworthy.

PAT FILLEY: "There were several guys on our team who were in the same boat. We had all been discharged for medical reasons. And we all heard the same thing: 'You son of a bitch. What the hell are you doing at home when our poor sons are fighting overseas?'

"But hell, we *wanted* to go. So, yeah, I did feel guilty being home. I felt miserable. I wanted to go and fight, and the government was saying I was unfit."

But during times of war, young men should be careful what they wish for. Consider Filley's teammate Bob McBride, who went overseas in October 1944. Only eight weeks later, he was captured by German troops at the Battle of the Bulge.

BOB MCBRIDE: "For about the first twenty-one days, they had us out walking. But most of the German soldiers were civil people. They were like neighbors of ours back in the United States. Only a few were mean and rotten to the core. If you just fell down while you were out walking, there were Hitlerites who would come up, put a rifle to your head and blow your brains out.

"I spent 123 days as a prisoner of war. Then, in April 1945, American forces liberated our compound. The first American doctor who I was privileged to meet was a young man named Schneider. He had gotten his pre-med at Notre Dame.

"Dr. Schneider said, 'Are you related in any way to the Bob McBride who played football at Notre Dame?' I said, 'Yes, I am.' He said, 'What relation?' I said, 'I'm him. I'm Bob McBride.'

"He just looked at me. He knew I'd played guard and

weighed about 210. And here I am, this stick, 104 pounds. The first word that came out of his mouth was 'Bullshit.' "

Back in the United States, Notre Dame went 8–2 in 1944 despite dozens of their upperclassmen now being in the service. One of those two losses was 59–0 to Army at Yankee Stadium. Halfback Bob Kelly, who scored 13 touchdowns that season, led the team in rushing and receiving, and made All-American, recalls the worst defeat in Notre Dame history.

BOB KELLY: "We were extremely young and Army was loaded. And Army just kicked the living shit out of us. They ran up the score on us, too.

"Yeah, you're goddamn right that humbled us. Humbled us and pissed us off."

Leahy wasn't present for that shellacking. He'd joined the Navy as a lieutenant before the season. So the joke around South Bend was that Leahy fought in World War II so he could escape the pressure of coaching Notre Dame football.

In 1944, with Leahy on active duty in the Pacific, his assistant Ed McKeever served as interim head coach. Irish guard Ed Fay recalls McKeever, and what happened the week before the Illinois game.

ED FAY: "McKeever was a tough guy. You either loved him or hated him. He would be talking to you and call you a 'piss ant.'

"In 1944, Illinois had this great runner Buddy Young. Buddy was black, and black players were rare during that era. The Big Ten had a few, but there were no black players yet at Notre Dame.

"The week before we played at Illinois, McKeever and his assistants were talking about Buddy Young. They knew this kid was fantastic even though he was a freshman. So one of their goals was to knock him out of the game."

ED MIESZKOWSKI: "Buddy and I were both from Chicago. I competed against him in high school, college, and pro. Buddy could really move, and you could never get a clear shot at him. So McKeever picked out this little Italian kid from Jersey. This kid wasn't fast like Buddy Young, but he was quick.

"Then McKeever sent one of our managers into town. The manager came back with a blue-and-orange Illinois jersey with Buddy Young's number on it. The coaches put this Italian kid in the jersey. Then they took a burnt cork and blackened his face.

"While all this is going on, McKeever is telling our great linebacker Marty Wendell: 'Wherever Buddy Young goes Saturday, I want you to follow him.' "

ED FAY: "The first time Buddy Young touches the ball, he goes 70-plus yards for a touchdown. The second time he touches it, our big tackle 'Tree' Adams scoops him up. While 'Tree' drives Buddy Young into the turf, Marty Wendell comes along and cuts him in half."

ED MIESZKOWSKI: "There was nothing dirty about the hit. Marty's not that kind of guy. But Marty was a big hitter and he creamed him."

ED FAY: "Buddy didn't come out for the second half. We ended up beating Illinois 13–7, and their athletic director was real upset. He said afterward, 'This will be the last time Notre Dame and Illinois play.'

"Actually, we played them two more times. Because it was in the contract. But after 1946, Notre Dame didn't play Illinois for many years."

In 1944, despite being targeted by his white opponents, Buddy Young scored 13 touchdowns as a freshman. In 1946, after serving a year in the Army, he led Illinois to a 45–14 win over UCLA in the Rose Bowl.

As for Buddy Young and Notre Dame, Terrence Moore puts the incident in perspective. Moore, who is black, was born and raised in South Bend. He is now a sports columnist for the *Atlanta Constitution*.

TERRENCE MOORE: "We can all sit here today and be idealistic: Well, the University of Notre Dame with all its high ideals should have been more sensitive than that.

"But when did Harry Truman integrate the Armed Forces? That wasn't until around 1948. Do we really expect Notre Dame to be more racially conscious than the United States government? In 1944, those were pretty racist times throughout this country."

Moreover, American bigotry wore many faces. Which the Irish were reminded of one season later, during a road trip they made in October 1945.

ED MIESZKOWSKI: "We went down by train to play Georgia Tech. When we got off the train in Atlanta, we walked up to street level. We saw two telephone polls with a rope tied between them. There were 11 dummies dangling by their necks. They even had our names and numbers on them."

ED FAY: "It was Southern anti-Catholicism. We heard the remarks all weekend from Georgia Tech's fans. Then we heard them Saturday from their sideline: 'Catholics beware. Mackerel snappers go home. Did you bring your holy water in a bucket, or do you have it piped in?'"

Despite this crude reception, Notre Dame routed Georgia Tech 40–7. Five weeks before this, on September 2,

1945, Americans had celebrated the Japanese surrender ceremonies on the U.S.S. *Missouri*. But while this marked the official end of World War II, it would still be several weeks before Leahy and most servicemen would be sent home. So in 1945, the team's interim coach was former Irish captain Hughie Devore.

Much more well-liked than McKeever, Devore had joined Leahy's staff in 1943. He led Notre Dame to a 5–0 start in 1945, although Lujack and most other stars still had not returned from military duty. Freshman fullback John Panelli recalls Notre Dame's next game against unbeaten Navy.

JOHN PANELLI: "The Navy guys were always physical. But this game went beyond physical. Navy had a linebacker named Dick Scott, and this guy had something taped beneath his jersey sleeve. I don't know what it was made of. But it was wounding our players. It was mutilating them.

"Our leading rusher that season was Elmer Angsman. Elmer, in my opinion, had the fastest first two steps in college football. Well, Dick Scott got Elmer real bad. Elmer came back to the huddle spitting out teeth. A couple were embedded in his tongue."

ELMER ANGSMAN: "Actually, I got hit by an elbow. An elbow that had a cast over it.

"It was still the first quarter. I broke to the outside after running a trap play, and while one guy tackled me and spun me around, Scott came over the top and hit me in the mouth. My upper four teeth were sheared off. Four of the bottom teeth were driven into the top ones.

"But I didn't have a concussion or anything. And it was a real big game. So I wanted to keep playing.

"But first they looked me over on the sidelines. I had a few live nerves, so they drenched some pieces of gauze in something that freezes you. I carried the gauze in my pants. Then I'd pop them into my mouth and freeze the nerves."

In this brutal defensive battle, Notre Dame tied Navy 6–6. But the game is mostly special for Elmer Angsman's iron-man performance. He would end up losing nine teeth, and his lacerated mouth would require 26 stitches. Still, after getting injured *in the first quarter*, Angsman played 54 minutes against Navy.

Against No. 1-ranked Army the next week, the young and banged-up Irish never had a chance. They lost 48–0 at Yankee Stadium—their second straight humiliation by the Cadets.

Notre Dame ended the season 7–2–1, a brave performance by a team so green it had just eight monogrammed players. Leahy returned to South Bend in late November, amid rumors his close friend George Halas would snatch him from Notre Dame to coach the Chicago Bears.

If the offer was real, however, Leahy declined it. With all the prodigious talent coming back, this was hardly the time to leave South Bend.

4

THE GLORY BOYS
1 9 4 6

FRANK TRIPUCKA GREW UP CATHOLIC IN BLOOMFIELD, NEW Jersey, dreaming of the moment when he would play Notre Dame football. But when the quarterback arrived in South Bend in 1945, it wasn't the football program that most impressed him. It was the sheer beauty of Notre Dame's campus.

FRANK TRIPUCKA: "Oh my God. I felt chills run down my spine. I loved the Golden Dome. I loved the Grotto and the Log Chapel. I loved the leaves changing color in the fall. I was so delighted to be there, I didn't even mind all those darn rules."

The rules. At a private university governed by priests, here were just a few in the 1940s:

No cars allowed on campus. No fraternities. No female students. No women at all on campus except for support staff and nuns. No lights on in any dorm room past

10 P.M. No say in the matter, since all dorm lights were shut off by one main switch.

Even if a Notre Dame student was brash enough to risk expulsion, to sneak out his dorm-room window after bed check, dash down the fire escape and sample the nightlife, options were pretty slim around South Bend. There were a handful of movie theaters and bowling alleys, a few bars and dance clubs. Much closer to campus—right across the lake—there were the female college students at Saint Mary's. But their rules were even stricter than the men's.

FRANK TRIPUCKA: "Yeah, but not much stricter. Every Notre Dame dorm had its own chapel, and three mornings a week they had a mass check. That meant you had to be there by 6:30 A.M., because they'd have a guy sitting there who'd check your name off. Then, if you missed any mass checks, you couldn't get what they called a 'midnight pass.' That was your one night a month to stay out late.

"That's why I've always said that Leahy had it easy. He didn't have to keep us from carousing. The Holy Cross fathers took care of that, you see."

Halfback Jack Connor knows about tight ships. He attended a rigid Catholic high school, graduated cum laude from Notre Dame, served in the U.S. Marine Corps, and worked as a special agent in the FBI. Connor also wrote the 1994 book, *Leahy's Lads*, the most intimate account of the Irish football teams of the 1940s.

JACK CONNOR: "In 1946, Notre Dame was like a monastery. Not only was it all boys, but there were priests all over the place. Many of the classes were taught by priests. The rector of every dorm was a priest. Then, on every floor of every dorm, you had a prefect. He was another priest.

"One night we had a little cocktail party in my dorm room. There were maybe fifteen guys. Whatever you wanted to drink, we had it all. Then there's a knock on the door. It's the rector of our dorm. He's one of the younger priests. It's just his first year there.

"Well, my roommate had been in the service. He was a gutsy guy. So he asked the father in. Then my roommate asked if he would like a drink. Now there was no alcohol allowed on campus. So we could have been automatically thrown out. But the father ended up drinking a beer with us.

"Then, as he was leaving fifteen minutes later, he stopped and turned around when he was at the door. He said, 'Gentlemen, have a good time. But please stop throwing the empties out the window. I've been getting complaints.'

"So it really just depended on the priest. Some turned their heads and others didn't. But in 1946, they really had no choice. All these guys were returning from World War II. They'd been prisoners of war and fought in all these battles. You couldn't treat these guys like they were kids. So even the priests loosened up."

Bill (Moose) Fischer, the All-American guard and winner of the 1948 Outland Trophy as college football's best lineman, says even Leahy bent in his first season back after two years in the Navy.

BILL FISCHER: "Well, he changed as much as Frank Leahy could. He was still very hard-nosed. In fact, in 1946 when Leahy returned, we had an assistant coach named Marty Brill. Marty and Leahy played for Rockne together. But when Marty became an assistant, he called Leahy 'Frank' a couple times. Well, no one called Leahy 'Frank.' And Marty Brill was gone after that season.

"On the other hand, we also played Tulane in 1946. We took a train to New Orleans, beat them 41–0, then had postgame parties lined up all over the French Quarter. We ended up staying out until the wee hours. Then we went to mass at eight in the morning. Then we started again with champagne brunch.

"When we finally got back on the train, we took over the club car. Suddenly, Leahy walked through. He was trying to ignore us. But Ziggy Czarobski was our team comedian. And Ziggy had this girl sitting on his lap. So Ziggy said, 'Coach Leahy, I want you to meet my friend.'

"Leahy nodded and started for the door, and some of our guys booed him. They were still half in the bag. Still feeling the oats.

"Now what would you do to the team if you were head coach? You gotta kill 'em, right? Leahy let it go. He never said a word. That's something I couldn't see happening before the war."

Leahy even flashed his dry wit on the October 11, 1946 cover of *Time* magazine. "Prayers work better when the players are big," Leahy's quote read.

The long profile inside captured Leahy at practice, fretting because a halfback got dragged down after gaining 40 yards. However, the story added, "Such talk does not fool Notre Dame's millions of subway-circuit alumni. Every butcher boy, beer salesman and politician knows that Notre Dame is loaded."

Just how talented was postwar Notre Dame? This is how *Sports Illustrated* later put it: "Notre Dame fielded the greatest college football team in history, but which unbeaten Irish juggernaut was it: the '46 or the '47 squad?"

In 1946, Notre Dame had 53 ex-servicemen on its roster. Lujack was returning at quarterback. The linemen included four all-time Irish greats: the 1946 Outland Trophy winner George Connor, the 1948 Outland Trophy winner Bill Fischer, the 1949 consensus All-American Jim Martin, and the 1949 Heisman Trophy winner Leon Hart. In 1946, Hart was only a 17-year-old freshman, but already scaring the daylights out of opponents.

The running backs were also amazingly deep, with future Notre Dame coach Terry Brennan, Jim Mello, Emil (Red) Sitko, John Panelli, Cornie Clatt, and a host of running backs who barely ever played, but would have been major stars in any other program.

And yet, despite this mighty collection of talent, Leahy still poor-mouthed Notre Dame's chances that season. Some have said Leahy learned this while playing for Rockne, whose pregame gloom had also been legendary. But while Rockne was actually a world-class salesman, Leahy's pessimism was no con. He was born to be a worrywart.

JACK CONNOR: "I swear to you it was real. Leahy dreaded every team we played. But then we'd win that week by four or five touchdowns. So after a while, none of the writers believed him. That's how he got the nickname 'Crying Frank.'"

Along this same vein, Jack's older brother George recalls the 1946 opener with Illinois.

GEORGE CONNOR: "Illinois had already played one game against Pittsburgh. So Leahy scouted the game and Illinois won 40–0. Then we had our team meeting on Monday in the Law Library.

"Leahy said, 'Lads, I want to tell you about this Illinois team. We fit about eight players on a bench. They are so huge, they only fit four players on a bench. They have a middle linebacker by the name of Lester Bingaman. I had him to dinner in my Long Beach, Indiana, home. Lads, I have eight children. Four of them went away from the table hungry.'

"It sounds like malarkey and maybe it was. But Leahy believed we could lose. Which is one good reason why we whipped Illinois. Leahy worked our asses off at practice, rather than taking them lightly. Leahy was the best coach I ever played for."

JIM MELLO: "Sometimes he got so excited during pep talks, he foamed at the mouth."

FRANK TRIPUCKA: "Some of the younger guys—like me and Terry Brennan—would almost be in tears during his pep talks. Especially whenever we played Army. And, see, that was our biggest game in 1946. Because we were national champs in 1943. But in 1944 and 1945, when all our guys were gone including Leahy, Army destroyed us 59–0 and 48–0.

"So now it's 1946. And Leahy won't let us forget how Army killed us. He kept saying, 'Lads, we all know Army picked on our youngsters. What will happen on Saturday when they face men?' "

"The college gridiron battle of the century," is how the *Los Angeles Times* described the coming showdown. *Time* deemed it Notre Dame's "holy crusade." And it did seem to have the ingredients for an epic. The No. 1-ranked Cadets had won 25 straight games and two straight national titles. They had two Heisman Trophy winners in their backfield: Doc (Mr. Inside) Blanchard and Glenn (Mr. Outside) Davis.

The No. 2-ranked Irish had payback on their minds. They had outscored their first five opponents by a staggering 177–18. They had Leahy's animus for his coaching rival, Colonel Earl (Red) Blaik.

GEORGE CONNOR: "Leahy and Blaik hated each other. Some people tried downplaying it, but it was true. Most college coaches would exchange game films. It was standard operating procedure. Leahy and Blaik never did it."

JIM MELLO: "Leahy was always suspicious. But he was twice as suspicious that week. He kept all our practices closed. He wouldn't let in reporters. He wouldn't let in our parents. He had student managers standing on top of the fences, to make sure there were no spies outside the fences. If a plane flew overhead, Leahy would only call conservative running plays."

FRANK TRIPUCKA: "Man, the buildup to that game got out of control. Everyone and his brother wanted tickets, tickets, tickets. And with the game being played at Yankee Stadium? With those scalpers in New York? We heard they were selling tickets for up to a thousand bucks.

"Our players were selling ours, too. We each got three or four tickets. But we were only getting a hundred a pop."

JOHNNY LUJACK: "How many people were at Yankee Stadium that day? About 75,000? Well, I've met 175,000 who told me they were there."

Those who truly got in saw cautious football, as Notre Dame and Army tied 0–0. Even odder than the score was the head coaching. For example:

- Lujack entered the game with a sprained ankle, got kicked in the head early on, and wasn't his usual magnificent self. But Leahy never played George Ratterman, the number two quarterback who was having a great year.

- Leahy played virtually none of his powerful second unit, even though he had been using them all season in the second and fourth quarters of each game. The second team, in fact, ended up scoring 28 touchdowns that year compared to the first team's 12. This was partly owing to the second team's talent and partly because when the second team came in, the first team had already worn down the opponent. So why not also run fresh players at Army?

- Both Notre Dame and Army had scoring opportunities inside the 16-yard line. Both could have won the game—and probably the national championship—by kicking a field goal. But neither team even tried one. This included the series in the second quarter when the Irish had a first down at the Army 12. Then, on fourth-and-one at the three, Billy Gompers came up short on a running play.

JIM MELLO: "Leahy didn't believe in kicking field goals. If you couldn't ram it in, he thought taking three points would be an insult. He thought Notre Dame was too tough for that.

"I thought that was all wrong. Let's just win the damn game."

GEORGE CONNOR: "I think both coaches choked. They hated each other so much, they didn't coach the game they normally would. They were too damn uptight."

JIM MELLO: "Want my honest opinion? We would have won that game if Leahy had stayed in South Bend."

These are the blunt words of a hard-nosed fullback. But according to the *South Bend Tribune*'s Joe Doyle, who has covered Notre Dame football since 1949, even Leahy felt remorseful later on.

JOE DOYLE: "It was 1952 or 1953. I would always go into the coaches' room before practice while they were getting ready to go outside. One day Leahy was sitting there. He was just lost in thought. Then he said out loud, 'If only we'd kicked the field goal.'

"Six or seven years later, and he's thinking about the goddamn scoreless tie."

So there it was again. Leahy the tactical genius during the week, Leahy the fire-and-brimstone pregame speaker, wasn't a very good bench coach. He had just showed that in the biggest game of his career.

Still, Notre Dame went on to finish undefeated at 8–0–1. And while Army (9–0–1) was also unbeaten, and won an additional game, the Irish were voted national champions for two main reasons:

- Notre Dame defeated USC 26–6 on the season's final weekend, while Army was squeaking by Navy 21–18.

- Notre Dame may have tied Army, the two-time defending national champs, but the Irish had dismantled everyone else. They had allowed just 24 points all season, while scoring 271.

So the Associated Press had voted correctly. Army wasn't robbed. Notre Dame was college football's strongest team—in 1946 and maybe ever.

5

THE DYNASTY
1 9 4 7 – 1 9 4 9

EXCEPT FOR GEORGE RATTERMAN, WHOM THE NOTRE DAME priests suspended for breaking curfew, almost everyone returned in 1947 from an undefeated team a year before. The Irish, in fact, were so loaded that 42 of their players went on to pro careers.

Lujack, a senior, won Notre Dame's second Heisman Trophy. He completed 61 of 109 passes (56 percent) for 777 yards and nine touchdowns. He only rushed 12 times, but averaged a gaudy 11.1 yards per carry. Lujack also led Notre Dame with three interceptions, and his former teammates say he was their best defensive back.

BILL FISCHER: "People talk about Joe Montana. He has those championship rings from the NFL. He and Bill Walsh had a lot of success together in San Francisco. But Montana, very frankly, couldn't carry Johnny Lujack's shoes."

FRANK TRIPUCKA: "He's probably the greatest all-around athlete I've ever seen in college football. See, Lujack wasn't even all that big. He was six foot and maybe 180. But he was just a very tough guy from western Pennsylvania. It probably showed the most when Lujack played defense. He'd come up and hit people head-on. You take Bertelli, myself, or Ratterman? We'd get killed if we went to hit somebody."

To go with his football skills, Lujack also had a large dose of charisma. In 1947, while making his run for the Heisman, he received nearly 300 fan letters a week in his room at Sorin Hall.

JACK CONNOR: "People were tired of war, so they couldn't get enough sports. And since Notre Dame was winning all those games, we were a big attraction. And Lujack was our biggest star.

"This was also before television. So Lujack became a star on the radio. You could hear him make a great run, but you couldn't see him. So you had to use your own imagination. That meant there was some mystery to him. And that made Johnny Lujack even more famous."

JOHNNY LUJACK: "I realize this sounds odd, but I never gave winning the Heisman a single thought. I mean, we played USC in our last game that season. I was calling the plays, and I think I ended up throwing 11 passes. Why should I throw more passes? We ran them to death and won 38–7.

"All our guys felt that way. All the honors that came to people like George Connor and Bill Fischer? Nobody followed that stuff. Nobody talked about it after practice. Hell, I didn't know until I graduated what my stats were. I didn't know my punting average. I didn't know if I threw for 50 percent. But I knew we won 'em all at Notre Dame."

Almost, but not quite. In Lujack's two and a half seasons as a starter—1943, 1946, and 1947—Notre Dame went 20–1–1 and won three national titles. For this, say many Fighting Irish buffs, Lujack still remains the finest quarterback in Notre Dame history.

In 1947, Lujack's last year, not even Army could make the Irish sweat. In a game moved from New York City to South Bend because of the millions of dollars gambled on the 1946 game, Terry Brennan ran back the opening kickoff for a 97-yard touchdown. Army never recovered and lost 27–7.

As Paul Zimmerman wrote in *Sports Illustrated:* "That game would be the last in a 34-year Notre Dame–Army series, whose cancellation by West Point would become a sore point with the Irish." But why did Army abandon this glamorous rivalry? According to several Irish players, Red Blaik feared he might never again beat Leahy.

Then again, not many coaches could. After routing Army in 1947, Notre Dame finished 9–0 and won its second consecutive national title. This gave Leahy a stunning five-year record of 41–3–3.

By the fall of 1948, Leahy had turned 40. Lujack, George Connor, and 13 more ex-seniors were earning NFL paychecks. Coming back, however, were Bill Fischer, Leon Hart, and Jim Martin. With that menacing trio blocking for Terry Brennan, John Panelli, and Emil Sitko, there was no doubt that Notre Dame could run. The biggest preseason question was Frank Tripucka, who had spent the last two seasons behind Lujack.

So much for preseason chatter. In Tripucka's only year as starter, the senior completed 53 of 91 passes for 660 yards and 11 TDs. Tripucka, to Leahy's delight, also threw no interceptions.

Still, the 1948 campaign ended shockingly. Going into

the season finale against 28-point underdog USC, the 9–0 Irish seemed to have a third straight national title all but sewn up. But in front of 100,571 roaring Trojans fans, Notre Dame lost six fumbles. Then, with the score tied 14–14 in the fourth quarter, Leahy thought the Irish were winning and ordered his offensive players to run out the clock. They argued for a moment in the huddle and then wasted a crucial time-out while someone informed Leahy of the right score. The game ended 14–14, and 9–0–1 Notre Dame finished second behind 9–0 Michigan.

In this, his last college game, Tripucka took a crunching blow from a USC defender just before halftime. Tripucka left the field on a stretcher and spent all of December in a Los Angeles hospital, where he feared not only for his pro career, but whether he would ever walk again.

FRANK TRIPUCKA: "See, I got hit in the spine. And I couldn't feel my legs after it happened. They felt like they were gone. So I thought I would be crippled. I mean, because of the spinal cord and all the horror stories.

"As things turned out, they said I was very lucky. I had seven broken bones in my back, and two dislocated ribs. Well, the tip of one of those ribs had broken off. But instead of disrupting the spinal column, it went *around* it and fell back into place. Had the tip of that rib cut *into* my spinal column, they said I would have been paralyzed for life.

"So, you see, God has been very good to me. I played fifteen years of pro football and I never had one problem with my back. And although I was sorry, of course, that we blew the national championship that season, I had the greatest time of my life at Notre Dame. I mean, here it is fifty years later. And I still get the shivers when I step on that campus."

In 1949, while Tripucka and his guardian angel went to the NFL, Notre Dame's Leon Hart became only the second lineman in history to win the Heisman Trophy. Still, it wasn't the bellicose Hart most Irish players looked up to. The team's emotional leader was senior and All-American tackle Jim Martin.

A Marine reconnaissance swimmer in World War II, Martin had won a Bronze Star for swimming 1,000 yards among deadly floating mines to determine where U.S forces could best invade Japanese troops on the island of Tinian. After 30 months in the Corps and three years at Notre Dame, Martin was 25 by his senior year. Four of his younger teammates—halfback Jack Connor, fullback Jack Landry, left end Jim Mutscheller and right end Chet Ostrowski—recall one of the school's most magnetic players.

JIM MUTSCHELLER: "Jim Martin did things that other people don't. Even in the Marines, how many guys had the nerve to swim beneath enemy ships and try to blow them up?"

JACK CONNOR: "Nobody lifted weights in those days, but Jim Martin was like a Greek Adonis. He was maybe 6 feet 2 inches and 204 pounds, with a 32-inch waist. And Martin wouldn't hit you, he would kill you. Then he would smile and help you get back up."

JACK LANDRY: "Jim had these tree stumps for legs from all that swimming. His calf muscle measured 17 inches around. He was kind of a ladies man, too. He would sneak out of his dorm, but instead of going back there, he'd bang on my window at 2 A.M. See, I lived on the first floor. So Jim would just climb up and crash on our floor."

CHET OSTROWSKI: "Jim had this big tattoo across his arm. It was a sword cutting through a big dragon, and it said

Death Before Dishonor. That always stuck with me. I mean, Jim was a man and we were just kids.

"He was a wonderful guy, though. You know, as Notre Dame athletes, we never received any special privileges. There were no athletic dorms. There were no training tables. We lived with Notre Dame's students. We ate whatever they ate. And I don't know why exactly, but on Fridays the food was always terrible. Not that it was any good to begin with. But Fridays were the worst. The older guys would call it shit on a shingle.

"Since no one wanted to eat at school on Friday, Jim Martin would take us down to the American Legion hall in South Bend. We'd have a nice meal and then there'd be a dance. We'd all be going after the young girls. Jim Martin would be dancing with their mothers.

"I don't know. Maybe I was just young. But Jim Martin seemed bigger than life. He also represented the end of an era. He was in Notre Dame's last batch of servicemen."

In 1949, behind Martin, Hart, and yet another star quarterback, Bob Williams, Notre Dame breezed to a 10–0 record and Leahy's fourth national title.

This also concluded the program's most glorious era. Between 1946 and 1949, the Irish played 38 consecutive games without a defeat. They won three of four national championships. The one season (1948) they didn't win it all, they finished No. 2.

It was a dazzling run to finish the decade. However, behind closed doors, trouble drew near.

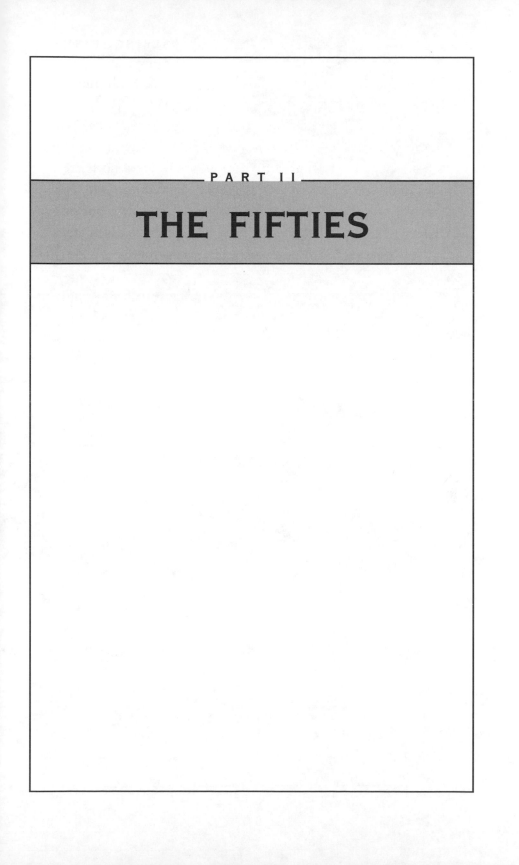

PART II

THE FIFTIES

6

POWER STRUGGLE

1 9 5 0

SHORTLY AFTER THE 1949 SEASON—EVEN AS NOTRE DAME reigned over college football—Leahy told some of his players he might leave for the pros. According to his biographer Wells Twombly, Leahy also informed school officials.

"I told Father John I might leave after the 1949 season," Twombly quoted Leahy in his 1974 book, *Shake Down the Thunder*. "The Los Angeles Rams had made inquiries as to my availability and I was tempted. Oooh, I was sorely tempted. But I considered it an honor to be head coach at Notre Dame. To me it was a sacred trust."

The "Father John" Leahy referred to was Father John J. Cavanaugh, who as Notre Dame's then vice president, had wooed and hired Leahy in 1941. By 1949, Father Cavanaugh had been named president.

Bob McBride, who joined Leahy's coaching staff in 1949, says this had a dramatic impact on Cavanaugh's relationship with Leahy.

BOB MCBRIDE: "It changed everything. Because when Father Cavanaugh was vice president, he had a gentlemen's agreement with Leahy to give him thirty to thirty-three scholarships a year. These were the years when Big Ten schools like Michigan and Ohio State gave out forty-five to fifty. So that thirty to thirty-three range was entirely reasonable.

"But in 1947, President Cavanaugh cut football scholarships down from thirty-two to eighteen. Meaning he purposely tried to deemphasize Notre Dame football. Because that's the main thing you do when you deemphasize. You reduce scholarships.

"I'm not sure what changed Cavanaugh's feelings. But once he became president, I think he might have envied Leahy's stature. And I'll give you a for instance.

"When General Eisenhower ran for the presidency, he was on his way to the national convention. But first he stopped in South Bend. He had a limousine pick him up at the airport. The limo then took him directly to Leahy's office. Later, when Eisenhower got the nomination, it was Leahy who made his first seconding speech.

"I think those kind of things irked Father Cavanaugh. I think as he went around to make his many speeches, he got tired of people asking about football. And although I don't understand it, I think he became ashamed of winning. That's why he wanted someone to rein in Leahy."

To implement his plan, Father Cavanaugh chose Father Theodore M. Hesburgh, a dynamic, handsome, scholarly young priest with middle-class roots from Syracuse, New York. After four years of teaching theology at Notre Dame, he became its executive vice president and athletic chairman in 1949. Father Hesburgh was only 32.

In his 1990 autobiography, *God, Country, Notre Dame,* he confirms that Father Cavanaugh charged him with restraining Leahy. But not for the same reasons Bob McBride cites.

"As the newly appointed executive vice president in 1949," Father Hesburgh wrote, "my first assignment was to go out there and reorganize the athletics department of Notre Dame. . . . The problem, as Cavanaugh explained it to me, was that while the administration theoretically controlled athletics, and had its own representative as an overseer, the reality was that Frank Leahy was doing whatever he pleased. Not that he was doing anything wrong, only that he was operating independently of the university administration. In other words, he was running what amounted to an autonomous fiefdom."

Father Hesburgh expounds here on his early dealings with Leahy, one of the nation's most celebrated coaches.

FATHER HESBURGH: "I came in and installed a lot of rules. So it was tense at first. But that was understandable to me. He was a very important guy. He was a power coach, and power coaches run their own domain. So I realized, early on, that it would have to be established: Either I had the ultimate yes or no—or I didn't.

"Well right away in 1949, Leahy and I had a little disagreement. It was regarding how many players he could take on a road trip, and it turned out Father Cavanaugh backed me. After that was established—that I had the ultimate say—Frank and I became very good friends. And when he would have difficulties of one sort or another, he used to call up and say, 'Let's walk around the lake.' That always meant consultation, counseling, et cetera. So we had quite a few walks around the lake. And we got along just fine."

By 1953, say several insiders, that dynamic had changed. Contrary to Notre Dame's official explanation, some feel Father Hesburgh fired Leahy.

In April 1950, spring practice ended ominously in South Bend. These events are recalled by All-American quarterback Bob Williams.

BOB WILLIAMS: "Every spring at Notre Dame, the upcoming team would play a team of ex-players. Later they called it the Blue-Gold game. Back then we called it the Old-Timers game.

"That year, 1950, it was a blood game. There was a lot of talking and mouthing off. Plus, their team was loaded. They had George Connor and Lujack and Bob Dove—all these NFL stars—plus they had a bunch of seniors from 1949.

"Well, they beat the hell out of us. And right then and there I thought: This is going to be a very long season."

On September 30, the Irish opened against North Carolina, a team they had routed 42–6 the previous season. This time they won 14–7, and only on a late touchdown pass by Williams.

The following Saturday, Notre Dame faced Purdue under dreary South Bend skies. The Irish, who hadn't lost in 39 games, came in as 20-point favorites.

Not only did Purdue win 28–14, but it could have been worse. The referees called back an 86-yard Boilermaker touchdown—on what many observers considered a phantom clip.

Three key players recall that historic game: Notre Dame's first defeat since December 1, 1945.

JACK LANDRY: "It was very somber afterward. There were a lot of tears in our locker room. We were embarrassed to be the guys who broke the streak."

CHET OSTROWSKI: "When someone plays Notre Dame—and I don't give a shit if they're a last-place team—they play like a million bucks. Notre Dame was so good in the late forties, it didn't usually matter. But not in 1950. We didn't have the horses."

BOB WILLIAMS: "It was 1947 when they first started cutting scholarships. Then it reached its apex in 1950. We only had about fifty football players. And since our freshman class had been so small, we didn't have many seniors. Well, that lack of experience showed on the football field. We went 4–4–1.

"Now at some schools, 4–4–1 isn't that bad. But at Notre Dame, it's terrible."

In the 1950 season, Leahy surrendered more than his glamorous streak. He lost more games than he had in the *past seven years.*

Dr. Nicholas Johns was Notre Dame's long-time team doctor and Leahy's personal physician. He recalls how Leahy reacted to losing.

DR. NICHOLAS JOHNS: "He was so unbelievably intense, he would seem to be in a form of shock. Even from time to time, Leahy would vomit.

"There was a game they lost that season at Southern Cal. Leahy didn't make the trip because he had some kind of viral problem. So he asked me and my wife Doris to come to his home for lunch and to listen to the ball game. Leahy was upstairs before the kickoff. Doris and I were downstairs, talking to his wife Floss while she made lunch. When Leahy finally came down just about game time, he barely acknowledged me. And Leahy and I were close.

"During the USC game, someone made a long run for Notre Dame, but the referees called it back on a penalty. Leahy got up, pointing his finger, and started walking slowly toward the radio. He said, 'You sons of bitches! You bastards! You hate Notre Dame! You hate Notre Dame!'

"Leahy was talking to this radio. Then he must have realized what he was doing. Because he turned and walked upstairs and never listened to the rest of the broadcast. Jesus, was Leahy intense."

BOB WILLIAMS: "That was our senior year at Notre Dame. And after seeing the heights we saw the years before, it was a very upsetting way to end a career.

"The administration wasn't unhappy about it, either. This fit right into their plans. They wanted to put Leahy in his place. They wanted Notre Dame to be known for something other than football. So if you look at it from a historical perspective, this is really when Leahy started going downhill. Not in terms of winning—because he won again—but in terms of who held the power at Notre Dame."

7

PAYING THE PRICE
1951 — 1952

DURING THE WINTER OF 1951, AFTER HIS FIRST .500 SEASON AS a head coach, Leahy signed a brilliant class of freshmen, including three future All-Americans, in quarterback Ralph Guglielmi, end Dan Shannon, and tackle Frank Varrichione. But while all this seemed promising for Notre Dame's near future, Leahy was much too driven to bide his time. And so at Cartier Field, where Irish practices were violent to begin with, Leahy and his assistants cranked up the volume.

Joe Heap, a speedy freshman halfback from New Orleans, describes spring practice 1951.

JOE HEAP: "Brutal. Cruel. Punishing. Severe. You're not supposed to lose at Notre Dame. Not even one game. And Leahy was coming off a four-loss season.

"I'll give you a good example of what it was like. One afternoon, I had a hemorrhoid operation. But I knew I dare not miss practice, so I went out on the field just to watch. It was freezing outside. I had on this big parka. The anesthesia still hadn't worn off.

"But this coach ran up and said, 'Where is your uniform?' I said, 'Coach, I just had an operation. Doc Green just cut my hemorrhoids out.' He told me, 'You don't run on your ass. Go get your uniform on.'

"That was Joe McArdle. His nickname was Captain Bligh. But he wasn't even Leahy's toughest assistant. That was Bob McBride. He went into World War II as a 200-pound tackle. He got captured by the Germans and came out skin and bones. Well, by the time McBride put that weight back on, he was real mean. Sometimes he would take on guys at practice, and afterward those guys would quit the team."

DAN SHANNON: "He was sort of Leahy's top enforcer. If somebody slacked off, or needed some extra incentive, McBride would take him out to Bunker Hill. That was a little mound of dirt on Cartier Field, where disciplinary action would be taken.

"Normally, Bob McBride would go on defense. He'd say to the player, 'Okay, block me.' Then, for ten or fifteen minutes, McBride would beat the heck out of him. Sometimes when they were through, that player couldn't get up off the ground. But none of us could help him. He had to get to the locker room himself."

CHET OSTROWSKI: "The name Joe Katchik pop up yet? He was this real big end. Maybe 6 feet 7 inches and 255 pounds. So Joe was supposed to be another Leon Hart. But Leahy was on him so bad, Joe couldn't catch the ball. It would hit him right in the hands and he would drop it, because he was so nervous and uptight. After that fifty-one season, Joe quit playing ball at Notre Dame.

"See, Leahy was a great coach right after World

War II. He was dealing with men. War veterans. Leahy could work the shit out of them. And they could handle that pressure. But all the war vets were gone by 1950. The younger players had different temperaments. And Leahy ruined a lot of those young guys. They couldn't take the pressure he put on."

This was not the case with future Heisman winner Johnny Lattner, the sophomore running back who had grown up poor and resilient on Chicago's tough West Side. In Lattner's senior year at Fenwick High School, he had averaged a monstrous 18 yards a carry. Soon after came a slew of scholarship offers. But Lattner was predisposed toward Notre Dame.

JOHNNY LATTNER: "When I was still in elementary school, I was educated by the Sisters of Mercy. Well, those nuns were very pro–Notre Dame. They'd sit around Saturdays and listen to Notre Dame games on their radio.

"Of course, I also grew up on Chicago's West Side. It was a melting pot—Irish, Italian, German, Polish, Greeks—but everyone seemed to be a Notre Dame fan. In fact, at the Marborough Theatre, they showed all the Notre Dame games on closed-circuit TV.

"That was a real big deal to all those West Siders. They thought it was the greatest thing since Tammany Hall."

In 1951, with Lattner showing flashes of his brilliance, and with several more underclassmen gaining experience, the Irish finished 7–2–1, a substantial improvement over 1950. But the young team also had its embarrassing moments. On November 10 in East Lansing, for example, Michigan State destroyed it 35–0.

JOE HEAP: "Leahy came into the locker room during half-time. He was literally foaming at the mouth. First he called us gutless. Then, in so many words, he accused us of throwing the game."

JOHNNY LATTNER: "That was the worst defeat that Leahy ever suffered. Not only as a head coach but as an assistant. Man, that's going all the way back to the 1930s.

"A few weeks after we lost to Michigan State, we went to Los Angeles to play USC. Well, that Friday afternoon right after practice, about seven or eight of us went to RKO Studio. They were filming *Clash by Night,* with Barbara Stanwyck, Paul Douglas, and Robert Ryan.

"But Marilyn Monroe was also in it. And that's why *we* were there.

"At first, the RKO people told us no. But we had this kid with us named Bobby Joseph. He was a good B.S.er. Bobby said, 'We're all Notre Dame football players. We're all here in L.A. for the big USC game.' Blah blah blah—and Bobby talked our way in.

"So then we're sitting there with Marilyn Monroe. We sat in her little star hut for maybe two hours. We were just nineteen years old, but she was probably only twenty-four. And, man, was this girl pretty. Not only pretty, but nice. She had no put-on at all.

"While we were sitting there, Marilyn Monroe pulled out this publicity photo. Then she said to me, 'Do you want a picture?' I said, 'Yeah, I do.' She said, 'What do you want me to put on it?' I said, 'Dear John, thanks for the wonderful night we had together. Love and kisses, Marilyn.' So that's what she wrote down—with her phone number on it!

"We called her from our hotel later that night. We wanted her to come to the USC game. We even had some field passes for her. But she said, 'Gee, I'm sorry. I won't be able to go. I'm meeting another athlete at the airport.'

"She was meeting Joe DiMaggio.

"Well, the next day we upset USC and Frank Gifford, 19–12, on national television. It was the first game ever televised coast-to-coast. So that was a dynamite weekend out in L.A. Then, as soon as we got back to Notre Dame, I put up my picture of Marilyn Monroe. But the priest who ran our dorm made me take it down."

In 1952, the following season, Lattner finished fifth in the Heisman Trophy voting, and Notre Dame went 7–2–1 for the second consecutive year. But with victories over four Top Ten ranked teams—Texas, Purdue, Oklahoma, and USC—the Irish ended up ranked No. 3.

Leahy, meanwhile, kept raving on the sidelines. The first incident occurred on November 11, during a 22–19 home loss to unranked Pitt. After snapper Jim Schrader botched a key extra point, Leahy grabbed him and yelled, "Oh Jim Schrader, you'll burn in hell for this!"

Two weeks later, in a 34–14 win over North Carolina, sophomore quarterback Tom Carey felt Leahy's wrath.

TOM CAREY: "Leahy never liked the passing game. He loved jamming the ball right down their throats. So before he sent me in against North Carolina, Leahy told me to keep the ball on the ground.

"First we ran some counters and options. But then we got hit with a fifteen-yard penalty. That gave us a third down with twenty-five yards to go. So I threw a long pass and we scored a touchdown.

"Now I'm proud as hell as I come off the field. Next thing I know—Bam!—I get hit in the back by Leahy. I turn around and he screams, 'You're a disgrace! You're a disgrace to those beautiful nuns who taught you! You are a disgrace to the Blessed Mother!'

"He followed me around, shouting like that. He didn't

even care we scored a touchdown. It was all about me disobeying him."

Still, the Schrader and Carey events were relatively minor compared to what happened at Southern California in Notre Dame's controversial season finale. The 9–0 Trojans came in ranked No. 2. The 6–2–1 Irish were No. 7. With the score tied 0–0 in the second quarter, Notre Dame had third-and-three at the USC nine. But instead of running a play when quarterback Ralph Gugelielmi yelled, "Hike," the Irish shifted into another formation. USC jumped offsides, Notre Dame got a first down, Lattner scored a touchdown a few plays later, and the Irish went on to upset the Trojans 9–0.

There was a price, however. Leahy's detractors charged him with dirty tactics. The "sucker shift," they said, violated the spirit of the game.

Leahy countered, correctly, that the Irish hadn't broken any rules. Furthermore, Leahy said, both Iowa and Pittsburgh had used the shift that year against Notre Dame.

Of course, this didn't satisfy the critics. And making a bad situation even worse, the NCAA rules committee was headed during this time by Leahy's old Michigan nemesis Fritz Crisler. After the season ended, Crisler and his committee not only outlawed the shift, they publicly scolded Leahy for its use.

8

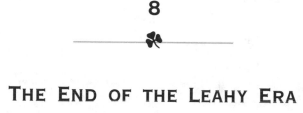

The End of the Leahy Era

1 9 5 3

It was a glorious season in many respects. Lattner set a school record for all-purpose yardage, won the Heisman Trophy, and graced the cover of *Time*. As the NCAA ended free substitution, and college players resumed going both ways, Guglielmi threw eight touchdown passes and made five interceptions. Notre Dame entered the season ranked No. 1, stayed there for eight weeks, and ended up undefeated at 9–0–1. Even with that one tie, which cost them the national title, many Irish players felt they were the nation's best team.

But this was hardly a season where everything went smoothly. The first crisis arrived on October 24 against Georgia Tech. With his team winning 7–0, Leahy collapsed in the locker room at halftime.

Bob McBride: "All the coaches were back in the equipment room, talking about what we'd do in the second half. Leahy fell to the floor from a sitting position. He was on the deck. We thought he was dying."

JOHNNY LATTNER: "Our captain Don Penza comes in crying. He says, 'Leahy's dying, Leahy's dying!'

"I'm sitting next to a guy named Bob Rigali, whose father had played for Rockne. Rigali had heard his father talk about Rockne, how he would make all these dramatic halftime speeches. 'Win one for my son' and all of that.

"So when Penza comes in crying, Rigali gives me a nudge and says, 'Don't believe him. Leahy is pulling a Rockne.'

"I just started laughing. Meanwhile, they were giving Leahy his last rites."

DR. NICHOLAS JOHNS: "I was in the dressing room at halftime, and somebody came in there yelling, 'Doc!' I went in a small private room and Leahy was on the floor. He was conscious, but in shock. He felt cold, clammy, sweaty. It looked like a classical heart attack.

"Then his blood pressure came up, and he had pretty much stabilized by the time the ambulance came. So we took him in for some tests at the hospital. Electrocardiogram was normal. As it turned out, he had acute pancreatitis. His children had had gastroenteritis . . . intestinal flu. It manifested in Leahy with this attack."

After being hospitalized most of that week, Leahy curtailed his activities for three games. He returned as sideline coach on November 23, as the 7–0 Irish hosted Iowa.

Notre Dame trailed 7–0 late in the first half when it drove to the Iowa 14. Then, with no remaining time-outs and just two seconds left, Frank Varrichione crumbled as if he'd been injured. The officials stopped the clock, Varrichione left the field, and Guglielmi hit Shannon for a touchdown. Notre Dame went inside tied 7–7.

The tactic worked again late in the fourth quarter. Trailing 14–7 with six second to go, no more time-outs, and the ball at the Iowa six, the Irish faked not one but several injuries. The officials killed the clock once again, and again Guglielmi hit Shannon with a TD pass. Notre Dame escaped with a 14–14 tie, instead of its first defeat.

Varrichione, already an outstanding junior tackle, would make All-American the following season. He would play 14 years in the NFL. But it was his sudden swoon that made him famous.

FRANK VARRICHIONE: "We used to practice it. And we never thought anything of it, because everybody else was doing it. I mean, it was the kind of thing you learn in high school. If you want to stop the clock, someone goes down.

"Okay, so we work on it during the week. Then we come up against a real tough Iowa team. We need to stop the clock to score before the half. But nobody really hits me on the play before that. So I faint dead to the world. Naturally, everybody gets suspicious. But what other choice does the ref really have? I'm just lying there prone. He has to do something, right? So he blows his whistle.

"From that moment on—and for the rest of my life—I was dubbed 'Fainting Frank.' They called me a thespian and everything else. In fact, a week or so later, there was a picture in a sporting magazine that showed the Harlem Globetrotters 'pulling a Varrichione.' One of the Globetrotters was lying on the court."

But others displayed a more hostile attitude. As Murray Sperber wrote in his superb 1993 book, *Shake Down the Thunder:* "The headline writers called Leahy's last team the 'Fainting Irish,' and the administrators in the Golden Dome received letters from fans decrying the tactic as unworthy of the Catholic institution as well as from anti-N.D. individuals mocking the school and its football history."

JOHNNY LATTNER: "Oh, yeah. It became this huge story. The newspaper guys loved it. They always had that love/hate thing with Notre Dame. And those articles were so serious. For a Catholic school like ours, with its Christian attitude, to fake an injury? That was terribly wrong.

"That's how they looked at it. Our attitude was: We're gonna burn in hell just for that?"

Jack Lee, a scrappy noseguard from Boston and one of Leahy's favorites, was rooming with Varrichione at the time.

JACK LEE: "Not only were Frank and I roommates, we were also the mailmen for Dillon Hall. And honest to God, we were getting bags of mail for Frank. I mean, *bags* of mail. I remember one guy sent him flowers. The note on it said, 'Rest in peace, you bastard.' "

RALPH GUGLIELMI: "We heard what was being said, and we didn't like it. But when you play for Notre Dame, you have just as many detractors as people who are for you. So you hear all this bullshit: You got those rosary beads. You guys are so lucky. You got a break from the refs.

"But it ain't all luck, believe me. Because people forget what happened before that fake injury play: We marched about 65 yards in less than a minute. That ain't luck, okay? That's fourth-quarter guts."

DR. NICHOLAS JOHNS: "The Monday after the Iowa game, I was in Leahy's office and he had all these headlines. Leahy said to me, 'Doctor, I can't understand it.'

"He was honestly baffled by the reaction. But the criticism began in the Iowa papers. Then it absolutely absorbed the entire nation.

"This did not help Leahy, by the way, in his relationship with Notre Dame. The school didn't want this kind of controversy."

TOM CAREY: "I would agree with that. I don't think it would help him. They were very, very conscious of their image and reputation."

According to Leahy's biographer Wells Twombly, the situation worsened when the Notre Dame alumni joined the chorus of fans and headline writers. "The alumni howled in self-righteousness," Twombly wrote.

But Father Hesburgh, who was then in the second year of his Notre Dame presidency, has an entirely different recollection.

FATHER HESBURGH: "No. No. No. I don't recall a lot of alumni reaction. But even those times when I did get calls and letters, I never got really tied up in things like that. Because I had a lot of other things on my mind that were frankly more important. Like building a great university.

"So the person you should ask is Father Ned Joyce. He was vice president in 1953. So he was in charge of overseeing athletics. Just as I had been when Father Cavanaugh made me vice president."

FATHER JOYCE: "I was a little surprised at how the press reacted, although I shouldn't have been. Because any time the press can smell a little controversy, they're into it with both feet.

"As far as alumni reaction is concerned, I don't think anybody in the Notre Dame family held it against Leahy. It certainly didn't change my own feelings toward him. In fact, it meant absolutely nothing. Because the tactic, as far as we knew, was rather common in intercollegiate football at that time. So under the circumstances, we thought Leahy did the smart thing. We thought he did what any coach would do."

Still, after their infamous tie with Iowa, the No. 1-ranked Irish fell to No. 2. That's where they ended their season two weeks later, with a final record of 9–0–1.

By then Irish fans had seen a strange few months. On October 24, Leahy had suffered his pancreatic attack. On November 21, the Fainting Irish furor had erupted.

Then, on January 31, 1954, Leahy held a press conference with Father Hesburgh and Father Joyce. Leahy, at age 45, was coming off an undefeated season. He still had two years remaining on his contract. And yet he announced his resignation.

In his official statement, Leahy said he was acting upon the recommendation of his doctors. "The doctors advised me, after my experience between halves of the Georgia Tech game, to give up coaching," he said.

Father Hesburgh stated, "The university of Notre Dame regretfully announces the resignation of Mr. Frank Leahy for reasons of health."

Following the lead of Leahy and Hesburgh, *Newsweek* reported, "Leahy resigned as head coach on the advice of doctors who had indicated that another attack of acute pancreatitis—an abdominal disturbance which caused his collapse during the Notre Dame–Georgia Tech game last autumn—could be fatal."

Time wrote, "Last season, stricken with acute pancreatitis, he was even given last rites. This week, on doctors' orders to take life easier, forty-five-year-old Frank Leahy resigned."

As time and history passed, the shorthand version became: Leahy's doctors told him retire or die.

But many Irish insiders still don't believe it. They feel Leahy was fired.

Fathers Hesburgh and Joyce respond.

FATHER HESBURGH: "Leahy voluntarily resigned. I wasn't about to fire him, which I could have done by paying off his contract. But the point was, Leahy collapsed at a game. He was hardly breathing. He could have died.

"Even well before this, back in forty-nine, I would find him walking the halls at night in our hotel. It happened the night before we played Indiana. Lord, we could have played them with our fourth team. Yet here is Leahy walking the corridors. Worrying. Always worrying.

"Well, that catches up with you after a while. Nobody's got an iron-clad nervous system. So I thought it was my duty to explain to him, in an honest way, that he was on a downward trajectory. I told him he had come close to hitting the bottom, and that I didn't want to have him die on me. I also said he had a wife and eight kids, and they were his number one responsibility. So I suggested that it would be better for his health, and for his responsibility to his family, if he would just resign.

"Leahy thought about it and said, 'I guess you're right. I'll quit.'

"So that was how it happened."

FATHER JOYCE: "I think Father Hesburgh and I felt exactly the same way. That it would be a tremendous loss to us and to our football program, but that the man's health was far more important than the Notre Dame football program. And it wasn't just us. Leahy spoke with close friends who advised him to retire before he killed himself. And we didn't put up any objection to that. So, in that sense, we encouraged it. But all those other people who think we eased him out—because he was winning too much and all those other things—there is absolutely no truth to that."

One of those skeptics is Professor Robert Burns. After receiving his Ph.D. from Harvard, Burns taught history at Notre Dame for more than 20 years. He spent another ten years as a history department administrator. He is now researching the school for his forthcoming book, *Being Catholic, Being American: The Notre Dame Story, 1842–1934.*

PROF. ROBERT BURNS: "There was the famous sucker shift against Southern California in 1952. Notre Dame got a lot of bad publicity over that. But that was nothing compared to the Fainting Irish. That was extremely embarrassing to Notre Dame. And embarrassing the university is the worst thing you can do. That is the absolute unforgivable sin.

"So I'm not too convinced his health was the reason. I don't really know how serious it was. He did have the attack in the Georgia Tech game. But the fact is he was back coaching by the Iowa game. Then, after he resigned, Leahy lived for another twenty years.

"I joined the Notre Dame faculty in 1957. When Leahy's name came up then, the faculty consensus was that he'd been fired. Even if you look at the statements made at the time, Father Hesburgh was saying how wonderful Leahy was. He was saying that Leahy projected Notre Dame's values. But Hesburgh wasn't mentioning the Fainting Irish. He wasn't mentioning the sucker shift. Well, I think he was trying to avert public relations damage. Because he had just gotten rid of the most celebrated football coach in the country."

DR. NICHOLAS JOHNS: "His health, basically, was fine. But Leahy was so intense that he would drain himself. Have you ever been really concentrated on something? You get an adrenaline rush and then you get exhausted. But that is a functional problem. That is not organic. The difference between organic and functional is just like in a car. When you lift up the hood and something is cracked, that's a change in the structure. So it's organic. Functional is when your motor is jumping. Functional means it's just out of tune.

"Leahy had a functional problem. Because he was so intense. And from a physical standpoint, I felt he could have kept coaching."

This raises an interesting question. If Dr. Johns, his personal physician, did not feel it was time for Leahy to retire, where did the famous quit-or-die story come from?

DR. NICHOLAS JOHNS: "I suppose he could have talked to other doctors, and they could have given him their medical views. But Leahy never said a word to me.

"In fact, I got a call one Sunday from Chicago. Leahy was there with Father Hesburgh, Father Joyce, and *Chicago Tribune* sports editor Arch Ward. They were calling me from the Stephens Hotel, which is now the Hilton. I can't recall if it was Joyce or Hesburgh or Arch Ward. But one of them said, 'Hello Dr. Johns? How are you?' I said, 'Fine, how are you?' Then that same person told me who was there. Then he said, 'We'd like to have you to talk to Coach Leahy.'

"Frank got on and asked me if he could use my name. He said he was resigning for reasons of health. He wanted to say that I had told him to. He wanted to say he was resigning because his doctor told him to.

"I said yes. I said he could use my name.

"Then we talked in generalities about his wife Floss, and how his children were. He asked about my wife Doris and I said, 'Fine.' Leahy said, 'Well, I want to thank you, doctor. I'll get together with you when I get back.'

"I knew at that time that he was being fired."

RALPH GUGLIELMI: "I think they made him an offer he couldn't refuse. Either quit or be fired. Most of the guys on the inside feel the same way."

JACK LEE: "My dad was the manager of the Boston Garden. He worked there sixty-five years. He knew everybody. Well, he and my mother got to be friends with Coach Leahy.

"In 1954, the year after Leahy left, I was still a senior. My parents came to one of the final home games. They stayed at the Morris Inn right there on campus. I went up to the desk after the game, looking for what room my parents were in. Suddenly Leahy walks in with a guy named Arch Ward.

"Leahy says, 'Hey, Jackie, how are you?' We talk and I tell him my dad is out somewhere, but my mom is up in her room. Leahy says, 'I want to see her. I've got something to do, but I'll be up there.'

"I told Leahy the room number and I went up. My mom was there with some of my friends from Massachusetts. Then there's a knock on the door and in comes Coach Leahy and Arch Ward. So we're all chit-chatting. Then my mother says, 'Frank, what happened? Why did you leave Notre Dame?'

"Leahy said, 'They didn't want me anymore.' Then he got so emotional, he couldn't talk. He actually started crying. So my mother took Leahy into the bathroom and wet a face cloth so he could dab his eyes. I think he was embarrassed. And it was a little pathetic, to be honest.

"Now, when I had first heard Leahy was leaving Notre Dame, I thought it was based on his health. But what tied it up for me was that day at the Morris Inn. I thought that told the whole story. Leahy didn't want to leave. He was fired."

GEORGE DICKSON: "I don't think too many of us were fooled by the thing. I asked Leahy myself about his health. He said, 'You know, George, I'm perfectly fine.'

"The truth is, he was pushed out. It isn't surprising either. It's a pattern as old as mankind. Leahy and Hesburgh felt threatened by each other."

ED MIESZKOWSKI: "I don't think it's any secret. Hesburgh was trying to get rid of Leahy. He was looking for an excuse. And when Leahy had that abdominal problem, that was Hesburgh's cue.

"The campus wasn't big enough for them both. Leahy wanted to run the program his way. As for Hesburgh, he was a prefect on our floor when I was a senior. He was a very likable guy; we all loved him. But once he became vice president at Notre Dame, he felt football was getting too big. He wanted to make the university a scholastic institution. Well, a few times when Hesburgh called Leahy to his office, Leahy sent an assistant coach instead. Because Leahy figured: Let Hesburgh come and see me."

GEORGE DICKSON: "The name of that assistant was Bernie Crimmins. And Bernie was really the guy who caught a lot of shit. Because Leahy sent him over there to do battle with Hesburgh."

ED MIESZKOWSKI: "Then, in 1953, before Leahy's last season, Father Hesburgh hired Terry Brennan to be the freshman football coach at Notre Dame. I had coached for four years with Terry in Chicago, at Mt. Carmel High School. Terry called me up on a Monday morning. He said, 'Guess who was over at my house last night? Father Hesburgh.' I said, 'What did he want?' Terry said, 'He wants to know if I want the freshmen coaching job at Notre Dame.'

"Terry didn't know what to do. His aim was to go to law school, because his father and brother had a nice firm in Milwaukee. But then here comes Father Hesburgh and offers him the freshman coaching job at Notre Dame. So that turned Terry's head a little bit.

"Now look at this thing from Leahy's viewpoint. Here comes Terry Brennan, an extremely successful head coach at Mt. Carmel, getting all this good publicity, winning the city championship three years in a row. Now he's taking a pay cut to coach the Notre Dame freshmen?

"So I think Leahy knew why Hesburgh hired Terry. Hesburgh wanted Terry to replace him. And Leahy saw the writing on the wall."

TERRY BRENNAN: "Frank Leahy was fired. But I'm not going to put in print why he was fired. Forty years ago, I promised Father Hesburgh I wouldn't do that. And I intend to keep that promise to him."

TOM CAREY: "I played quarterback for Terry at Mt. Carmel. At the time, my father knew some Notre Dame trustees. And when Notre Dame began recruiting me, my father told me what would happen. He said they would de-emphasize Notre Dame football, and that Terry would go down there and replace Leahy.

"That's exactly what happened. Notre Dame wanted to become the Harvard of the Midwest. And that was partly why they moved out Leahy. They couldn't de-emphasize with Leahy still there."

FATHER HESBURGH: "I put in some pretty strict rules. Some of our rules were stricter than the Big Ten's. And thanks to Father Joyce, those rules were kept and enforced. But there was no conscious effort to deemphasize football. Deliberately deemphasize? No way."

FATHER JOYCE: "I don't think we were doing that at all. I think it was all just talk. Certainly during the time I worked with Ted Hesburgh, we never talked about de-emphasizing football. We wanted to be successful at everything we did. That included athletics and academics."

But the question of deemphasis aside, another significant issue must be raised. If in fact Leahy was forced out, was Notre Dame justified? Had Leahy stayed at the table too long?

Even some players who loved him seem to think so.

JACK LEE: "I sincerely believe that Leahy, in some way, felt he was above the dictates and the desires of the administration. That's ultimately why he left Notre Dame. He wasn't paying attention to his bosses."

BILL FISCHER: "Leahy had gotten so powerful by then. And then you had that fanaticism of his. Some years Leahy had players coming in early, practicing off-campus, beating the rules. Why, some guys were working out on a farm in Cleveland. This was in the preseason. They were practicing before they came back to school."

TOM CAREY: "I felt he would kill himself if he kept going. Because he was a basket case by the time he stepped out. There were halftimes when his friend Fred Miller, the guy who owned Miller Brewing, would practically hold Leahy up while he was giving us his halftime speech. That was hard to watch."

JACK LEE: "Leahy always dressed well. He always wore a dark suit, a bow tie, and a large hat. We called it a 'hood' hat. Because it had the wide brim like the hoods in Chicago wore.

"Well, Leahy was always famous for stomping on his

hat. One time he took the hat and flung it out onto the field. But it was so blustery, the hat turned around and came back just like a boomerang. It hit Leahy right in the head. He looked down and said, 'Where did that thing come from?'

"I'm not saying the guy was cracking up . . . but he just didn't have it together quite as much."

JOHNNY LATTNER: "I don't think Leahy wanted to retire. But I do think it was time. Leahy was kind of out of it during the games. He was kneeling and praying and getting very distraught.

"I know he was always emotional. But I think he became psychotic toward the job. He loved Notre Dame so intensely, he felt his mission in life was coaching its football team. Because as long as he was coach, Leahy felt that Notre Dame would win."

Before stepping down in 1954, Leahy led his alma mater to four national championships, six undefeated seasons, a 39-game unbeaten streak, an 87–11–9 record, and an 11-year winning percentage of .855. This is still the second best mark in the history of college football. Rockne, at .881, is still ranked first.

During his 35-year reign (1952–1985) as president of Notre Dame, Father Hesburgh was also remarkably productive. Under his firm hand, 40 new buildings went up on campus. The student body doubled and the faculty tripled. The once all-boys university admitted females. Notre Dame's endowment grew from $6 million to over $500 million.

In the process, wrote Kevin Coyne in his compelling 1995 book, *Domers*, Father Hesburgh changed Notre Dame "from a small sectarian college into a leading national university." In addition, Coyne wrote, "Hesburgh had counseled seven presidents and four popes, collected enough honorary doctorates to earn a place in the *Guinesss Book of World Records*; spoken loudly and internationally for the causes of civil rights and human rights . . . and emerged as the nearest thing American had to its own pope."

Coyne concluded by stating that everything about Hesburgh was so large that any successor was bound to seem small by comparison.

Many who knew Frank Leahy felt the same way. Which Terry Brennan would learn quickly enough.

9

❧

TWO STUBBORN IRISHMEN
1 9 5 4 — 1 9 5 5

ON FEBRUARY 2, 1954, TWO DAYS AFTER LEAHY'S FIRING/RE-
signation, Terry Brennan was given the toughest job in
college football. Brennan, 25, was the youngest head coach
in Notre Dame history, and except for his one year on
Leahy's staff, his only experience had been coaching
high school.

FATHER JOYCE: "Father Hesburgh knew Terry better than I
did. He had taught him in a class at Notre Dame, and he
was very high on his integrity and intellect. So we had
thought in 1953: Let's get Terry in here. Frank's not going
to last forever. Let's get Terry seasoned by learning from
the great master.

"Well, we had no idea that Frank would be going out
at the end of 1953. So then, what could we do? We would
have preferred that Terry had far more experience in college coaching, but we thought: Let's gamble on it.

"Which is really what we did. Hiring Terry was a cal-
culated risk."

FATHER HESBURGH: "He had won three high school championships in the Chicago Catholic League, which was probably as tough as any in the country. But when I first called Terry about the job, I said, 'You're a little young for this. It's a pretty fast league. Normally, I would think the best thing for you would be to go on being an assistant coach here. We replace Leahy for a few years and then you're next. I'll give you first crack at it.'

"He said, 'No, I can do it. I want to do it now.' I said, 'Well, okay.' And that's how it happened."

PROF. ROBERT BURNS: "In its early years, that administration did not put great value on experience. Because here were two relatively young, relatively inexperienced guys themselves: Father Hesburgh and Father Joyce. Yet both were very bright and very hard-working, and they had recently taken over the running of this university. So I think they believed that any young, bright, hard-working person could manage almost anything at Notre Dame. Case in point: Terry Brennan."

Despite Brennan's modest coaching credentials, he was well-known to Irish fans as a clutch and versatile halfback on two national championship teams (1946–1947). In the '47 grudge match against Army—the season after the 0–0 tie—Brennan returned the opening kickoff for a 97-yard touchdown. The Irish won that day 27–7.

But in 1954, even though Notre Dame finished 9–1, Brennan had a difficult rookie year. Brennan says Father Hesburgh cut back on scholarships, while also toughening academic standards. But while Brennan knew this would affect him later on, his most immediate problem was Frank Leahy.

GEORGE DICKSON: "I came back Terry's first season to coach the quarterbacks. Well, Leahy was still in South Bend. And Terry felt the old man was interfering."

ED MIESZKOWSKI: "You know what's funny about it? Leahy used to love Terry Brennan. I mean, Terry was Leahy's fair-haired boy. When Terry and I coached together at Mt. Carmel—whether it was game films or strategies or equipment—we would get it from Notre Dame with no questions asked. Only because Frank Leahy loved Terry Brennan.

"But in 1953, when Terry got hired as Notre Dame's freshman coach, that put a wall between them. Because Leahy wasn't the one who hired Terry. Father Hesburgh did. So Leahy snubbed Terry that whole 1953 season."

GEORGE DICKSON: "My understanding is, you're probably right on the money. I don't know for a fact that the old man didn't speak to him. But there was a coolness."

TERRY BRENNAN: "No. My relationship with Leahy was perfectly fine the year I was an assistant. There was never any problem that I was aware of.

"But when I became head coach in 1954, I knew that Leahy had been fired. And I knew he wasn't feeling good about what happened. So I tried to smooth things over. Before our season opener against Texas, I asked Leahy to talk to the team. I really thought I went the extra mile. I mean, how much can you bend over backward to try and make it smooth for the guy who just left?

"Leahy was doing cartwheels. He wanted to do it. But actually it was a dumb thing to do. Because there is no smoothing things over with Frank Leahy. It's gonna be his way or no way. So Leahy made his speech a half hour before game time. Well, you don't do that rah-rah stuff until you're ready to run out the door. So it ended up disrupting everything. It was a disaster. But I'm not blaming him. It was my own bad judgment. Fortunately, we beat Texas anyway."

RALPH GUGLIELMI: "Up to that point, I had no problem with Brennan. Tom Carey and Dan Shannon had played for him in high school. They liked him and that was good enough for me.

"But something took hold of him after that Texas game. Leahy, I felt, had made a damn good speech. And we beat Texas 21–0. But when we had our team meeting that next Tuesday, Terry Brennan says this is *his* football team. He says what happened last Saturday will *never* happen again. And he goes on and on. And here are something like seventeen Notre Dame seniors, who have just gone through three years with Frank Leahy.

"Well, just take a look at our next game. Purdue comes into our place. We're a three-touchdown favorite. Purdue kicks our ass 27–14. Then Brennan blames the seniors for the defeat. Man, I'll never forget that. I'm our starting quarterback. I'm a senior. And that third week of practice, Brennan had me holding practice dummies. Brennan had Joe Heap doing it, too. Hey, you can say what you want about Leahy. But when a Leahy team lost, he took the blame. I never heard him blame it on his players."

JOE HEAP: "Our relationship was strained. But it was strained between him and a lot of guys. Terry seemed to have a chip on his shoulder. I remember one meeting after a game. Terry jumped off the stage and offered to physically whip anyone there. You know what I mean? This is your new head coach, getting down to that level."

The *South Bend Tribune*'s Joe Doyle also recalls that season's turbulence.

JOE DOYLE: "Brennan didn't want Leahy looking over his shoulder. But one week after Notre Dame beat Texas, Leahy came into the locker room again. Brennan didn't invite him this time, either. Leahy came in the back door, literally. The guy working the door just let him in.

"Then Brennan walked in and he was irate. He didn't grab Leahy and physically throw him out. There was no great outburst. But Brennan clearly didn't want him in there. Then Notre Dame went out and got upset by Purdue. So the guy who let in Leahy got reprimanded. And that was it for Leahy. He never came into the locker room again."

GEORGE DICKSON: "Terry said to me after the Purdue game, 'He has no business being in here. This is our ball club now, not his.'

"Well, I was a little bit caught in the middle there. Because I always liked them both. One night I even said to Terry, 'You were a great football player for Notre Dame. Goddammit, of anybody, I'd think you'd think Leahy was something pretty special.'

"Terry said, 'I don't. Would you want him coaching your kid?' I said, 'Damn right.'

"I tried talking to Terry a few more times. I tried to make some peace between those two. But this was Brennan and Leahy. Two stubborn Irishmen."

RALPH GUGLIELMI: "We beat Texas, we lose to Purdue, and then we go into Pittsburgh. Brennan benched me that game. He started Tom Carey instead. Then he went and benched some other key seniors.

"One of Brennan's assistants walked up to me in the first quarter. He said, 'Get ready. You're going in.' I said, 'Fuck you. I'm not going in.'

"I'll tell you what pissed me off. If the man wants me

to play, he should tell me himself. If he was the one who benched me, then he should have enough guts to send me back in.

"That's the way I felt. I was pretty pissed off. But then Joe McArdle spoke to us at halftime. He had coached for Leahy. He was old school. McArdle took the seniors off to the side. And McArdle got to us. We went out and kicked ass in the second half. We ended up beating Pitt 33–0."

After finishing 9–1 and ranked No. 4, the Irish lost both Guglielmi and Carey to graduation. In 1955, their starting quarterback was junior Paul Hornung.

Recruited by 100 colleges out of high school, Hornung chose Notre Dame to please his Catholic mother. But according to his close friend Sherrill Sipes, there was great pressure on Hornung to stay in his native Kentucky.

SHERRILL SIPES: "We were high school teammates in Louisville. We won the state championship our senior year. Well, Bear Bryant was coaching Kentucky at the time. Naturally, he really wanted Paul. So one of Bear Bryant's assistant coaches told us: 'If you guys play for Kentucky, we'll take your whole high school team.'

"There was another guy we met in Louisville. He was a businessman with close ties to Bryant. He took us for a ride in a brand-new Cadillac. Then he said, 'This car is yours. You don't even have to commit to Kentucky. Just don't take that recruiting trip to Florida.'

"Paul and I were both poor. We were impressed by that. But Paul's mother was Catholic—God bless her, very Catholic. And I already had my heart set on Notre Dame. So Paul and I agreed to take a visit."

DAN SHANNON: "I was assigned to them when they came down. But if you were under twenty-one at the time, you weren't allowed in bars. Even if you were caught drinking Pepsi Cola, you could be kicked out of school.

"So Hornung and Sipes come down as a tandem from Kentucky. Tom Carey and I take them out to the usual places: a movie, a hamburger place, a tour of the campus. The first thing Hornung says is, 'Where are the girls?' We say there are no girls at Notre Dame. Hornung says, 'Well, where can we get a drink?'

"That's the way it went all afternoon. So then we went back to Leahy. We said, 'Forget it. You're not getting this guy.' "

Hornung's mother prevailed, though. And according to three team captains—end Dick Prendergast, halfback Jim Morse, and tackle Chuck Puntillo—Hornung wasn't exactly stymied by Notre Dame's limitations.

DICK PRENDERGAST: "Let me put it this way. The women were after him like mice on cheese. He was a good-looking guy. He had this full crop of hair. They called him the Golden Boy."

JIM MORSE: "Hornung and I roomed together for three years on the road. But I was already married. Paul was young, handsome, not married at all. He probably had more girlfriends than any guy in Notre Dame history.

"I mean, there weren't any girls *at* Notre Dame. But there were St. Mary's girls. There were South Bend girls. In Paul's case, there were probably Chicago girls and Los Angeles girls too."

CHUCK PUNTILLO: "Hornung was just plain lucky. One of the luckiest guys I ever met. He could fall in a pile of shit and come up smelling good."

In 1955, Hornung led Notre Dame to an 8–1 record going into its season finale at USC. But the unranked Trojans shocked the No. 5-ranked Irish 42–20.

Afterward, Jim Murray took a shot at Brennan in a struggling new magazine called *Sports Illustrated.* "By no means did Notre Dame play as badly as the score indicates," Murray wrote, "but Notre Dame was not the superbly prepared crew Frank Leahy used to bring to the Coliseum either."

DICK PRENDERGAST: "We weren't really up for USC. We went out to Los Angeles one day early. Then we allowed ourselves to be wined and dined. Not that we were necessarily drinking, but we weren't serious enough about USC. We looked at it like a vacation to California. Truthfully, we blew that football game."

This is an intriguing observation, since by 1958, Brennan's final year at Notre Dame, several insiders felt that he'd lost control of his team. And the seminal event that made them feel this way—and which some say contributed to Brennan's firing—would also occur on a trip to Los Angeles.

10

❧

ROCK BOTTOM

1 9 5 6

IN 1956, WHEN NOTRE DAME PRODUCED ITS WORST RECORD ever, outsiders were stunned. How could the Irish possibly go 2–8? How could a powerhouse collapse so quickly?

Notre Dame players and coaches cite three main reasons:

- A crippling string of injuries that year.

- A remarkably hard schedule, even by Notre Dame standards. At the time the Irish played them, Oklahoma was ranked No. 1, Michigan State No. 2, Iowa No. 3, USC No. 17, and Pittsburgh 20.

- Deemphasis.

TERRY BRENNAN: "A couple of Notre Dame professors told me that when Father Hesburgh was hired in 1952, he wanted to be the education president. He was friends at the time with the head man at Princeton. And his friend from Princeton said, 'What you have to do is make a strong statement.'

"Hesburgh did it by cutting scholarships and by raising the academic standards. I never argued the academic side. I didn't want to bring in any bums. But it bothered me when they cut the scholarships. It was like being put on probation by the NCAA. Except your own school was doing it.

"Other recruiters jumped all over it, too. They said, 'Notre Dame's deemphasizing. Notre Dame is going to join the Ivy League.' That made it hard on us for a few years."

FATHER JOYCE: "There may be some truth to the scholarships going down, and that it was starting to show in 1956. But I don't know whether this was just accidental.

"I do know, again, that we were not deemphasizing football. I came from an athletic background. I always enjoyed being Notre Dame's head of athletics. We *never* talked about deemphasizing football. We wanted to be successful."

These statements have been supported by Murray Sperber, the respected historian and author of *Shake Down the Thunder*. "Because Father Hesburgh had started to transform the school into a modern university," Sperber wrote, "critics charged that he also wanted to 'deemphasize football.' In fact, he was merely acting appropriately as president of Notre Dame, attempting—with greater vigor, intelligence, and determination than any of his predecessors—to emphasize the academic side of the institution but still preserve its athletic heritage."

Of course, not everyone from Notre Dame agrees. Some still sound irritated four decades later.

DICK PRENDERGAST: "When I came into Notre Dame, they just started cutting back to eighteen or nineteen rides. So here you bring in a new coach, a young man, wet behind the ears, and you cut him back to eighteen rides. You do it two years in a row. But you keep playing the same hard schedule.

"Now, all of a sudden, this guy who went 17–3 his first two seasons has a bad year in 1956. And people start saying, 'Well, he's a bad coach.'

"Bullshit. It's a lousy administration for putting a guy into that situation."

BILL FISCHER: "I coached the line for five years while Terry was there. Those first few years, we didn't have enough kids. I remember one day Hunk Anderson came down. He was the head coach after Rockne died. Just a fabulous character who loved Notre Dame.

"Hunk says to us, 'Where's the freshman team?' We pointed to a small handful of guys. He says, 'Come on, don't shit your old friend Hunk. Where you hiding them?' We say, 'No, that's it.'

"Hunk says, 'You guys are gonna get slaughtered. You can't run this program with those numbers. And I'll tell you what else. When the shit comes down, you'll be the fall guys.' "

SHERRILL SIPES: "We started 1–3 in 1956. Then we were going to play at Oklahoma. Well, we all heard about this real big bettor. He was from Oklahoma, and the word got back to us that he was willing to lay twenty-five points. That was completely insulting. They might beat us, but never by twenty-five points.

"So Hornung and I started gathering money. We were backing freshmen into corners, getting all the money we could to go and bet this guy. But when we went looking for him, we couldn't find him. We would have blown our money if we had. Oklahoma beat us 40–0. Can you even believe that? They destroyed us in South Bend."

Besides getting routed by top-ranked Oklahoma, Notre Dame lost five straight games for the first time since taking up football in 1887. When the Irish beat North Carolina to snap the embarrassing streak, but then were crushed by Iowa 48–8, Leahy emerged as Brennan's loudest critic.

"It's not the losses that upset me," Leahy told the Associated Press a few days before Notre Dame played USC. "It's the attitude. What has happened to the old Notre Dame spirit? Those great fourth-quarter finishes. That old try right down to the final whistle even if there was no chance of winning?"

Leahy's blunt remarks got national play, and Elmer Layden instantly backed Brennan. "Leahy's publicity crazy," the former Irish coach said. "He's only trying to keep his name in the newspapers. He should remember that his 1950 team lost four and tied one."

Leahy shot back, "If any Notre Dame man is critical of what I've said, I can only reply, 'Isn't it true?' Notre Dame can lose games, but in the past they have always gone down swinging. . . . The team just quit last week against Iowa."

That was the biggest bombshell: calling the Fighting Irish a team of quitters. Then, as other Notre Damers lined up behind Brennan or Leahy, the *Chicago Tribune* called it an "Irish Feud."

TERRY BRENNAN: "I didn't say much at the time. It's not my style to battle it out in the papers. But here's what really happened.

"Leahy had a TV show. He called me the week before

the USC game. He wanted Hornung on his show the night before the game. "I told him, 'No way. Just think about it, coach. Back in 1947, when Johnny Lujack and I were playing together, would you have wanted Johnny Lujack, or me, or any of your players, to do something like that on the night before the last game of the year? You would never do that, but you want me to? Well, I'm not going to.'

"So I stood up to him, and Leahy didn't like it. Then he hung up with me and called Father Hesburgh. But he told Leahy no. He wouldn't intervene.

"That's when Leahy started taking his potshots at me. That's when he started doing everything he possibly could to try and hinder my performance at Notre Dame. Yeah, I was pissed off. But what was I going to do? You don't get into a pissing contest with a skunk.

"See, Leahy was very Machiavellian. He was still mad at Notre Dame for firing him. But he was smart enough not to criticize the school. So he comes after me and vents his spleen. But it looks like he's defending Notre Dame.

"Well, you don't expect things like that from a former coach. Notre Dame prides itself on loyalty. By doing what he did, Leahy showed he didn't know how to spell the word."

With Brennan privately seething, and Leahy and Layden sparring in the press, Notre Dame ended its year with a 28–20 loss at USC. Hornung, in his final college game, had to play halfback because of two dislocated thumbs; he couldn't properly the handle the snap from center. But he still gained 215 all-purpose yards, including a 95-yard kickoff return for a touchdown.

After that dazzling performance, Hornung won Notre Dame's fifth Heisman trophy. But Hornung didn't deserve it. Not with three touchdown passes and 13 interceptions. And not on a 2–8 team.

The 1956 Heisman should have gone to Jim Brown. The magnificent Syracuse fullback averaged 6.2 yards per carry, gained 986 yards and scored 14 touchdowns. But in 1956, Jim Brown had the wrong color skin.

Meanwhile in South Bend, Brennan had just completed his three-year contract, and disgruntled fans and alumni screamed for his job. So did some members of the school's athletic board. But Father Hesburgh gave Brennan another year.

According to *Sports Illustrated's* John Underwood, Father Hesburgh also began curtailing deemphasis.

"It had done precious little for Notre Dame's spiritual or financial needs," Underwood wrote. "Recalls an alumnus who has remained close to his alma mater for 40 years, 'Fund-raisers were not mad, they were furious.' It's not likely that Hesburgh will make such a mistake again. For one thing, he's too alert to fiscal needs."

Underwood isn't alone in his assertion. From the Terry Brennan era to Gerry Faust's, many observers have said it's a fact of Notre Dame life: Alumni donations go down when the football team loses.

And the two men in the best position to know?

FATHER HESBURGH: "Not really. It never seemed to change things. We had a number of losing seasons here. But even during those terrible seasons, under Brennan, under Faust, we always raised more money than the year before."

FATHER JOYCE: "Everybody asks this question. Well, as far as Notre Dame goes, it's totally ridiculous. Donations never went down. They kept going up and up. Why, when Joe Kuharich was coach, our donations were triple or four times what they had been. Those Kuharich teams were very poor. So it obviously had nothing to do with football. What it really involved was our growing sophistication at fund-raising.

"That isn't to say we never got complaints. I always got letters complaining about the coaching, or the team's record. But very few of them came from alumni. And none from important alumni. Then, every once in a while, you'd get this letter that said, 'I'm never going to give you any more money.'

"Out of curiosity, I would always check to see what he had done. And it would make you laugh. It would be from some fanatic subway alumni. Some guy who had never sent more than ten dollars. But now he's telling you to fire the football coach."

11

NOTRE DAME UNDER FIRE
1957 – 1958

THE FIGHTING IRISH, ON PAPER, COULD NOT BEAT OKLAHOMA in 1957. There was no discernible reason the game should even be close.

Notre Dame, 4–2, was coming off two straight losses in which it had been outscored 54–12. Brennan was already rumored to be on his way out.

The Sooners were led by the legendary Bud Wilkinson. Their 47-game winning streak was the longest in college football history. They had routed Notre Dame, 40–0, the season before in South Bend. Now the Irish had to play at Norman—in a raucous stadium awash in Sooner red.

DICK PRENDERGAST: "Me and a guy named Ed Sullivan were co-captains. Well, because they had beat us 40–0, we did a lot of talking that week about payback.

"But we also had no illusions. Oklahoma had seven or eight All-Americans. They were the defending national champions. And we had just gone 2–8."

ED SULLIVAN: "Nobody gave us a chance. Bud Wilkinson was the king of college football. Oklahoma was overpowering. The week before they played us, *Sports Illustrated* put them on its cover.

"Yeah, well, guess what happened? That was the birth of the *Sports Illustrated* jinx."

DICK PRENDERGAST: "The Friday before the game, we found all this graffiti in the visitor's locker room. It wasn't anti-Catholic. More along the lines of: You will get your ass kicked tomorrow. Don't take it personally. Oklahoma does it to everyone.

"So we're looking around at this and we're getting mad. Then we upset Oklahoma 7–0. And we won that game on spirit. We were extremely pissed off."

ED SULLIVAN: "Oklahoma hadn't lost in forty-seven games. So their fans didn't leave for twenty minutes. They didn't even stand up. They just sat there, stunned.

"Man, was that fantastic."

Don White, the sophomore quarterback who started as a senior, recalls the team's reception back in South Bend.

DON WHITE: "The airport was packed when we flew in. We could hardly board our bus. Then we arrived on campus and there were thousands of people on Notre Dame Avenue. It was just this swarm of pure emotion.

"A few weeks later, we played at Southern Methodist. That was another big game. They had Don Meredith at quarterback, and Meredith was having this great season.

"Well, Meredith was numbered. There was a price on his head. If one of our defensive players knocked him out, there might be a little reward. A little incentive. Maybe a sports jacket or something.

"Meredith did wind up leaving that game. He kept

getting sacked and hit and finally went out. And we routed SMU to finish 7–3. Now, that wasn't as good as we wanted. But it sure beat the hell out of 2–8. So most people were feeling optimistic. It seemed like Notre Dame football was back on track."

BILL FISCHER: "Earlier that year, the decision had been made that Terry would be replaced. Notre Dame even had dinner with Joe Kuharich and asked if he wanted to be the next head coach. They were gonna let Terry go at the first opportune moment.

"But then we beat Oklahoma. And it was such a tremendous victory, such an emotional thing, they didn't have the courage to let him go. They gave Terry another one-year deal."

FATHER HESBURGH: "Actually, Terry asked me for one more year. He said, 'I really need one more year.'

"I said, 'OK. I don't think you're going to make it, Terry. But if you want one more year, you've got one more year.'"

Brennan had high expectations before this season. In 1956, when his sophomore-laden squad had gone 2–8, he had told the press: "Wait until these boys are seniors. Then you'll see something."

In 1958, Brennan had 25 lettermen returning from a 7–3 team that had shocked Oklahoma. Fans and alumni spoke of a national title. Every major poll ranked Notre Dame in its preseason top five.

Although the Irish looked shaky while starting 2–0, they figured to fatten up with three straight games in South Bend against so-so opponents. But Notre Dame lost 14–2 to Army, barely beat Duke 9–7, and fell 29–22 to Purdue.

This humbling 1–2 stretch at Notre Dame Stadium started the rumor mill churning. Brennan was sure to be sacked, insiders claimed.

By the November 29 finale at USC, Notre Dame had slipped to 5–4, Brennan had been hung in effigy by the students, and Leahy had charged Brennan's Irish with underachieving.

Notre Dame, ranked No. 18, beat unranked USC 20–13. But what happened that night in Los Angeles may have killed any small chance Brennan still had.

Three Irish players recall that momentous road trip: guard and future captain Ken Adamson; halfback and future leading scorer Bob Scarpitto; and tackle and then captain Chuck Puntillo.

KEN ADAMSON: "Not everyone at Notre Dame had a halo. And a couple of our guys tore up their hotel room."

BOB SCARPITTO: "Remember the old Ambassador Hotel? We stayed out in the cottages they had. Well, the grass in between these cottages was almost like a putting green. And somebody took a car and drove it over the lawn. You could still see the tire tracks afterward.

"Then someone took all the glass patio furniture and put it up on the roof. I think there was also some damage inside the rooms—to some lamps and pictures and things.

"I believe the school found out as we were checking out. Then after we got back home, the hotel must have notified them what the total damages were. If I remember the numbers that were thrown out, it was eight thousand dollars. Which was a lot of money during the fifties.

"Also, that thing in L.A. was not the first time it happened. We had a couple seniors that year who were out of hand. These guys roomed together. They should have split them up, but they never did. They'd walk into a hotel and say 'I don't like that picture.' Then they'd drop the picture over the bedpost. Or they'd break a lamp for no reason. Crap like that."

CHUCK PUNTILLO: "I don't think the USC thing ever made the papers. But after we got back to school, the next thing I knew Brennan was fired."

When asked about the episode in L.A., any similar ones, and whether they played a role in his dismissal, Brennan says he does not remember any of this.

Which is a little odd, since just about everyone else— including Father Hesburgh, legendary sports information director Roger Valdiserri, and several Notre Dame players—says these events happened. All they differ on is how much the incidents mattered.

ROGER VALDISERRI: "There were a couple of incidents off the field. So they felt Terry didn't have good control of the team. I think that might have contributed to his firing."

CHUCK PUNTILLO: "Maybe he would have lost his job regardless. But if he was on the edge, this could have pushed him over."

DON WHITE: "Even before it happened, there was this feeling that Terry was not a strong enough disciplinarian. That he wasn't big on rules and regulations. That he was too young and liberal with us.

"Personally, I felt that was a bad rap. I think Terry figured: This is Notre Dame. These guys have been hand-picked. They can regulate themselves.

"But I do think this USC thing hurt him. In fact, I really think it did him in. Because these were big-name players who were involved. And once this all got back to Notre Dame, it was a black mark for Terry."

FATHER HESBURGH: "There were a couple of episodes where hotels or motels were torn up a bit. One time, I think it happened in Baltimore. But it also could have been Los Angeles.

"But, no, I don't think it was a very big deal. The simple thing around here is, You want a coach who can give great leadership to the football program. Now there have been a number of guys who have shown that immediately. Frank Leahy did. Certainly Ara Parseghian did. Lou Holtz did, although Lou did lose five or six games his first year here. But he was obviously in control of things.

"So, that's what really drives it. Can he be a great leader for the program? And after Terry had been here several years, it didn't really seem like he would make it."

FATHER JOYCE: "Terry had a young coaching staff. This was part of his problem. He won the first few years, we think, because he still had Frank's staff. And they were doing a lot of work.

"And then Terry began bringing in his own friends. Coaches like Bill Fischer, Bill Walsh, Jack Zilly. They're all wonderful men. They're great Notre Dame people. But they were all young like Terry.

"And so, when we looked to the future, we thought it would probably continue on this mediocre basis. Today it might not seem so mediocre. But in the 1950s, after having gone through the Leahy era, to lose four games in one season was rare. Losing eight games in one season was unheard of."

ROGER VALDISERRI: "When Terry was fired, he handled it with class. But the publicity was unreal. Terry was a very attractive subject. He was twenty-five years old when he took the job. He had a law degree. He was a great-looking guy. He'd been a great football player at Notre Dame.

"But the main reason the story got so big was the timing involved. I think they let him go on December 16. Well, people jumped on that: 'This guy has a family, and they're firing him right before Christmas.' That just resulted in all kinds of criticism. Everybody took a shot at us."

Notre Dame, in fact, had never been so ferociously attacked. In addition to the timing of Brennan's firing—which actually wasn't announced until four days before Christmas—most writers had no inkling of the 1958 team's discipline problems. All they saw was an earnest young coach whose teams won 64 percent of their games.

Arthur Daley wrote in his influential column in the *New York Times*: "No college in the country, in all probability, has as many or as unrestrainedly devoted followers as Notre Dame. Here is the 'People's Choice,' in a most sentimental form, all of it packed in the roseate glow of pure idealism. Yet this was the school that gave the sack to the 30-year-old father of four children for Christmas."

Notre Dame alumnus Red Smith wrote: "A startling dismissal of (an) honest, personable, conscientious, and able young man."

At *Sport* magazine, even though Dick Schaap turned in a balanced piece on Brennan's firing, his editors headlined it, "SHAME, SHAME ON NOTRE DAME."

Meanwhile, back in South Bend, the Irish players themselves were more divided.

DICK PRENDERGAST: "I grew up in an Irish neighborhood on the South Side of Chicago. Notre Dame was the dream. Notre Dame walked on water.

"But when Brennan got fired, it really turned me off to Notre Dame. I didn't go to games for eight or nine years. Because they really took a dump on Terry Brennan. They cut back the scholarships and made him the scapegoat. And then they bring in Joe Kuharich? First you dump a guy? Then you replace him with a shitty coach?"

ED SULLIVAN: "I think Terry was a nice guy. But the university probably made a mistake when they hired him. Especially the year when we went 2–8, it seemed like we changed our strategy almost weekly. If another team ran a series of plays against us—and had success with it— then we'd run that series of plays in our next game. We were grasping at straws."

ED MIESZKOWSKI: "The funny part about it? They fired Terry at the wrong time. He was a better coach when they fired him than when they hired him. Because Terry wasn't ready when they hired him. That's a helluva move: coming out of high school to the most prestigious coaching job in the country.

"That's why they should have given him more time. By the end of 1958, he was a seasoned coach who'd been through some stuff. He had all the scars you'd want."

BILL FISCHER: "Everybody said, 'You fire the guy at Christmas?' I said, baloney. What the heck is the difference when it happens? The fact is, we weren't given the tools to work with. You can't get enough top players without the scholarships.

"But Joe Kuharich put the heat on them. Remember what I told you? They were going to hire Kuharich after we went 2–8? But then they kept Terry when we beat Oklahoma? Well, after we went 6–4 in 1958, Kuharich told them, 'Look, it's either now or never.'

"So Father Joyce asked Terry to resign. Just like they asked Leahy to resign. But Terry didn't do it."

TERRY BRENNAN: "They told me it was all over. Then they offered to have me resign. My response was I didn't want to do that. I just wanted to show what really happened. Just let them print the truth.

"Yeah, I was disappointed. I mean, they created the problem. They took away the scholarships. Then they wanted me to build things back up quickly. But it isn't going to happen immediately. Look at any other school that loses scholarships. It's going to take some time.

"But I enjoyed being coach at Notre Dame. We were a Top Ten team three years out of five. We played some pretty good football. Sure, there were frustrations. But who said life is fair?"

12

"A HARDHEADED CROATIAN"

1959

BORN AND RAISED IN SOUTH BEND, JOE KUHARICH ONCE TRIED sneaking into old Cartier Field to watch his beloved Notre Dame play football. He was caught by a Norwegian fellow named Knute Rockne.

Kuharich played guard for Notre Dame in the mid-1930s and got his first head coaching job in 1947 at the University of San Francisco. His four USF teams went 25–14, including a 9–0 record his final season, which led to a job in the pros as head coach of the old Chicago Cardinals. In December 1958, Kuharich was the fourth-year head coach of the Washington Redskins when Notre Dame brought him back home to replace Brennan.

Father Joyce recalls what made Kuharich attractive.

FATHER JOYCE: "I knew Joe. He was one year behind me at Notre Dame. He was a good student, fine football player, intelligent guy. He had a good college record at San Francisco, and he was doing quite credibly with the Redskins.

"After Brennan, we also wanted someone seasoned. And we wanted a Notre Dame graduate, because that's all we were hiring back then. So we went after the most seasoned coach in the country who was also an alumnus. It turned out to be Kuharich.

"Of course, he was worse than Brennan. Kuharich was a disaster."

Father Joyce doesn't say so, but he also made a classic coaching change: from the overpermissive Brennan to the strictly old-school Kuharich. But Father Joyce went too far. Kuharich was so taciturn he rarely spoke to his own players.

KEN ADAMSON: "Kuharich was a disciplinarian. He believed in working you to death. He kept saying that first spring: 'We don't know how far we can push these bodies.'

"We had a kid on our team named Jim Colisimo. He collapsed during sprints and had to be hospitalized. Those were the days when you couldn't drink water at practice. You just ate those salt pills. Frankly, it's a wonder nobody died.

"I was captain that year, so I heard a certain amount of bellyaching. But there were no major rebellions against Kuharich. It was a different era. Athletes did what they were told."

In 1959, the Irish weren't averse to working hard. With future NFL players such as Adamson, Nick Buoniconti, Bob Scarpitto, Monty Stickles, Red Mack and Myron Pottios on the roster, they also had talent. So why did Notre Dame finish 5–5?

JOE DOYLE: "Kuharich. I could tell that first spring he wasn't the man for the job. He never had quarterback meetings, for example. Leahy had quarterback meetings.

Ara had quarterback meetings. *Everybody* had quarterback meetings. But Joe didn't believe in it. It was just plain dumb.''

BILL FISCHER: "Kuharich was a meathead. I played for him in the pros. He was head coach when I was with the Cardinals. Do you know we never had a screen play in our whole repertoire? The screen play wasn't even in our book! I can't tell you what a hardheaded Croatian that guy was."

Late in Kuharich's regime, John Underwood began covering college football for *Sports Illustrated.* Underwood's memorable stories—along with those of Dan Jenkins—helped popularize the sport and also transform *SI* into one of the country's finest magazines.

JOHN UNDERWOOD: "When I was a little boy, I remember reading about Johnny Lujack. I remember Notre Dame as this grand and glorious presence.

"But that was appreciating it from afar. When you get a little bit closer, you don't see it quite so gloriously, and you don't see it without some stains. But by and large, from my standpoint, it's still a wonderful example of what you can do with a college sports program. Because they try to keep the school a beacon of education. They try so hard to be upright.

"What does make you stop and wonder is their choice in coaches. Because Leahy wasn't selected by Hesburgh and Joyce. The first coach they hired was Brennan. He was twenty-five, so that was a strange choice to begin with. Kuharich was an absolute disaster. Well, I don't want to use the word *disaster*, because losing football games should never be a disaster. But Kuharich was certainly an unfortunate selection. He was the image of the beleaguered football coach. As he would explain defeats with his long-suffering demeanor, he seemed willing to go on forever being 5–5."

ROGER VALDISERRI: "There was another reason why the controversy over Brennan's firing wouldn't die quickly. Because of his successor, Joe Kuharich. He was here four years and never had one winning season. That 5–5 finish in 1959? That was as good as his record ever got."

So there it was. Brennan had been no Leahy and Kuharich was no Brennan. And as the 1950s ended, and Notre Dame joined the ranks of the formerly great, its fans had nothing to dine on but past glories.

PART III

THE SIXTIES

13

ONCE THEY WERE KINGS
1960 — 1962

IT WAS THE YEAR ROGER MARIS HIT 61 HOME RUNS. CHARLES Van Doren lied to a grand jury about his role in recent quiz show scandals. Teenage girls swooned over Elvis Presley's "It's Now or Never."

At Notre Dame in 1960, Father Hesburgh announced plans for a splendid new library. Five St. Mary's women were allowed to enroll in a Notre Dame English class. There was cheering in the streets when the country elected John Kennedy its first Catholic president.

On September 30, even the football campaign started with promise. Notre Dame beat California 21–7 and jumped from being unranked to No. 12. But one week later the Irish got taken apart, 51–19, by unranked Purdue. It happened in South Bend, and it was the worst home loss in school history.

JOE DOYLE: "Afterward, somebody asked Kuharich if he thought his players might be shell-shocked by the Purdue game. He said, 'No. It won't bother them at all.'

"Hell, they never recovered. They were gun-shy all season. They not only went 2–8, they lost eight games in a row. No Notre Dame team had ever done that before."

Ed Burke, the son of Irish immigrants, played offensive line at Notre Dame from 1960–1962. He admits he's "very jealous" of teammates who later played for Ara Parseghian. But Irish players say Burke never surrendered.

"He was in the middle of everything," says All-American linebacker Jim Carroll, a 1962 teammate of Burke's who did get to play for Parseghian as a senior. "If there was a fight on the field, Burke was the guy who always watched your back."

ED BURKE: "The early Sixties was a difficult time to play football at Notre Dame. In 1964, Ara came in and lit the place up. But Kuharich had no emotion. His teams had no emotion. It was like playing behind the Iron Curtain.

"In 1960, our captain was Myron Pottios. I was only a sophomore and he was senior. But one day I ran my mouth off at him. I didn't think he gave a shit at practice. I didn't think he was showing much leadership. But then I realized: He was probably gung-ho when he was a sophomore. But by now he'd been ground up by Kuharich's regime."

Steve Kolski played end the same three years Burke played tackle.

ED BURKE: "Steve didn't play much at Notre Dame. But he's one of those Notre Dame guys who took his degree and became extremely successful after football. You should talk to him. If there was any humor in the Kuharich era, Kolski would probably remember."

STEVE KOLSKI: "After going 2–8 in 1960, we went 5–5 in 1961. But we did have one big win against Syracuse. You remember how good they were? They had John Mackey, Walt Sweeney, Ernie Davis. All fantastic players.

"Syracuse was winning 15–14. There were only three or four seconds left in the game. So our kicker Joe Perkowski tried a 56-yard field goal. But it was a cold and blustery day in South Bend. You could tell right away the kick wouldn't make it.

"So the game is over, right? But now there's all this confusion and hollering. Because one of the Syracuse ends ran into our holder. And there's a flag on the ground. The ref is marking off the 15 yards.

"Then Purkowski lined up again and kicked the damn thing straight and beautiful. We win 17–15. Well, shit, there was pandemonium. The Syracuse sideline went crazy. They thought *they* had won.

"I was standing next to a guy named John Murray. Back when he was a freshman, John spent the first half of that year in the seminary. Then when he decided not to be a priest, he accepted a football scholarship to Notre Dame.

"John was a very regular guy in all respects—except he didn't swear. I don't say that negatively, either. I guess he should be admired for it.

"So John and I are standing on the sideline. We just beat Syracuse on this disputed field goal. John and I see this Syracuse cheerleader. She's running straight at our bench. She looks very attractive. We don't know what the hell she's gonna do.

"She stops about five yards from me and John Murray. She says, 'You dirty Christians! You dirty Christians! You stole that game!'

"I'm just standing there. I'm a little shocked. John Murray looks at her and says, 'Fuck you.' "

Angelo Dabiero, Notre Dame's leading rusher in 1960 and 1961, recalls the aftermath of the Syracuse game.

ANGELO DABIERO: "It turned into this giant controversy. Some people said that time already expired, so there should never have been a second kick. Some people wanted Notre Dame to forfeit the game. Then our captain Nick Buoniconti came out and said, 'No. We will not give this victory to Syracuse.' "

ED BURKE: "There was a feeling on campus—and also among the players—that Theodore Hesburgh was going to give the game to Syracuse. And Nick Buoniconti lost his mind over that."

The Notre Dame administration didn't forfeit. Father Hesburgh deferred to the NCAA rules committee, which let the victory stand. But reflecting the inconsistency of the Kuharich years, Notre Dame followed its upset of tenth-ranked Syracuse with two embarrassing season-ending losses: 42–21 to Iowa and 37–13 to Duke.

Duke? A basketball school? Routing the once-proud kings of college football?

ED BURKE: "Nobody gave a shit, to be quite honest. Again, football is such a game of emotions. And we were emotionless. Joe Kuharich was emotionless. By Duke, we were just playing out the season. The football team had been gutted. Nobody cared."

In 1962, the apathy extended to the fans. Though Notre Dame Stadium held 59,075, only 35,553 showed up on November 17 to see the 3–4 Irish defeat North Carolina.

Norm Nicola and Ken Maglicic were sophomores that

year. Nicola would start at center his next two seasons. Maglicic, a 5 foot-10 inch, 215-pound linebacker, would lead the Irish in tackles in 1964. Both respected team leaders, they shared the unique distinction of playing for three head coaches in three years: Joe Kuharich, Hughie Devore, and Ara Parseghian.

Here the ex-teammates recall 1962.

KEN MAGLICIC: "The Big Ten was powerful during this time. And since we scheduled a number of Big Ten teams, there was talk that Notre Dame could not compete. So some people felt Notre Dame should be more realistic. It should play Stanford, Northwestern, Rice, Duke, Boston College—schools with higher academic standings. It should not play the Michigan States, the Purdues, the USCs.

"There was also a feeling that Notre Dame wasn't keeping up with the times. They had made poor coaching decisions. They were too much tied into old traditions, like only hiring coaches who were Catholic and Notre Dame grads. The program was losing its stature rapidly."

NORM NICOLA: "I always felt that Joe Kuharich really meant well. But you could also see the pressure he was under. The press just tore him a new one. The stands weren't full at home games. There was a lot of insider fighting among his assistants."

In the December 1 season finale, 5–4 Notre Dame lost 25–0 at top-ranked USC. But even before this game, *Sports Illustrated* wrote that Kuharich was "reported to have accepted a $35,000 job as coach of the Los Angeles Rams. Another story said that a Chicago alumni group was buying up his Notre Dame contract, which has three years to run."

Kuharich called both rumors "ludicrous."

In fact, the second one was. Notre Dame alumni clubs, no matter how zealous, don't exert that kind of influence over athletics. Every dollar of every alumni contribution goes into the university's general fund. Then those donations are earmarked by administrators. Therefore, the money can't go directly to football, or even to Notre Dame's athletic department.

"This is why Notre Dame will never be like a Georgia," says the *Atlanta Constitution*'s Terrence Moore. "Georgia's booster club has such a direct line into the football program, it's more powerful than the university's Board of Regents."

The first rumor—Kuharich to coach the Rams—also proved untrue, albeit slightly closer to the mark. Four months after the season, on March 13, 1963, Kuharich did return to the NFL. But he came back as its supervisor of officials.

With a 17–23 record, Kuharich was the only losing coach in Notre Dame's long football history. Since he had departed with three years left on his contract, the *Chicago Daily News* asked: "DID KUHARICH JUMP? OR WAS HE PUSHED AT ND?"

Sports Illustrated stated it more bluntly: "Joe Kuharich resigned under pressure."

Kuharich's former players tend to disagree. So does Joe Doyle of the *South Bend Tribune*.

JOE DOYLE: "I think he left voluntarily. By 1962, Kuharich had lost control of the football team. In one game he sent in a player with a play. Daryl Lamonica waved his hand at the guy coming in, like 'Go, get outta here.' The player still came into the huddle, but Lamonica changed the call. When I talked to Lamonica later he said, 'Ah, we're not paying any attention him.'

"So by then I think Kuharich wanted to get the hell out of Notre Dame. I also don't think Notre Dame would have gotten rid of him before his contract was up. But when he said he was leaving, they might have had a few drinks in celebration."

FATHER JOYCE: "We were not unhappy about him leaving. And if he would have come to talk to me, I probably would have said, 'Yeah, I think it would be good for you to go.'

"But we didn't initiate any kind of push. I don't even remember giving him a little nudge, frankly."

STEVE KOLSKI: "You have to look at the timing. Kuharich didn't leave until just before spring practice. If they were gonna push him out, they would have done it much earlier. With Kuharich leaving in March, they got caught in a tight situation: Now who the hell's gonna coach in sixty-three?"

ED BURKE: "I don't know if he was forced out. But I think he was happy as hell to get out of college football. Are you aware of his connection to Pete Rozelle? Kuharich's publicity man at the University of San Francisco was Rozelle, and Kuharich got Rozelle his first NFL job with the Los Angeles Rams. Rozelle worked his way up to Rams' general manager. Then around 1960, when the NFL owners couldn't decide on their next commissioner, they finally went with Rozelle after many votes.

"In 1963, when Kuharich was terminated or left Notre Dame, there were no coaching jobs open in the NFL. So there was a job created for him by his buddy Rozelle. Kuharich was named supervisor of NFL referees. Just a couple years later, Kuharich was hired as coach of the Philadelphia Eagles. That was also influenced by Rozelle."

Kuharich lasted five years as coach and general manager of the Eagles. He was criticized there, too, for trading Sonny Jurgensen to the Redskins. In 1970, Kuharich was diagnosed as having bone cancer. Doctors said he had 30 months to live. But Kuharich, bullheaded as ever, fought off the disease 11 years. Kuharich died on a Sunday at age 63. His loyal friend Pete Rozelle delivered the eulogy at his funeral.

14

REQUIEM FOR THE IRISH
1 9 6 3

PETE DURANKO, THE RUGGED TACKLE FROM JOHNSTOWN, Pennsylvania, calls the 1963 season "the winter of our discontent." To Maglicic, the stocky, erudite linebacker from Cleveland, it was, "comedy, melodrama, chaos." Affable John Huarte remembers it as "nonsense. Pure disarray."

The quarterback from Anaheim should know. As a senior in 1964, Huarte would win the school's sixth Heisman Trophy. In 1963, Huarte didn't play enough to earn a school letter.

Much of the madness centered around Hugh Devore, the true-blue Golden Domer who played as a freshman for Rockne in 1930 and was acting head coach in 1945 when Leahy entered the navy.

After Kuharich left in March 1963, Devore served as interim coach a second time. Devore's players loved him, just as the 1945 squad had. But the game had passed him by in those 18 years. So why did Notre Dame appoint Devore?

FATHER JOYCE: "It was already spring. It was too late to get another coach. So we promoted Hughie, who was already coaching our freshmen. Hughie was also a great Notre Damer, adored by everybody. So we just brought him in as an interim.

"Unfortunately, as a coach, he was over the hill."

PETE DURANKO: "Hughie Devore wound up in a real tough spot. He still had Kuharich's assistants on his staff. And those guys weren't in the mood to back him up."

NORM NICOLA: "That's because they were hoping to be head coach themselves. Once they got passed over, they weren't about to make Hughie Devore look good.

"But Hughie didn't help himself much either. He had a lot of mood swings. Which were probably dictated by his drinking problem."

STEVE KOLSKI: "I played for Hughie when he was freshman coach. He was known to participate in beverage taking."

TOM MACDONALD: "I grew up in Southern California. I had a summer job back there with Mike Garrett, the USC running back who won the Heisman Trophy in 1965. Mike was a sophomore in 1963. He told me that next summer after they played us, 'You guys almost got one of our coaches fired. He scouted Notre Dame against Purdue. The next week, you guys played us. You had all new players and a whole new system.'

"I said, 'Yeah, that was us.' "

JOHN HUARTE: "Hughie wasn't too organized. But, God, we loved him. Remember Yogi Berra? One time someone asked him what time it was. Berra said, 'Right now?'

"Hughie was our Yogi Berra."

KEN MAGLICIC: "Instead of being 'cat-quick,' we had to be 'double-cat quick.' One day he said at practice, 'We have too many French poodles around here. What we need are some mad dogs.' "

JOHN HUARTE: "We're preparing for Michigan State at Michigan State. All week long I play first string at practice. So I go up there fully expecting to start.

"Right before the game, I'm sitting next to Sandy Bonvechio in our locker room. Sandy's our second or third string quarterback. Sandy is relaxing, peeling an orange, knowing I'm going to start.

"Then Hughie Devore rushes in and goes through the entire starting lineup. When he gets to quarterback, I'm waiting to hear 'John Huarte.' But I hear 'Sandy Bonvechio.'

"Sandy looks up and says, 'Who?' And I go, 'You.' And he goes, 'Jesus Christ.'

"Sandy gave me his orange and played the whole game. I never got on the field at Michigan State."

KEN MAGLICIC: "There were no headsets back then. If a head coach wanted to speak with his assistant coaches in the pressbox, there was a regular phone that sat on the bench.

"Well, one game Hughie got terribly frustrated because we were losing again. I was standing there with Nicola when Hughie picked up the phone to call the pressbox. But he had the receiver upside down. The speaking part of the phone was in his ear. He kept saying, 'Hello, hello?' But he couldn't get an answer. Hughie thought he'd been deserted. He threw down the phone and yelled, 'Those bastards left me!' "

Somehow after four weeks, Notre Dame had managed to be 2–2. *Sports Illustrated* ran a story before game five, wondering "whether Notre Dame can achieve enough success this season to keep Devore on the job."

But regardless, the story went on, "The prospects seem splendid that for the remainder of the season (Notre Dame) will not be pushed around by anybody."

Nice call. The Irish went 0–5 the rest of the season. And on November 9, at Notre Dame Stadium, Devore showed signs of cracking under the strain.

KEN MAGLICIC: "We were losing badly to Pittsburgh. Hughie got mad at the team because we looked so rotten. But instead of yelling at us, he ran out and started arguing with an official. Hughie ran right on the field. Bob Lehman, our captain, tried to pull him off. But Hughie wouldn't come off. The poor guy just lost it.

"That was the low point for me at Notre Dame. I was embarrassed as a football player. I was embarrassed for Hughie. I thought the administration should hang its head, too. I was angry at what they'd done to Notre Dame football.

"I knew after Pitt that Hughie had lost his job. But maybe Hughie knew it even before that. Maybe that's why he wouldn't come off the field. He wanted to go down swinging."

On November 22, 1963, 13 days after Notre Dame lost to Pittsburgh, a discordant year became catastrophic.

NORM NICOLA: "It was the Friday before the Iowa game. We were still in South Bend, doing a light workout. Someone from Notre Dame came out to practice. He told Hughie something. Hughie called the team together. He said, 'Someone has tried to assassinate President Kennedy. They don't know what the extent of his injuries are.'

"We all said a prayer. Hughie called off practice. When we got to our locker room, we found out that Kennedy was dead.

"There was immediately talk of canceling Saturday's game. But we went through the motions of flying to Iowa City. We stayed there Friday night. Mostly stayed in our hotel rooms. Saturday morning we found out the game was canceled. We flew back to South Bend . . . and went through the pain just like the rest of the country."

KEN MAGLICIC: "Traditionally, on Saturdays, there's a lot of activity in the Notre Dame dorms. But everyone was in shock. We were reading the articles. Watching the news reports. There was little talking. There were many masses.

"It was like a shadow came over Notre Dame. Kennedy was Catholic. Now we had our own leader. And he got put down. Shot down. I remember feeling: What is it about Catholics? What did we do wrong?"

Six days after the tragedy in Dallas, Notre Dame ended its season by playing Syracuse in Yankee Stadium. Minutes before the kickoff, Devore made his players smile through their remorse.

KEN MAGLICIC: "Hughie came from the same mold as Rockne: He would get real worked up in his pregame speeches. This time Hughie was talking about his son Joey. He said before he would ever let Notre Dame lose a game, he would take Joey out to midfield and stab him. In other words: I'd rather kill my kid than lose to Syracuse.

"And so while Hughie is getting more and more passionate, his dentures fly out of his mouth. But then

Hughie catches them. He catches them, sticks them back in, and doesn't miss a beat. We all ran outside laughing."

Against Syracuse, Maglicic recovered a fumble and made his 88th tackle. Tom MacDonald caught a TD pass and grabbed his school record 15th career interception. The Irish physically dominated the Orangemen. But in this season from deepest hell, Notre Dame lost anyway 14–7.

The team's final record was 2–7 and could well have been 2–8 had the Iowa game been played. The offense was atrocious. With their best quarterback Huarte rotting on the bench, the Irish completed just 54 passes all season.

KEN MAGLICIC: "The players had lost hope. We felt the administration was really not interested in the football program. We felt the Notre Dame spirit was done and gone. We had no idea Ara was coming."

15

A New Messiah

1 9 6 4

Ara Parseghian was born to be in football, but his mother needed convincing. She had wanted a girl and found football too violent. So her dark, handsome son would sneak out to sandlot games in Akron, Ohio, until his mother ran out to the field and yanked him back home.

At South Akron High School, Parseghian starred at running back while his mother stood under the stands and prayed he wouldn't get hurt. In 1947, he led Miami of Ohio to an undefeated record, which earned him a roster spot with the Cleveland Browns. Then, early in his second NFL season, a severely damaged hip destroyed his career.

Parseghian had once told his brother Jerry, "Anyone who would get into coaching is nuts." But with his playing days suddenly over, he took a job in 1950 as freshman coach back at Miami under Woody Hayes. After only a year, Hayes left for Ohio State and Parseghian replaced him at age 27. His five Miami teams went 39–6–1.

That gaudy record led him to Northwestern, the only private school in the Big Ten, where the struggling Wildcats had won just seven games in the past four seasons. In Parseghian's first year in Evanston, Northwestern finished 4–4–1. His eight-year mark was 36–35–1, including 4–0 against Notre Dame between 1959 and 1962. This hardly went unnoticed in South Bend, considering the Irish had vastly more talent.

Still, it is interesting to note: When Notre Dame hired its first great coach since Leahy, it was Parseghian who made the first move. He called Father Joyce and asked two questions. Did Notre Dame intend to retain Hughie Devore, and would they ever consider a non–Notre Dame alumnus as their head coach?

FATHER JOYCE: "Before Ara came in, we felt it was important to hire Notre Dame graduates because we wanted them to know what the university stood for. We wanted devoted sons of Notre Dame. And that is how things had been done since 1917. Beginning with Rockne, every coach had been a Notre Dame grad.

"But in 1964, we changed our policy dramatically. Because there weren't any Notre Dame graduates who had proven themselves as coaches in big-time football. So in our minds, we had no choice but to change.

"Of course, it also helped that Ara was calling. He had beaten us four years in a row, and all four years he outcoached us. But we had a policy of not stealing coaches. So when he called and said he was leaving Northwestern, my heart leapt with joy. It was like a gift from heaven."

But what about Ara's religion? He was a French-Armenian Protestant.

FATHER JOYCE: "I don't even recall that being an issue. Not to me anyway. Most Notre Dame coaches are Catholic, but not all. Rockne wasn't Catholic, if you recall."

On December 3, 1963, the day Notre Dame hired Parseghian, Tony Carey was home in Chicago visiting his parents. Carey's father had gone to Notre Dame. His brother Tom played quarterback for Brennan.

But Carey was fed up. During the dismal season just ended, the hard-hitting cornerback had separated his shoulder and Notre Dame had finished 2–7.

TONY CAREY: "I was already going to be a junior. So I was thinking: Football might not work out here. But I'm gonna get my degree and go on with my life.

"Then one day over Christmas break, I was driving to a store to buy my mother a present. It was snowing lightly. I pulled into the parking lot and I heard on the radio that Notre Dame had hired Ara Parseghian. The next thing I remember, I'm standing outside on the hood of my car. I'm jumping up and down and yelling, 'THIS IS IT! WE'RE GONNA DO IT!' "

By the time Parseghian took the job, he had 75 collegiate wins. He had also learned his craft from three football legends: his college coach Sid Gillman, his NFL coach Paul Brown, and his Miami of Ohio boss Woody Hayes. Gillman was an innovative technician, Brown a fanatical organizer, Hayes a fiery leader whose teams played hard. All three worked like horses.

Whatever Parseghian culled, he supplemented with his own charisma. He came across as honest, principled, sincere. Yet he was also urgent and intense. "He communicates with his very pores," a friend once said.

Then there was his physical appeal. A former 190-

pound running back, Parseghian looked, at 41, as if he could still get out there and break tackles. But his most striking feature was his eyes.

TONY CAREY: "Very dark and piercing. Eyes that could inspire you. And also burn right through you when he was angry."

KEN MAGLICIC: "Ara's first team meeting was very memorable. He came right out and said no smoking and drinking. He laid out the rules. If those rules were broken, Ara said he wouldn't take any crap."

TONY CAREY: "We had a guy named Dave Pivec. He was the starting tight end the year before. He had great hands and he played in the pros for a while.

"But Pivec got into something at the Linebacker Bar. He ended up getting booted off the team."

KEN MAGLICIC: "With Kuharich and Devore, they had let most things go by the wayside. So we figured a couple of guys would try and test Ara. Pivec was one of those guys.

"You talk about shaking down the thunder? That shook down the thunder. Because there were other guys who got kicked out, but it was always by the administration. It was by Notre Dame. Now it's the coach taking charge. So we said, 'This guy is for real.' "

NORM NICOLA: "It was obvious in spring practice things had changed. Ara had every practice organized down to the minute. From 3:45 to 3:52, we might work on punt returns. From 3:52 to 3:59, we might work on short-yardage plays. Suddenly, we had a system we could count on. Suddenly we were prepared."

Future All-American Jim Lynch, one of the finest linebackers in Notre Dame history, was only a sophomore in 1964. But he fully realized what Ara's arrival meant.

JIM LYNCH: "You almost have to understand the time period. The country was still very rich in parochial schools. Notre Dame was still Mecca for most of those schools. So the feeder system was there. You still had tremendous athletes pouring into Notre Dame. But they weren't winning football games.

"So when Ara Parseghian came in, there was a little bit of thank God Almighty. Here comes the new Messiah."

During his first preseason, Parseghian made several key personnel moves. He switched Jack Snow from halfback to split end, where Snow made All-American and later All-Pro. He converted Duranko, a slow-but-punishing fullback, into a terrifying defensive tackle. Parseghian made Huarte, whose first two years had been wasted, the undisputed starting quarterback. Huarte threw for 2,062 yards, 16 touchdown passes, and won Notre Dame's sixth Heisman Trophy.

ARA PARSEGHIAN: "That was very dramatic. He went from being a non-monogram winner to being a Heisman winner.

"See, Huarte was a senior when I got there. But he had barely played. So he started to believe he wasn't any good. I wanted to dispel that. So I told John before our opener at Wisconsin, 'You're my quarterback. I don't care if you throw five interceptions in the first quarter. You're our best quarterback. You're better than any quarterback I've ever had.' "

JOHN HUARTE: "Yeah, I remember those words. And they were important to me."

At Madison, Huarte threw for 270 yards and two long touchdown passes to Snow. The defense held Wisconsin to a school-record –51 yards rushing. Unranked Notre Dame, which was coming off five straight nonwinning seasons, routed Wisconsin 31–7.

The next week the Irish returned to South Bend for their emotion-charged opener against Purdue.

ARA PARSEGHIAN: "The Friday night before Saturday's ball game, we wanted to get our players off the campus. Because we knew how much commotion there would be. So we started a new tradition. We began spending Friday nights at Moreau Seminary.

"It was a beautiful spot—directly across the lake from Notre Dame—and very few seminarians were living there. So every player and coach had his own room. The rooms were sort of austere, as you can imagine at a seminary. So it was a perfect place to concentrate.

"That first night we ever stayed there, I woke up in the morning and looked out the window. Out across the lake the ducks were quacking. The sun was coming up.

"It was very peaceful. But something also struck me at that moment: The magnitude of the job. The enormous responsibility I had undertaken. Which was being head football coach at Notre Dame."

Well-rested and well-supported by the seminarians, who had stamped BEAT PURDUE on each sheet of toilet paper, the Irish arose at Moreau on Saturday morning, attended mass together as a team, ate a hearty breakfast, and stomped the Boilermakers 34–15.

JOE DOYLE: "I became very close with Ara over the years. Three mornings a week, we would have coffee together at five A.M. But it was that first home game against Purdue when I first realized how tough he could be.

"Ara was calling all the plays from the sidelines. Notre Dame had first-and-goal at the Purdue one. Ara signaled a running play straight up the middle, but Huarte pitched out wide and the halfback scored. I was up in the press box, and I happened to have the binoculars fixed on Ara. He came off the bench and grabbed Huarte by the throat.

"I asked him later, 'You didn't like your quarterback changing that play?' Ara said, 'You're goddamn right. I told that son of a bitch if he ever waved off another play I sent in, he'll be looking for a scholarship somewhere else.'

"Ara had a temper. But he also had tremendous compassion. He was just a very emotional guy, and Notre Dame players have always responded to that."

As the pumped-up Irish kept beating their opponents, dozens of prominent writers flew into Chicago's O'Hare Airport, rented better cars than their editors wanted, wove their way through Windy City traffic, then sped east on Route 90, past Gary and Hammond, to suddenly revitalized South Bend. *Life*, *Newsweek*, even *The Saturday Evening Post* showed up. *Sports Illustrated* dispatched the great Dan Jenkins, whose article ("Wake Up the Echoes") was lively enough to land Huarte on *SI*'s cover. Parseghian, although reluctant, made the cover of *Time* three weeks later.

By Saturday, November 28, the Irish were 9–0 and ranked No. 1. With a victory at 6–3 USC, they could produce their first national title since 1949, their first undefeated season since 1953, and the most stunning turnaround in college football history.

Notre Dame led 17–0 at halftime. After USC scored to make it 17–7, the Irish apparently went up 24–7 on a fourth-quarter touchdown run from one yard out. But Irish tackle Bob Meeker was penalized for holding.

The points were nullified and Notre Dame failed to score. So the Irish still led with 1:33 left, but only 17–13. USC had fourth-and-eight at the Irish 15 when quarterback Craig Fertig looked for Rod Sherman over the middle. Sherman beat Tony Carey to the inside, caught the pass at the three, and scored the winning touchdown. At that dramatic instant—as Notre Dame lost 20–17—a *Life* photographer captured Parseghian in his raw anguish.

Kevin Hardy, the three-time All-American defensive tackle, is characteristically blunt as he relives that heartbreaking defeat.

KEVIN HARDY: "We got screwed. It was a home job. When we watched the game film afterward, it was horrid. That play where we scored, but they called Meeker for holding? Jack Snow was lined up at wide receiver. He took a step forward, and their cornerback stepped up and smashed him in the face.

"We kept running this back on our projector. So we can see the official throw his flag down. He's standing right near Snow, who is split wide to the right. So it looks like he's going to call unsportsmanlike conduct on the cornerback who hit Snow. He calls holding on Meeker. The *left* offensive tackle."

NORM NICOLA: "I have the tapes of the game. There is no doubt about it. We got hometowned. It wasn't one call, either. There was a series of them in the fourth quarter.

"In fact, I just read an article on that game. One of those anniversary stories? Well, their quarterback Craig

Fertig was talking about the ref who made that horse-shit holding call on Meeker. Fertig said, 'All I can say is thank God for Jack Springer.' That takes a lot of balls, doesn't it?''

ARA PARSEGHIAN: "I was out in Los Angeles ten years later. The TV guy who did their play-by-play was putting together a half hour show of that game. He went through and picked out all the key plays. So this guy says to me, 'Boy, you guys were screwed.' I said, 'It took you ten years to figure that out?' "

KEN MAGLICIC: "The guy who took it hardest was Tony Carey. He was covering Rod Sherman on their TD pass. We kidded him for years about that play, and Tony would always say it wasn't his man. Finally, twenty years later, he admitted it was.

'But Tony really had a great season for us. He led the nation that year with eight interceptions. And Tony was our hardest hitter. Tony, pound for pound, was the toughest football player I ever saw."

TONY CAREY: "Yes. I was terribly hard on myself. But sometimes good comes out of something bad. So let me tell you this story.

"Four years after this game, when I'm a lawyer, this Chicago policeman/bailiff looks at me during a recess from the courtroom. He says, 'Your case doesn't look good, does it, counselor?' I said, 'Nah, it doesn't." And I stick out my hand and I say, 'My name's Tony Carey.' His name was Peter O' Reilly or something like that. An Irish Chicago cop.

"So he stops in his tracks. He says, 'Tony Carey? Are you the guy that missed that pass to lose the Southern Cal game in sixty-four?'

"By now I'm used to this. So I go into my pocket and bring out some fives and tens. I tell him, 'Okay, how much did you blow on the game? I'll make it even.'

"He thought that was the funniest thing in the world. Now he's my best buddy. So I start explaining my case. I tell him I really believe my client is innocent. So he says, 'Let me see what I can do.'

"So he went to bat for me. He talked to the judge. My guy was still found guilty, but he got off on probation. Now, in my opinion, justice was done. But had I knocked down that pass, the poor guy would have ended up in jail. So out of bad came good."

KEN MAGLICIC: "Tony was crying his eyes out after that game. Everybody was. Because everyone knew exactly what it was. We were Cinderella minus one.

"Of course, since it was a road game, we also had our traveling team out there. So in our locker room, you had older priests and administrators. You had freshmen who were eighteen. And so from the age of sixty down to eighteen, the only sound you could hear was people crying. Some people cried loudly and some softly. But everybody shed tears.

"Ara also looked like he'd been crying. His eyes seemed wet, anyway. And Ara told everyone to gather around him. He said, 'I know what this game meant to you. I know what it meant to me. But your show of emotion here, your show of Notre Dame spirit, means more to me than winning this football game.'

"I was a senior. College football was over. But that was the greatest moment of my career. Because Ara taught me a lesson. It's not about wins and losses. It's not about houses or cars. It's about dignity. It's about how you live your life."

ARA PARSEGHIAN: "It was a shocking thing. You felt punched in the stomach. But they'd had a remarkable year and I didn't want that spoiled. Because even though we lost, and even though it hurt, 1964 was a huge season. Notre Dame hadn't been winners the past five years. Then in 1964, the same core group of players who went 2–7 came within a minute and some odd seconds of being undefeated national champions.

"So now the football program is turned around. There's new electricity. There's new confidence. Notre Dame is regaining its reputation. It's returning to greater days established by Rockne and Leahy."

16

❧

SHAKE DOWN THE THUNDER
1 9 6 5 – 1 9 6 6

WITH HUARTE GRADUATED, AND NO CLEAR-CUT REPLACEMENT, the Irish couldn't pass in 1965. Quarterback Bill Zloch, a converted split end and defensive back, attempted just 89 passes all season. Zloch completed only 36.

While finishing 7–2–1, the low point on offense came in a 12–3 home defeat to Michigan State. As Bubba Smith, George Webster, and friends stacked eight defenders up-front, they held the Irish to –12 yards rushing, 24 yards passing, and three first downs.

Being manhandled in South Bend was bad enough. But All-American halfback Nick Eddy says the Spartans added insult to defeat.

NICK EDDY: "The Michigan State game was ugly. They were pointing their fingers, hollering, spitting. They had players running right up to Ara Parseghian, getting into his face and cursing him out. And they did this at our house."

Parseghian doesn't recall being sworn at, but his offensive backfield coach Tom Pagna does. Pagna arrived with Ara from Northwestern. They coached 11 years together in South Bend.

TOM PAGNA: "Every football team has a personality. We were work-oriented. No starting pissing matches with our opponents. No strutting in the endzone. We believed in the old remark by Paul Brown. If you score a touchdown, act like you've been there before.

"Michigan State tried to intimidate you. They came running downfield on kickoffs like Kamikazees. They pounded on each other after they made tackles. They screamed at our sidelines: 'You Catholic mackerel snappers! You Catholic bastards!'

"Of course, Ara wasn't Catholic. But that wasn't the point. The point was to establish supremacy."

KEVIN HARDY: "I had back surgery that year, so I was on the sidelines. I heard two or three Michigan State guys say to Ara, 'Fuck you, man. We got your ass today.' "

"On third and nine, we were in jail," Parseghian told the *New York Times* after this pass-impaired season. In 1966, the passing game would hinge on Terry Hanratty.

At 6 feet 1 inch and 200 pounds, Hanratty looked like he could take a pounding. He'd shown a cannon arm during spring practice. He grew up in western Pennsylvania, the cradle of great quarterbacks such as Johnny Lujack, Johnny Unitas, Joe Namath, George Blanda, Dan Marino, Jim Kelly, and Joe Montana.

On the other hand, Hanratty was only an 18-year-old sophomore. And with freshmen ineligible during this era, Hanratty still hadn't taken a college snap.

Jim Seymour, another sophomore, won a starting position

at split end. Seymour came from just outside Detroit, grew up on Michigan football and planned on joining up. But Seymour's uncle the priest, Seymour's two aunts, who were nuns, and Ara Parseghian combined to change his mind.

Seymour, at 6 feet 4 inches and 205 pounds with the smooth strides of a sprinter, was bigger and faster than most defensive backs. He could also read a defense while running full-speed, a skill which many pro receivers can't master.

Seymour's background was affluent/suburban, Hanratty's poor/steel town. But in their college debuts, they each learned something important about one another.

TERRY HANRATTY: "Early in the game, we had a third and ten. I went back to pass and got hit as I threw. This thing just quacked and quacked its way downfield, but Seymour flew up in the air and caught it anyway. I thought: Holy Cow. This guy can make me look great."

JIM SEYMOUR: "I already knew Terry could throw. But he rifled in one pass the defensive back never saw. Well, every receiver loves a quarterback who gets the ball there fast. It's guys who float passes that get receivers killed."

In their auspicious first game, Hanratty passed for 304 yards and two touchdowns to Seymour, who also broke two school records with 13 receptions for 276 yards. Eddy ran back a kickoff for a 97-yard touchdown. Notre Dame won 26–14, bespeaking an end to its offensive problems.

The Irish were also loaded defensively, with returning All-Americans Hardy and Lynch and impending All-Americans Duranko, Alan Page, and Tom Schoen. Demanding and inspirational John Ray was considered the nation's foremost defensive coach.

The 1966 defense, subsequently, was one of college

football's all-time greatest. While shutting out six of ten teams, it allowed just 24 points all season.

But 158 miles away in East Lansing, there was another historic college defense. Though massive Bubba Smith drew most of the publicity and NFL scouts, the Spartans had three other players who actually hit harder: rover back George Webster, linebacker Charlie (Mad Dog) Thornhill, and safety Jess Phillips.

As the season progressed and Notre Dame and Michigan State emerged as powerhouses, the sports world couldn't wait for their November 19 showdown. By then Hanratty and Seymour had made the cover of *Time*, MSU coeds wore buttons reading KILL, BUBBA, KILL, the No. 1-ranked Irish were 8–0 and the No. 2-ranked Spartans 9–0.

JIM LYNCH: "We knew it would be a war. It was like when you were a kid and you got challenged by another kid who was just about your size. You knew you had to fight him, but you weren't real happy about it. That was Notre Dame and Michigan State. It was bone on bone."

Sophomore halfback Bob Gladieux gives his perspective.

BOB GLADIEUX: "It was Michigan State's final game. We only had one game left. So whoever won that day figured to win the national championship.

"But even without all that, Michigan State was still our biggest grudge match. They were bad-asses. They would hit the shit out of you."

Rocky Bleier started at halfback in 1966 and the following year succeeded Lynch as team captain. Bleier later served in Vietnam, where he was caught in a Viet Cong ambush while on patrol. Bleier got wounded twice—first by machine gun fire and then a grenade. After three leg operations, he won four Super Bowl rings with the Pittsburgh Steelers.

ROCKY BLEIER: "On the Friday before the game, we took the train from South Bend to East Lansing. I can remember seeing people holding signs. While we were still in Indiana, the signs said GO IRISH. As soon as we crossed the state line into Michigan, the signs said GO FUCK THE IRISH."

The next day's clash was billed as the Game of the Century. It was played, fittingly, under a slate-gray sky, in freezing temperatures, before 80,011 hearty fans in East Lansing. Another 33 million watched on television, which was the largest audience ever for a college football game.

What they witnessed was four interceptions, five fumbles, 16 punts, several key injuries, and savage hitting. When Notre Dame had the ball, the most lethal place of all was over the middle.

JIM SEYMOUR: "It was a running play. I wasn't paying attention and drifted into the middle. Mad Dog Thornhill drilled me. Knocked me right on my ass. Then he stood over me. He said, 'Don't ever come into my territory.' "

BOB GLADIEUX: "I got hit over the middle by Jess Phillips. I was in midair, reaching for a pass. It felt like getting hit with a sledgehammer. My right thigh had so much internal bleeding, it hemorrhaged to twice its size. The quadricep muscle looked like hamburger."

ROCKY BLEIER: "It was a pass play over the middle. I jumped up and caught it, and felt this searing hit in my lower back. It was from George Webster. He lacerated my kidney. After the game was over, I went into the urinal and passed blood."

Bleier and Seymour each stayed in the game. Gladieux couldn't walk, let alone play, but when he got hurt the game was nearly over and Gladieux had already scored the only Irish touchdown.

Hanratty wasn't as fortunate. He went down on Notre Dame's second possession.

TERRY HANRATTY: "Ara sent in a guy with a quarterback draw. Which I considered strange. Because we hadn't practiced that play in three or four weeks. And that was not like Ara. He was always very regimented.

"So I'm thinking: This is weird. But I'm also a sophomore, so what am I gonna do? So I take my five steps back and all I see is green jerseys. Charlie Thornhill hits me, stands me up. I look to my left and here comes Bubba Smith full steam ahead. Bubba plants me into the ground. Separates my shoulder.

"The first thing Ara says is, 'Why'd you call that draw?' I said, 'You called it.' He said, 'I called a *halfback* draw.' I said, 'Well, there's more bad news. There's something wrong with my shoulder.' "

Nick Eddy, the Heisman Trophy candidate, had never even played after reinjuring his own shoulder on Friday. Now with Eddy and Hanratty both sidelined—and All-American center George Goeddeke also lost early—Notre Dame trailed 10–0 in the second quarter. But the Irish didn't panic. They fought back to a 10–10 tie in the fourth quarter. Then, with two minutes left, the Game of the Century turned into the controversy that wouldn't die.

With fourth-and-four at their own 36, the Spartans' Duffy Daugherty played it safe. He punted rather than try for the first down.

Notre Dame took over at its 30, with two time-outs and 1:24 remaining. But as Bubba Smith and Charlie

Thornhill called the Irish "sissies," Parseghian called four straight running plays.

Nevertheless, that final running play was actually a gamble: It came on fourth-and-one at the Irish 39.

Coley O'Brien, Hanratty's replacement, got the first down. But when Parseghian finally called a pass with ten seconds left, Bubba Smith sacked O'Brien before he could even set up. The 285-pound Smith had beaten the 205-pound Tim Monty, the back-up center who replaced Goeddeke. Then, with Notre Dame looking at second-and-17, O'Brien ran into the line as time expired.

Final score: Notre Dame 10, Michigan State 10. But the jeering was only beginning.

TOM PAGNA: "As both teams are walking across the field to shake hands, this big son of a bitch is coming out of the stands. He says to Bubba Smith, 'Don't shake their hands. They played for a tie.' Bubba pulls back his hand and says, 'Yeah, man. They played for a tie.'

"The thought of not shaking hands never crossed their minds until this lummox started to incite it. I thought: What the hell? Didn't you see the game these teams just played?

"I mean, thirty-three of these guys were NFL draft picks. There were something like twenty-five All-Americans. Two great college football teams played their hearts out. But nobody cared about that. They just went after Ara."

JIM SEYMOUR: "Michigan State was in a prevent defense. So what happens if we pass and they pick it off and win it with a field goal? Then Ara gets crucified for doing that."

JIM LYNCH: "Let's just put the ball in the air and see what the hell happens? No. And I'll tell you what Ara

Parseghian was guilty of. He was guilty of being a very smart football coach."

ROCKY BLEIER: "All my game experiences up to that time, all my athletic contests, whether they be in the neighborhood, the backyard, in school . . . you always played to win. You played to win until the whistle blew.

"So I kept waiting for us to throw the ball. I kept wondering: Why are we doing this? What the hell is happening out here?

"I was very upset in the locker room. I went into the bathroom with tears in my eyes. That's when I started urinating blood."

BOB GLADIEUX: "I was thinking during the game: What are we doing running? We oughta be trying to get upfield.

"But then we're all sitting around the locker room with our heads down and tears in our eyes and bummed out and pissed and injured and bleeding and everything else, and Ara comes in and hollers, 'Get your heads up! You guys didn't lose that football game! You were behind 10–0 in foreign territory! You fought back and tied it! Nobody in this country knows who's number one now! Next week we play Southern California on national television! We can show the world we're number one!'

"You're still down after that. But now he's planted a seed. You're saying to yourself: Shit, he may be right."

Not according to Jim Murray, the brilliant and biting *Los Angeles Times* columnist. Murray's headline read: "TIS A PITY WHEN IRISH 'TIE ONE FOR THE GIPPER'." Murray wrote beneath it: "The Four Horsemen, indeed. The Four Rabbits! The Four Mice! 'Outlined against a blue-gray October sky, the Four Mice went into hiding again today . . .' May George Gipp never hear of it!"

Dan Jenkins wrote in his cover piece for *Sports Illustrated*: "Put the No. 1 team, Notre Dame, on its own 30-yard line with time for at least four passing plays to break the tie. A No. 1 team will try *something*, won't it, to stay that way?

"Notre Dame did not. It just let the air out of the ball. For reasons that it will rationalize as being more valid than they perhaps were under the immense circumstances, the Irish rode out the clock."

ROGER VALDISERRI: "I always liked Dan Jenkins. We've always been good friends and still are today. But that article took me by surprise. I considered it an unfair criticism—one which poor Ara hasn't lived down yet."

ARA PARSEGHIAN: "I have no remorse whatsoever about what took place on that sideline. I could have easily blown that game for those kids.

"We were on our 30-yard line. Our center had been replaced by a very small one. We were facing one of the top defensive teams for two years in a row. Our quarterback had missed his last six or seven passes. And one of those passes really bothered me. It was a short pass to Seymour. It was from here to there. But Coley threw it over Seymour's head.

"That was really the play that influenced me more than anything. Because I know Coley's a helluva passer. He brought us back to a 10–10 tie. But I also know he's a diabetic. And all of a sudden he's missing everything.

"So you have to think about your personnel. You have to look at field position. The other team's field goal kicker. Then you make your own decision.

"As for how many people are in the stands? How many viewers are watching on TV? You're gonna be influenced by that?"

The week after the game—reportedly to Dan Jenkins's delight—Notre Dame students burned 1,200 copies of *Sports Illustrated*. Then, on Saturday in Los Angeles, Notre Dame routed USC 51–0.

This time Coley O'Brien, who had not expected to play against Michigan State, and had gobbled orange juice and candy bars on the sideline, had the benefit of regulating his diet. He completed 21 of 31 passes for 255 yards. Seymour caught 11 balls for 150 yards and two TDs. Notre Dame's powerful defense posted its sixth shutout.

Parseghian held the game ball his players awarded him as the triumphant Irish left the Coliseum. On Monday in South Bend, it was announced at a campus pep rally that both wire services had voted Notre Dame No. 1 and Michigan State No. 2.

The crowd went haywire. Only three years after arriving, Parseghian had delivered the grand prize.

17

❦

TERRY, JOE, AND O.J.

1967–1968

AFTER NOTRE DAME WON ITS FIRST NATIONAL TITLE IN 17 years, priests on campus wore I LIKE ARA buttons. Jim Seymour, the voluble star receiver, had his own deejay gig on the campus radio station WSND. Even the annual spring Old-Timers game, which originated in 1929, was nationally televised by ABC-TV.

With greater fame came heightened expectations. In 1967, Notre Dame entered the season ranked No. 1 by *Sports Illustrated* and AP. But as Hanratty points out, "We lost Lynch, Duranko, Page, Nick Eddy, and several more All-Americans. In reality, we went from great to good."

After a 2–2 start, including a home loss to USC and O.J. Simpson, Notre Dame won six straight to finish 8–2 and ranked No. 5. In 1968, the expectations eased, but only slightly. The Irish entered their first game ranked No. 3.

They defeated Oklahoma 45–21, but lost 37–22 to Purdue the next week in South Bend. That was the basic pattern throughout the season. Notre Dame struggled on defense and rang up big numbers on offense.

On October 19, Hanratty became the school's all-time offensive leader during a 58–8 rout of Illinois. His 4,189 yards (passing and rushing) eclipsed the fabled George Gipp by 79. But only two weeks later, Hanratty's career at Notre Dame ended.

TERRY HANRATTY: "We were practicing in South Bend on a soggy overcast day. Well, at our practices the quarterbacks were live. When we led a sweep, we blocked. When we ran the ball, we got hit.

"I was running an option to the right. But somebody missed their block. A guy from the prep squad slipped in and took out my knee. Ara ran out and asked me if I could get up. I told him no. So they carried me off the field.

"It turned out I had torn ligaments. And the ligament I had torn was the medial collateral in my left knee. Now, do you know what happened at Alabama? The injustice Bear Bryant did to Joe Namath? Namath hurt his knee and Bryant kept him out a couple weeks. Then Bryant played Namath in the Orange Bowl. Bryant was doing the best thing for Bryant, and not necessarily the best thing for Namath. Well, Namath's knee never got better after that. Namath wore that brace the rest of his life.

"Ara could have done the same thing with me. With two easy games coming up, and then Southern Cal, Ara could have rested me for two weeks, put a big brace on my knee, and sent me out to play against USC. But Ara wouldn't allow that with my injury. He said, 'You have too good a pro career in front of you.'

"So they operated on me four days later. That ended my career at Notre Dame, but elongated it in the NFL.

"Did you know that's also how Theismann got his break? He took over at quarterback when I got injured. Hey, have you talked to Joe yet? Well, then you better give yourself plenty of time. Joe likes to run his mouth. He's got a bit of an ego. I'm not sure it could fit inside this room."

Hanratty says this smiling. Then he continues.

TERRY HANRATTY: "Actually, Joe needed to have a big ego. He was tiny when he got here. Joe looked like a bird who had just cracked his shell. This is definitely a guy who got better looking with age."

In 1967, when the 5 foot 11 inch, 148-pound Theismann announced he was leaving New Jersey for South Bend, a local paper ran a story headlined: "LITTLE JOE TO GET KILLED AT NOTRE DAME." Over the next several years, Theismann pumped enough iron to be a solid 200-pounder in the NFL.

Mike McCoy also recalls his early impressions of Theismann. An All-American defensive tackle, McCoy stood 6 feet 5 inches and weighed at least 275 pounds. He destroyed so many plays before they got started, he often found himself blocked by up to three men. Frequently one of those blockers would cut McCoy at his knees. This is the scourge of every tall defensive lineman. The Irish did it themselves to Bubba Smith.

MIKE MCCOY: "After a while I learned this little trick. While the guy was still down there, I'd grind his helmet into the ground with my knee. Then I'd stay there awhile and genuflect on his head. That would usually stop the cut-blocking.

"As for Theismann, he was a freshman when I was a sophomore. He was running the prep squad one day at spring practice. Well, I just buried him. I hit him as hard as I've probably hit anyone. And what did this kid weigh? About 155, 160? Well, not only did Theismann get up, he started mouthing off. I thought: Hmmm. Very interesting."

JOE THEISMANN: "They trounced me into the ground when I was a freshman. But they do it to everyone. A freshman football player at Notre Dame? You're the second lowest form of life. You're barely above an amoeba.

"As a sophomore, I was returning punts with Bob Gladieux. Hanratty was a Heisman Trophy candidate. Then Hanratty got hurt with three games left. I was nineteen years old. This skinny little shit. Now I'm the quarterback at Notre Dame.

"We played Pittsburgh and Georgia Tech. We had bigger and better football players. I just had to make sure the ship didn't run off course. And we won both weeks very easily.

"But then we played our last game against Southern Cal. They were defending national champs. They had O.J. Simpson as a senior. They were 9–0 and we were 7–2. Plus we gotta play them out on the coast. So this is the game that's gonna tell the tale.

"The first pass I threw was intercepted. Then, as I was walking toward the sideline, Ara started coming in my direction. But before he had a chance to say a word, I said, 'Don't worry about it. I'll get it back.' "

JIM SEYMOUR: "Not only was Theismann's first pass intercepted, USC ran it back for a touchdown. It was just a little square-out pattern to me. But Joe waited too long to throw the ball.

"I told him after the play: 'You might want to throw that out a little sooner.'

"Then, shit, Joe never looked back. He went on from there and played a great game."

After putting his team in a 7–0 hole, Theismann led touchdown drives of 86, 77, and 45 yards. Notre Dame led at halftime 21–7.

The Trojans rallied in the second half, primarily through the air, because Mike McCoy was doing a number on Simpson. After this game, in fact, he became known as the guy who shut down O.J.

MIKE McCOY: "Hate is too strong a word. But I never liked USC. I didn't like L.A. I didn't like their campus. I didn't like the arrogance of their players. I couldn't stand the galloping Trojan horse, especially when they brought him to South Bend. I mean, this thing defecated all over *our* field. Then they didn't clean it up. My goodness: Even the USC band was irritating.

"As for O.J. Simpson, he was gone if he broke through the line of scrimmage. But O.J. was never like a Walter Payton. Walter would hit you and stick you. And as great as Walter was at running the ball, he would also block.

"O.J. was just a runner. A great runner, obviously. But I never saw him block much. And he didn't fight too hard for extra yards. One or two good hits and the guy went down."

Simpson came into the Notre Dame game averaging 184 yards per outing. The Irish held him to a career-low 55.

So while Notre Dame wasn't thrilled with its 21–21 tie (or its final record of 7–2–1), it had just shut down the Heisman Trophy winner, found its own emerging star in Theismann, and damaged USC's chances of winning a second straight national championship.

18

RACE

IN EARLY SEPTEMBER 1968, AS NOTRE DAME STUDENTS RUSHED to their first day of classes, they were joined by five black freshman football players: Clarence Ellis, Tom Gatewood, Bob Minnix, Ernie Jackson and Herbert Hooten. By the standards of many other northern schools, adding five black new players would seem paltry. At Notre Dame in 1968, it represented progress.

Part of this story begins 15 years earlier, in December 1953, at Notre Dame's annual postseason football banquet. As sophomore tackle Wayne Edmonds received his varsity letter, he also made his mark on Notre Dame history. No black football player had ever monogrammed.

Edmonds grew up in western Pennsylvania, where his father worked in the coal mines. Edmonds had never experienced the South until Notre Dame played North Carolina his sophomore year. Upon the team's arrival at Chapel Hill, Edmonds worked out and ate dinner with his white teammates, but was not allowed to sleep at the same hotel. Edmonds spent the night at a bishop's residence.

WAYNE EDMONDS: "Dick Washington stayed there, too. He was our other black player in 1953. We were the first two blacks to play in a varsity football game for Notre Dame. Then Dick entered the army and I wound up playing three years.

"I was proud of what I did at Notre Dame. I knew the country was changing, and I felt black athletes were right there at the vanguard. But so many things that happened gave me mixed feelings.

"For example, we played at Miami. We had all our rooms booked at this brand-new hotel called the Fontainebleau. But in 1955, there were no blacks allowed on the beach properties. Notre Dame fought for it, and I stayed with my teammates. So that was positive. But then, after the game, one Miami player came up to shake my hand. I thought: Well, maybe this guy is sincere. And as I reached out to shake his hand, he said, 'Nice game, nigger.'"

In the midst of these racial epithets, there were also the stories in the papers, setting Edmonds apart as the "tan gridder," the "Negro slated to see gridiron action," and the player giving the Irish a "new look."

The racial climate had changed by 1966. Rosa Parks had refused to give up her bus seat. There had been dangerous Freedom Rides into the South. President Lyndon Johnson had signed the Civil Rights Act.

Yet at Notre Dame in 1966, there were only 60 blacks in a student population of six thousand. Among those one percent, Alan Page was Notre Dame's only black football player. This was one more black player than all-white Texas.

Terrence Moore recalls this era vividly. Moore, a sports columnist for the *Atlanta Constitution*, grew up in a large extended black family in South Bend.

TERRENCE MOORE: "But most of my relatives weren't Notre Dame fans. In fact, there were only four exceptions: My mother, my brother Dennis, my brother Daryl, and myself. We loved Notre Dame. My mother even dressed us in Notre Dame sweaters, just like Ara wore along the sidelines. After we watched their games on my aunt's TV, we'd play tackle football in her backyard. I would always be Terry Hanratty. Dennis would be Nick Eddy. Daryl would be Bob Gladiuex or Jim Seymour. We never even thought in terms of race. Our aunt lived a punt away from the Golden Dome. Notre Dame was our team.

"That's why I'll never forget the Notre Dame–Michigan State game. It was 1966. I was ten years old. My aunt's house was packed. But except for me, my mother, and my two brothers, everybody was cheering for Michigan State. It was the racial issue. Michigan State had a black quarterback. Most of its starting defense was made up of black guys. Notre Dame had Alan Page and that was it. So essentially, to my family, it was the white boys at Notre Dame against the black Michigan State team.

"That's the way it was when I grew up in South Bend. In the black community, Notre Dame was seen as a racist institution. And much of this came from the makeup of its sports teams. The long-time absence of blacks."

In 1966, Mike Oriard came to Notre Dame as a walk-on. He ended up a team captain, an All-American center and a Rhodes scholar nominee. He later wrote the 1982 book, *The End of Autumn*, a poignant reflection on his life in football. He is now an English professor at Oregon State.

MIKE ORIARD: "The irony of Notre Dame being slow to integrate was its extraordinarily progressive national image. Notre Dame was once the school of the little guy. It was the school of the ethnic minority. I'm talking about the Irish, the Italians, the Polish, the European immigrants, and so on. There were even some incidents during Rockne's time when Notre Dame was embattled by the Klan. And so by the mid-1920s, Notre Dame had acquired this national following. It had become the beacon for the non-WASP, the nonelite, the newly immigrated, the working-class.

"But there was a flip side to this. These second-generation immigrant groups have often been notoriously racist themselves. Take a look at the struggles in cities like Boston: the battles between the Irish and African Americans. These are very much a part of our nation's history. And I believe these larger social factors were also being felt at Notre Dame."

TERRENCE MOORE: "I'm not even sure I'd call it racism. But I do know race always matters. Race *is* an issue. So when you study Notre Dame, you have to look at the crowds who came to football games. You have to look at the alumni. In both cases, they were predominantly white. So maybe Notre Dame did not want to offend them by bringing in black players.

"Then you also have the fact that Notre Dame was generally successful. If you're winning football games without black players, then maybe it's not a high priority. And this is often how racism gets started. It isn't George Wallace, fire hoses, police dogs. It's usually more benign. Things fall through the cracks and then perpetuate.

"But I still think there is a real paradox here. During the fifties and sixties, Hesburgh was on all kinds of civil rights commissions. He worked with JFK and Lyndon Johnson. So on one hand, Hesburgh was big on race relations. On the other hand, Notre Dame was slow to integrate. It's really one of life's great mysteries."

FATHER HESBURGH: "I went on the U.S. Civil Rights Commission in 1957. I was sworn in at the White House by Eisenhower. From that time on, I was face-to-face with all the results of apartheid, lack of equal opportunity, and all the bad things going on in regard to race in America.

"I didn't come back home and forget all that. I was constantly pumping away at it. But it's not the kind of thing you cure overnight. Until 1965, there wasn't a single black cop in the FBI, or in the entire South. There were state laws keeping blacks out of southern colleges. In housing, administration, justice, employment, we were every bit as bad as South Africa. I mean, why did it take 200 years to get rid of slavery? Why did we go through World War II with 15 million guys in uniform, and without a single integrated unit? Why even as late as 1964, were there six million blacks who couldn't even register to vote?

"This was a tough, tough, deeply ingrained thing. And then something important happened in 1964. President Johnson put through the Civil Rights Act, which Kennedy wouldn't touch with a 10-foot pole, and it literally changed the face of America. And once those floodgates were open, things began moving faster everywhere. Including Notre Dame."

PROF. ROBERT BURNS: "That commission was a great education for him. It really opened his eyes. And he did send us a very stiff directive, telling us to hire black faculty members.

"But this was also a time when a Notre Dame faculty

member could still be fired for getting a divorce. The school had a very distinctive Catholic culture. And except for New Orleans and elsewhere in Louisiana, there were not many black Catholics. So when some black professors came to visit Notre Dame, they found the environment too foreign. So they would choose to go elsewhere."

ARA PARSEGHIAN: "I had some outstanding black players on my teams at Northwestern. And when I came to Notre Dame in 1964, we were recruiting black players from the beginning. But sometimes a kid would say, 'Well, where's the rest of the blacks? What kind of social life am I going to have here? Oh, you're a Catholic institution? Hey, where are the women?'

"We also had some problems with admissions. We'd find a black player whom we wanted—and who wanted us—and he would get turned down by the academics office. One time we had this kid, an excellent running back from Troy, Ohio. We had him all locked up. But then, at the last minute, they turned him down.

"Now, if I could avoid it, I didn't want him to play for a team on our schedule. So I called up Bo Schembechler at Michigan. Bo couldn't believe we couldn't get him in. I said, 'Boy, it's embarrassing, but we don't have any options.' So Bo took him up at Michigan. And this kid became a great player for them.

"Those were the kind of dilemmas we faced. Then one time Father Hesburgh asked me about it. It was a post-game party at my house in 1972. Father Hesburgh said, 'How come we don't have more blacks on our football team?' I said, 'Go to your admissions office. That's where you can find out. They'll tell you how many black kids we've had turned down.'

"So Father Hesburgh said, 'Well, let me work on that.'

By this time, I suppose, he was being criticized for not having enough minorities on campus. I'm sure that was a factor. And he started to open the door a little bit. Notre Dame became a bit more flexible.

"Then in 1973, one year after that conversation at my house, we wound up getting Ross Browner, Willie Fry, Luther Bradley, and Al Hunter. They helped us immediately. And we won the national championship that year.

CLARENCE ELLIS: "I arrived at Notre Dame in 1968. But I really wasn't that much into football. It was just a means to go to college, and there were only two colleges offering me full rides. That was Western Michigan and Notre Dame. I picked Notre Dame for its academics.

"Now, this was all a product of the late sixties. With the civil rights movement and all the social upheaval, Notre Dame was pushing to bring in more blacks. So in 1968, the football team brought in the five of us. That was considered a breakthrough. Up until 1968, there was usually one black player at a time.

"I grew up in Grand Rapids, Michigan. Notre Dame was only 130 miles away. But at first it was overwhelming. There were some people there who just weren't ready for us. My academic adviser, for example. The first time we ever met, he said, 'I don't understand why Notre Dame has to bring in all these niggers.'

"That was our last conversation. After that I found another counselor. He was a great individual. So I told him what happened with my other counselor. He said, 'This will be a transition for many people. It's unfortunate you had to sit through that.' "

BOB MINNIX: "I grew up in Spokane, Washington. In a city of about 185,000, there were maybe 2,000 blacks. So I was already used to being a small minority.

"What was harder to adjust to was the lifestyle. I came from a public school, and most of the kids at Notre Dame were preppies. They had nice clothes and nice stereo equipment. They could fly back home whenever they wanted. So that's what struck me the most: the snobbiness.

"As for racial incidents, I never had any. None of my fellow students—or my teammates—ever confronted me on any racial basis. And it wasn't because I shrunk into the background. I was very outspoken at Notre Dame. I had a secondary major in Black Studies. I was involved in the Black Student Union. I even had an afro.

"But you have to remember this, too. Notre Dame is a very conservative school, and that extends to its black athletes. So at Notre Dame, we might have seemed militant. But if you had enrolled us at Berkeley in 1968, we would have seemed more like Clarence Thomas."

19

INSIDE THE AMERICAN WHIRLWIND
1 9 6 9

ON JANUARY 20, 1969, RICHARD M. NIXON WAS SWORN INTO the White House. On April 3, United States combat deaths in Vietnam exceeded the 33,639 killed in Korea. On October 14, with Nixon still lying about our level of involvement, Rocky Bleier made his first return to Notre Dame.

Contrary to the legend, Bleier didn't come straight from Vietnam. After leaving Southeast Asia with bullet wounds in his left thigh, his right foot partially blown off by a grenade, and his pro career with Pittsburgh deeply in question, Bleier spent four months in an Army hospital in Kansas. The Army granted a leave one month into his stay, and as Bleier drove back to his native Appleton, Wisconsin, he stopped at South Bend to visit some friends.

MIKE MCCOY: "I remember when Rocky came back from Vietnam. He spoke at our pep rally before the USC game. He had crutches and half his foot was bandaged. It was in the old field house. When Rocky came out, the roar was deafening. It was very emotional. I'll never forget it."

ROCKY BLEIER: "I just went there to say hi to a few people, but I ran into this guy Colonel Stephens. He was associate athletic director under Moose Krause. But he used to be commander of Notre Dame's ROTC.

"I came out from seeing Moose and the Colonel said, 'Rocky, sit down. You know we're playing Southern Cal tomorrow. I'd like you to present the flag to the honor guard before the game.' I said that would be fine. Then he said, 'Would you also mind speaking tonight at the pep rally?' I said, 'Colonel, please don't ask me to do that. Thank you, but really, no.'

"The Colonel kept pushing. He went into this God and country and Notre Dame pitch. And so, in my mind's eye while the Colonel is talking, the American flag is slowly waving behind him. Softly in the background, Kate Smith is singing 'God Bless America.'

"Finally, I couldn't say no. But then I'm thinking: What am I gonna say? Southern Cal. Big game. And I'm not an orator.

"So we're up there at the rally on Friday night. There are four thousand students crunched shoulder to shoulder. The band comes marching in after snaking its way through the campus. There is this sea of humanity in front of you, all singing the Notre Dame fight song and shouting for Ara. 'ARA, ARA, ARA—WE LOVE YOU, ARA!'

"Finally Ara gets up and there is a hush. He gives this perfect little speech about beating Southern Cal, and I'm still wondering what I'm going to say.

"When Ara was done the team captain spoke. Then he introduced me as a former captain, coming back, after serving in that war.

"I said, 'It's been two years since I stood here before you as a team captain. Over that time, some good and bad things have happened to me. One of the good things is that I met a group of people much like yourself . . . with the same dreams and aspirations we all have when we are young. The bad thing is that, unfortunately, I had to leave some of those people on the battleground of Vietnam.'

"Then I got to thinking of some of those people. I started choking up. My stomach was in my throat. I said, 'What I would like to do is dedicate tomorrow's game in their honor and memory . . .'

"Then I started crying. And nobody said anything. Ara just came over and sat me down. There was a cheer, and the fight song started playing, and everybody dispersed at that moment in time. And I felt kind of bad, because I put a hush on their big game."

On Saturday afternoon, as Notre Dame and USC tied 14–14, sophomore safety Clarence Ellis put on a show. He saved the Irish from losing by breaking up four passes in the end zone.

BOB MINNIX: "Clarence was very visible that day. Not only did he play great, but he was black and fast. Normally, USC had all the fast black guys.

"That's why Clarence made such a dramatic impact. Up until he came in, Notre Dame's defensive backs were white, slow, and hard-hitting. But you have to catch the guy before you can punish him."

In 1968, Minnix admits he wasn't ready to start at half-back. But wide receiver Tom Gatewood, another black Notre Dame sophomore, was already emerging as a star.

Gatewood, unlike Ellis, wasn't fast. But he ran beautiful routes and had great hands. At 6 feet 2 inches and 208 pounds, he also ran through tackles like a halfback.

In 1969, as Gatewood and Theismann were getting to

know each other, Gatewood made 47 catches for 743 yards
and eight touchdowns. In 1970, his 77 receptions and 1,123
yards each set single-season Irish records. In 1971, Gatewood became Notre Dame's first black captain.

Here he recalls an unforgettable road trip.

TOM GATEWOOD: "It was November 1969. We were flying
to Atlanta to play Georgia Tech. So we arrive on Friday
and go to our hotel. Normally, at a hotel, we'd be prereg-
istered. Our hotel keys would be in envelopes with our
names on them. We'd get them and go to our rooms in
an orderly fashion.

"This time there's major confusion. No one under-
stands what's going on. Our team is in the lobby, but
we're not getting checked in. The problem is, this hotel
doesn't want us. We are being denied accommodations,
because we have three black players on our traveling
squad.

"This is 1969, which is not terribly long ago. This is
in Atlanta, this transition city. This emblem of the New
South.

"This was not the first time I experienced prejudice.
So what stands out in my mind is Ara Parseghian. I was
impressed how calmly—yet with contempt—Ara was able
to handle this situation. Staying very controlled, he let
these people know that he was vehement. Everyone on
our team was staying at that hotel."

ARA PARSEGHIAN: "See, something had happened when I
played for the Cleveland Browns. In 1949, the Browns
played against an all-star team in Houston. This new
Shamrock Hotel had just been built. It was an elegant
place. But our black players—Marion Motley, Horace Gil-
liam, and Bill Willis—couldn't stay in there with us.

"I was incensed, and it had an impact on me. It had

a big-time impact. Because the coaching staff in those days acquiesced.

"Two years later, I was head coach at Miami of Ohio. We took a train to Wichita to play Kansas. When we got to the hotel lobby, everybody was saying, 'Why the delay? What the hell's the wait?'

"Finally our athletic director walks up. He says, 'Ara, we got a little problem here. They won't take any blacks in this hotel.'

"It was 1951. I was twenty-seven. But I said, 'Either we all stay here or none of us stay. I don't know how you're gonna accommodate this. But you're athletic director. So it's your problem. And if we don't play the game, that's all right too.'

"So the standard was set in 1951. Then, at Notre Dame, I was backed up by Moose Krause. Moose was athletic director. He felt the same way I did. It's not gonna happen. We travel as a team."

TOM GATEWOOD: "Then we played Georgia Tech on Saturday night. There were three black faces in that stadium: the three black players who came with Notre Dame.

"While we were still in the tunnel, waiting to be introduced, their fans were jeering and pointing at our black guys. But not every slur was racial. We were Yankees from the North. We were Catholics traveling through the Bible Belt. So our white players had their own bones to pick.

"We went out and trounced them, but it still turned out to be a horrible night. The fans were throwing Coca-Cola bottles. They were throwing dead fish. You know those cards the fans bring to spell out words? Those things were whipping across the field like Frisbees.

"I scored a touchdown that night. So did Clarence Ellis. He intercepted a pass and ran it back for a long touchdown. Normally when a player scores a touchdown, he'll run all the way through the back of the end zone. He's jubilant, he's jumping up and down. But on the highlight films of the Georgia Tech game, you see Ellis barely run into the end zone. He steps two feet inside, and then he stops. Because the way this stadium was set up, the fans sat very close to the end line. Ellis didn't want to get anywhere near that crowd."

After rocking Georgia Tech with a 31–0 lead, Notre Dame won 38–20. On that Monday, with one remaining game left against Air Force, school officials made a shocking announcement. If the Irish defeated the Falcons, they would play in a bowl game.

The last time Notre Dame had appeared in a bowl game, it was January 1, 1925. Knute Rockne and his Four Horsemen took a train to Pasadena, where Notre Dame beat Stanford in the Rose Bowl. But Notre Dame's round-trip excursion took almost a month, as Rockne stopped in several cities to showcase his team and expand its national fan base. The following season, when Rockne and others pushed for another bowl game, the administration wouldn't budge. They said extending the season would interfere with academics.

This policy stood for 45 years, until 1969, when Notre Dame reversed it for three main reasons:

- The academic calendar had changed. Rather than final exams running into January, they were now complete by mid-December.

- Notre Dame wanted to use the bowl game proceeds to finance a scholarship program for minority students.

- Bowl games were growing in importance. Until as late as 1967, the Associated Press had been taking its final vote before the bowl games were played. Then, in 1968, final rankings were tabulated after the bowl games. This meant Notre Dame needed to join the twentieth century if it wanted to compete for national titles.

In its first bowl appearance in four decades, Notre Dame would meet Texas in the Cotton Bowl on January 1. The Irish, 8–1–1, arrived in Dallas ranked just No. 9. The Longhorns were 10–0 and No. 1.

MIKE ORIARD: "Supposedly, we didn't have a chance. Texas had more talent. We were playing in their backyard. Texas was going to kill us."

MIKE MCCOY: "Dallas was cold when we got there. Dallas had no trees. Dallas was where Kennedy was killed. Our attitude was: Let's not worry too much about seeing the sights. Let's just get to work."

BOB MINNIX: "Texas was still being coached by Darrell Royal. When we arrived in Dallas, someone asked him why Texas had no black players. Royal said that he had won without 'em, and that he would continue to win without 'em.

"I found that statement very interesting. Because Dallas had such a large black population, and because of the social consciousness of the time. I just didn't expect Royal to say that."

CLARENCE ELLIS: "We viewed Royal's quote as pretty outrageous. And all our guys—white and black—played Texas very tough. We led 17–14 in the fourth quarter, but they won 21–17 on their final drive.

"The only reason they won is that I got beat. Texas had this huge fourth-and-two at our ten. I was covering Cotton Spreyer. I didn't want him catching a pass in the end zone. So there was only one play I would give him. That was an out.

"Well, they threw an out. I missed it by two inches. They scored a few plays later and we lost. I swore coming off the field that I would get even with Texas."

MIKE ORIARD: "I was crying after that loss. Then LBJ walked into our locker room. The former President. But I didn't give a shit. I felt the locker room was our inner sanctum. He was just an intruder."

MIKE McCOY: "I felt the same way. We were incredibly sad and LBJ starts talking real loud. I said, 'Who let him in here? What is he doing here?' "

After narrowly defeating Notre Dame, Texas finished 11–0 and ranked No. 1. But the 1969 Longhorns have another legacy: They were college football's last all-white national champions.

As for Notre Dame, the heartbreaking loss in Dallas closed out a momentous decade. From the ennui under Kuharich, to the bedlam under Devore, to the astounding transformation under Parseghian, the sixties had been a long strange trip indeed.

PART IV

THE SEVENTIES

20

KENT STATE TO DALLAS

1 9 7 0

BY THE SPRING OF 1970, MARTIN LUTHER KING, JR., AND ROBert Kennedy had been murdered within a span of eight weeks. Chicago policemen had bludgeoned protestors with nightsticks a few miles away from the Democratic convention. San Francisco State had been shut down for three weeks, and Harvard students had taken over University Hall.

Even at Notre Dame, with no history of activism to speak of, there had been campus protests against the invasion of Cambodia, the recruitment of Notre Dame students by the CIA and Dow Chemical, an on-campus speech by right wing senator Strom Thurmond, and the still-meager number of blacks in Notre Dame's student body and faculty. But the greatest tremor was felt on May 4, 1970, when four students at Kent State were killed by National Guardsmen.

In the aftermath at Notre Dame, stunned and angry students boycotted classes. *The Scholastic*, the university's student magazine, dedicated that week's issue to "all those men and women who have died in Vietnam, Laos, and Cambodia; and to Allison Krause; Sandy Scheuer; Jeffrey Miller and William Schroeder, killed at Kent State College on Monday, May 4, while demonstrating so that the killing might stop."

MIKE ORIARD: "I grew up in the fifties, in a small town in the Northwest. I grew up thinking my country had never done a bad thing.

"So Kent State was a kind of an awakening for me. Not that I suddenly became radicalized. My experience, I think, was more typical of most students from that generation. Most of us never went through those dramatic swings, where we were lunatic anarchists in 1968, who became lunatic stockbrokers in 1996. Gradually, thoughtfully, we started taking a harder look at our country.

"After the Kent State massacre, my guess is that mainstream America did the same thing. Kent State was a galvanizing moment—the most explosive moment—because mainstream America began to realize: Something has gone horribly awry. American soldiers are killing American students."

BOB MINNIX: "I saw kids getting killed at Kent State. I saw people getting blown away on TV in Vietnam. I saw a prominent black man, Martin Luther King, get killed while trying to better things for everybody. But when I wanted to demonstrate and voice my concern, some people at Notre Dame would frown on that.

"So I used to get into it with them. I'd say, 'You went out and found the best and the brightest. Now you want us to pretend we don't have any questions?

Asking questions is how we became good students. Well, right now I have a *lot* of questions. And I'm not hearing any good answers on why I should not be allowed to demonstrate.'

"In the spring of 1970, about seven football players, white and black, actually went to Ara and asked if we could skip a day of spring practice. We wanted to participate in a moratorium march against Vietnam. Ara didn't get into the politics of it. But he warned us not to miss practice.

"About half of us went anyway, and half the guys got cold feet. It was a peaceful demonstration. We marched, we sang, we went home. Ara called us in the next day. He wasn't happy. But instead of taking our scholarships away, or running us until we dropped, he made us pick up paper at Notre Dame Stadium. For one Saturday, we had to help the maintenance guys clean up.

"That was the end of it. So to me it wasn't political at all. Ara was just showing us who was boss."

ARA PARSEGHIAN: "I don't recall that specific event with Minnix. But geez, there were a lot of things happening from 1964 to 1974. We coached through the Vietnam years, the hippie years, the dissenting years. And I tried to move with the times. Nobody really respects a dictator.

"So I would tell the players: 'You're here at Notre Dame to get an education. So you better go to class. That's number one.

" 'Number two, if you're gonna be a part of our football program, you're gonna come to our practice sessions. Then if you want to demonstrate, that's your decision.'

"Above all, I tried to be fair and consistent. Whether a guy was a star player or he was a prep team player, he got the same discipline. Because when you show favoritism, you're really not a leader. And college kids see right through that."

DR. NICHOLAS JOHNS: "Ara and I spent a lot of time together. His daughter Karen had M.S., and he was head of the M.S. Society. Any time any new research would come out, we would evaluate it together. We were very close.

"We also argued like hell. One thing we argued about was politics. One time, we were on vacation in Acapulco. We were playing golf. Ara said that Nixon had raised the money to help get George McGovern nominated. I said, 'Ara! This is America! That can't happen! God Almighty!'

"And we argued like hell through eighteen holes. Well, later on, with Watergate, I called Ara and said, 'I want to apologize to you. You were right about that guy.'

"So the truth is, Ara was a liberal. But he always knew what the hell he was talking about."

On the field in 1970, Theismann and Gatewood led Notre Dame to an eye-popping 510 yards per game. Clarence Ellis anchored a defense that allowed only 108 points all season.

The Irish were 9–0 and ranked No. 4 going into the regular season finale at Southern Cal. At 5–4–1, John McKay's Trojans were having a rare off year. But in a stunning repeat of 1964, USC wrecked a perfect Irish season.

BOB MINNIX: "We had a Heisman Trophy candidate in Theismann. We had a veteran team. For once, we had more talent than USC. But we just came out flat. They came out fired-up and knocked our socks off."

CLARENCE ELLIS: "USC won 38–28. But it wasn't even that close. They were winning at one point, 38–14. Then Theismann got hot and we scored two late touchdowns. But USC was already playing its scrubs. Everyone and their Mama was playing by then.

"To be honest with you, I really think we dreaded going out there. I remember when I was still a freshman, and I first saw Southern Cal run out on the field. These were the biggest people I'd ever seen. They looked like an NFL team. Their fullback Sam Cunningham was bigger than some of our linemen. I think USC had us psyched out."

After dropping to 9–1, the No. 6-ranked Irish prepared for their second straight Cotton Bowl showdown with No. 1-ranked Texas. Greg Marx, a defensive tackle who would later become a consensus All-American, recalls that month of practice before the Cotton Bowl.

GREG MARX: "Our defense had been dominating people. Then suddenly USC scored 38 points. So for that entire December, we felt humiliated and embarrassed.

"We also knew how strong Texas was. They'd won thirty straight games. They were defending national champs. Their wishbone was killing people. When Texas had the ball, it looked like a track meet.

"Plus we all remembered what happened the season before. Texas beat us 21–17. And their fullback Steve Worster had a huge game. He gained over 150 yards. Not many players have done that to Notre Dame.

"So going into the rematch, our defense had a plan.

We would punish Steve Worster. I mean, we wanted to do some damage."

Backing up Marx at tackle was Pete Schivarelli. Described by Mike McCoy as "the real Rudy," he played his high school football in Chicago. He even received some college scholarship offers, but since none came from his beloved Notre Dame, he put off going to college and opened a hot dog stand. Four years later, with enough money stashed to pay for his own education, Schivarelli arrived on campus as a 22-year-old freshman.

MIKE McCoy: "I think I was the first guy ever to talk to him. And here's this very Italian guy dressed in black shoes, black socks, black pants, black shirt, and his hair greased back like John Travolta. I mean, who is this guy? And what is he doing here at Notre Dame?

"But everybody loved him. Then Pete made the team as a walk-on. Well, nobody ever worked harder during practice. We'd be saying, 'Man, they're killing us.' He'd be saying, 'No, this is great! I love it! Oh boy!'"

Schivarelli is now the manager for the rock band Chicago. But he is still a diehard Golden Domer.

PETE SCHIVARELLI: "We were extremely pumped-up for that Cotton Bowl. I mean, Texas was No. 1. But we knew we could beat them.

"Before we left for the game, we got word from our alumni in Dallas that the Cowboys were playing the Lions in the NFL playoffs. They were playing at the Cotton Bowl on the same day we were arriving. So our alumni in Texas had tickets lined up for us. They also said they'd introduce us to the Cowboys.

"We got off the plane in Dallas. We checked into our hotel. We were all excited about the Cowboys game. But

Ara called this meeting right away. He said, 'We didn't come here to see a football game. We came to play one.'

"So we did end up at the Cotton Bowl. But we went after the Cowboys already played. We went in full uniform. They turned on the lights for us. Ara had us scrimmaging full-speed. This was our first night in Dallas. But Ara was setting the tone."

Evidently, it worked. Before 73,000 fans at the Cotton Bowl, No. 6-ranked Notre Dame shocked No. 1-ranked Texas 24–11. Steve Worster finished the day with 42 yards rushing, four fumbles, and one broken nose.

PETE SCHIVARELLI: "This guy Worster came in as everybody's All American. But our defensive tackles were Greg Marx and Mike Kadish. They weighed 500 pounds. Every single time Texas ran its option, Marx and Kadish hit Worster. Even if Worster didn't have the ball."

CLARENCE ELLIS: "Worster was all bloody. He looked like he'd been in a boxing match. By early in the third quarter, that boy did not want that football. I actually felt sorry for the guy."

To Ellis, who blamed himself for the 21–17 loss to Texas one year earlier, the game was especially sweet. Ellis won defensive MVP and even played some split end when Gatewood got injured. So terrified was Texas of his speed that their defensive backs played 10 yards off him. Yet Ellis still caught a pass for 37 yards.

After snapping Texas's 30-game winning streak, Notre Dame wound up ranked No. 2. Theismann, who left South Bend with a school record of 5,479 total yards, finished second in the Heisman Trophy voting.

But for all the good feelings enveloping South Bend,

it was impossible to ignore top-ranked Nebraska's final record: 11–0–1. This meant 10–1 Notre Dame had lost more than its perfect record at Southern California. The Irish had surrendered a national championship.

21

BOWL GAME MADNESS

1 9 7 1 — 1 9 7 2

IN THE 1971 PRESEASON, ALMOST EVERY FOOTBALL POLL IN THE country placed the Irish among the nation's top five teams. Notre Dame, after all, had 16 starters back from a 10–1 team that won the Cotton Bowl. The only mystery was at quarterback, where the program had gotten spoiled by Huarte, Hanratty, and most recently Theismann. Still, after Notre Dame crushed Northwestern 51–7 in the season opener, *Sports Illustrated* headlined its story: "A CHEERLEADER COULD RUN THE TEAM."

SI was correct, but only to a point. The Irish could win games with the quarterbacks they had: Pat Steenberge, Bill Etter, and Notre Dame's first black quarterback, Cliff Brown. But they couldn't win them all. Notre Dame finished 8–2, including losses to USC and LSU.

In late November, the Irish were still 8–1 when the Gator Bowl invited them to play Penn State. But to the surprise of fans, alumni, and Ara Parseghian, Notre Dame's players voted to turn down the bid.

Tight end Dave Casper and kicker Bob Thomas, two future stars who were then sophomores, recall their opposite viewpoints.

BOB THOMAS: "I was thinking: What's the decision here? I wanted to play. I felt it was an honor. I didn't even see why there was a controversy."

DAVE CASPER: "I voted against it. I considered us a very average team. I mean, we played four quarterbacks that year. I was about the fastest guy on our offense, and that's not all that fast. We were lucky to go 8–2. We only won that much because we were well-coached."

BOB MINNIX: "That was my senior year, and I was very much involved in us not going. One, we weren't playing for a national championship. Two, we'd be playing in Jacksonville, Florida. Why waste Christmas with our families for that? Three, I was seriously unsure whether the money that Notre Dame was making on bowls was really being used for minority scholarships. In my last three years there, I didn't see any significant increase in black enrollment. I didn't see much increase in the Black Studies program, either. So I added it all up and said it's not worth it."

CLARENCE ELLIS: "I voted against it, too. But I don't recall race playing any part at all. I felt the biggest factor was our seniors. There were eight of us on our way to the NFL. Three of us would get drafted in the first round.

"So we were thinking NFL. We were getting big heads. We thought: Everyone else will have fun down in Florida. The band, the coaches, the administration. But the players will be stuck doing all the hard work."

ARA PARSEGHIAN: "I think they voted no twice. And particularly after the second vote, I wasn't going to try and influence them. It wasn't complicated. I told Father Joyce: 'I don't want to coach a team that doesn't want to go a bowl game.'

"It was that pure and simple. You know the old saying about leading a horse to water? Well, you can take them to the bowl game. But it doesn't mean they're gonna play."

The Saturday after the vote, Notre Dame's season ended with a 28–8 loss at LSU. That embarrassing defeat, on national television, was made even grimmer by the hostile atmosphere in Baton Rouge. Two outstanding sophomores, punter Brian Doherty and safety Mike Townsend, recall that southern road trip

BRIAN DOHERTY: "It started when our bus pulled up to the hotel. Someone had written in soap on every window: GO TO HELL, NOTRE DAME. Then we go inside the hotel. The guy behind the desk takes a tray full of keys and flings them onto the floor. Then he turns and walks away.

"Now it's Saturday night. We take these two big Greyhound busses to Tiger Stadium. We can see all these bonfires burning outside. Now the LSU fans start rocking our busses. Our bus driver won't keep moving. So Ara tells him, 'Get going. You keep these busses moving. Or I'm letting my players out to deal with this crowd.'

"I'm sitting there thinking: Who is he talking about? The punters or the linemen? I'm not moving an inch without the linemen.

"Then we get in the stadium. You know that Bengal tiger they have at LSU? They put the microphone in the tiger's mouth. Then they hit him in the groin with a cattle prod. That thing lets out a roar you wouldn't believe.

"Finally, we leave our locker room. We're going to play the game. We open the door and see the tiger. He's inside his cage. Devouring some meat. Blood is all over his face. We literally have to tiptoe around his cage."

MIKE TOWNSEND: "We got treated like trash basically. Their fans were pelting us with beer bottles. They were throwing anything hard they could find. And the referees weren't *acknowledging* this fact. They were pretending it wasn't going on."

BOB MINNIX: "Typical LSU fans. They'd been drinking since that morning. Then they'd finish a whiskey bottle and throw it. I clearly remember fearing for our safety. Just from the pitch of their voices, they seemed very capable of leaving the stands."

CLARENCE ELLIS: "It was the only time in my life that I got called a nigger almost every time I turned around. Their players, fans, it didn't make a difference. It was just something that rolled out of their mouths. It was my worst experience in college football."

Though it never became public, Townsend says the drama continued later that evening.

MIKE TOWNSEND: "It was our last game of the season. So our plane wasn't leaving until Sunday. There was no practice on Monday, no films to review. So some of our players checked out the local bars. At this one establishment, there was a fight.

"It started over a beer. One of our players was drinking down his last one, getting ready to hit the next club. Well, this local guy accused him of drinking *his* beer. One word led to another, and pretty soon it was a scuffle.

"There were only four Notre Dame players, and maybe fifteen of these local guys. But these local guys picked on a linebacker, a defensive end, and two defensive tackles. Well, our guys cleared out the bar.

"Ara gave us a scolding on that Sunday. He waited until we were flying back to South Bend. Then he talked to us like a father who had caught his son doing wrong. Ara said the police had called him late last night. He said, 'This will not happen again while I'm coaching at Notre Dame.' "

Parseghian recalls being upset over the loss. He calls it a lousy way to end a season. But he says he doesn't remember this event. "I'm not saying it didn't happen," Ara adds. "There were many incidents over the years."

Yes, there were. And according to Parseghian and others, a significant number of them featured Art Best.

Best was a wild child from Gahanna, Ohio. After picking Notre Dame over 50 other schools, he earned a reputation as a brawler, drinker, and magnet for young women. In this last respect, Best had perfect timing. When he arrived in 1972, Notre Dame went coed after 130 years of being all-male.

On the field, the brash young halfback had 9.7 speed. A solid 6 feet, 1 inch and 200 pounds, Best was also willing to run people over. In 1972, the first season since the Korean War that freshmen could play varsity athletics, Best ran 56 yards for a touchdown on his first college carry. Two games later he scored from 57 yards out.

ART BEST: "My first year at Notre Dame, my goal was to start on the junior varsity squad. But then I got moved up to varsity. Then right away I scored a few long touchdowns. After that, everyone knew me. That was both good and bad.

"The good was that Notre Dame let in three hundred women that year. But since there were eight thousand guys, the odds still weren't so great. So being well-known was helpful. It made it easier, basically, to get laid.

"The bad aspect of my notoriety was the fighting. I didn't learn to fight until I got to Notre Dame. I would spend a lot of time in town. Well, a lot of the townies were jealous of football players. So I learned very quickly to take guys out with one punch.

"Sometimes on the weekends I'd have a couple drinks. Or I'd smoke a cigarette. These were things that other guys were doing. But since I was famous for that kind of behavior, people would pick up the phone and call Ara Parseghian. I was in Ara's office quite often, in fact."

ARA PARSEGHIAN: "He's a piece of work all right. I spent more time counseling Art than I did my own son. I'd bring him in, talk to him, he'd be remorseful as hell. Next thing you know he'd be down in a bar getting drunk. So frankly, Art was difficult to coach. He got into trouble with me. He got into trouble with Devine. He also got into some trouble with the Bears. Art was a wild hair.

"But I'll tell you what was ironic. At our twenty-year reunion, the least likely person to organize it was Art Best. But he's the guy who pulled the thing together!

"So that was funnier than hell. And I told this to the guys when I stood up to speak. I said, 'The last guy we figured to organize this was Art Best. Well, it took twenty years. But all that stuff I poured in his head finally sunk in.' "

As the 1972 season began, Notre Dame had been hit hard by graduation. Ellis, Walt Patulski and Kadish were all first-round draft picks. Gatewood went in the fifth round to the New York Giants. Eight seniors in all joined the NFL.

For eight regular season victories, it didn't matter. But Notre Dame's two defeats were all-time shockers.

On October 21 in South Bend, the Irish lost 30–26 to 28-point underdog Missouri. On December 2 at Southern Cal, Notre Dame trailed the No. 1-ranked Trojans just 25–23 with five minutes left in the third quarter. Then USC scored 20 straight points and won in a 45–23 landslide. Anthony Davis not only scored six touchdowns, he kept mocking the Irish by dancing in the end zone on his knees.

The 11–0 Trojans ended their year at the Rose Bowl, where they routed Ohio State and won John McKay's third national championship. The 8-2 Irish landed at the Orange Bowl, where they received their third and final humiliation.

Part of this story is known. Notre Dame came in ranked No. 10. Nebraska (8–2–1) was one spot higher. The Irish defense keyed on Heisman Trophy winner Johnny Rodgers, but the dazzling little tailback still scored four touchdowns. Nebraska coach Bob Devaney, the tough Irishman with the winningest percentage in college football, retired after the game. Notre Dame got shellacked 40–6, in Parseghian's worst loss since coming to South Bend.

What has never been publicized is what two star players say happened the night before the Orange Bowl. One of them is Art Best. The other is Gerry DiNardo, who started three years at guard and earned All-American honors as a senior. DiNardo is now in his fourth year as head coach at LSU.

GERRY DINARDO: "This was 1972 and I was a sophomore. Now just three years before this, Notre Dame had first gone back to playing bowl games. But things had evolved very quickly. The first two years, guys were excited to play Texas. They were excited just to play in a bowl game. The next year it was already: 'The bowl games are only for coaches and their wives. They bring their families, we work our asses off, and the university keeps all the bowl-game money.'

"The result of that was the Gator Bowl controversy, when the Notre Dame players voted not to go. So now go back to 1972. We're invited to the Orange Bowl. But this time there is no vote. Ara just says, 'We'll find twenty-two guys and go.'

"So we went to Miami to play Nebraska. But all year long we'd had poor leadership. I hate to say this, but it was a bad group of seniors. And the night before the Orange Bowl, a good majority of the seniors were out in the ocean. I guess they had been drinking. They were out there having a party. Then we went out and got destroyed by Nebraska."

ART BEST: "I don't know about the seniors, but we were definitely partying. The Orange Bowl was played on New Year's Day. So the night before the game was New Year's Eve. Well, we had beers in our bathtub chilling on ice. We had girls in our hotel room. We were bouncing around in our underwear, just raising hell.

"The next night, against Nebraska, we had guys taking handfuls of aspirin before the game. Some guys were so hung over, they were doing white cross. Just so they could wake up.

"So we weren't in too good a shape to play that game. And Nebraska had a good team and they just whomped us."

ARA PARSEGHIAN: "Well, that's news to me. And I don't know if you're talking about two or three guys or twenty-two. But I suppose it could have happened. Some guys could have gone out. But if they did or not dissipate, I don't think it changed the outcome in any way. After coaching that game, after watching the film, it was evident that we weren't up to Nebraska's standard.

"You also had the fact that it was Devaney's last game. Devaney had turned Nebraska into a national power. He set the stage for Tom Osborne. So going into Devaney's last game, those kids were gonna win come hell or high water.

"So that's really what it was. We were outmatched. But after the game, I got our players together. We knew what just happened. We were all embarrassed. I still remember my statement. I said, "We will rise from these ashes.' "

GERRY DINARDO: "Ara was relentless after that. At every practice he worked the dog out of us. Ara did not back off for one entire year—until we beat Alabama to win the national title.

"So that was really when Notre Dame won its national championship: The night we got our ass kicked by Nebraska."

22

❧

"REACHING FOR THE STARS"
1 9 7 3

BY 1973, HIS TENTH YEAR AT NOTRE DAME, PARSEGHIAN WAS
widely considered to be one of college football's elite
coaches. He had turned around the moribund Irish program, winning the national championship in 1966 and
narrowly missing two others in 1964 and 1970. His nine-
year record in South Bend was 74–15–4.

Still, Parseghian's ledger showed a recent decline. In
both 1971 and 1972, Notre Dame had finished outside the
Top Ten. The last campaign in particular had been galling,
with its three stunning defeats to Missouri, USC, and
Nebraska.

In 1973, befitting a solid but not invincible program,
Notre Dame entered the season ranked No. 8. But this
was a ballclub that might get interesting. DiNardo and
Frank Pomarico, two intense New Yorkers from the
same Catholic high school, were among college football's finest guards. Tight end Dave Casper could bury
a linebacker while run-blocking, then beat a safety deep

THE CHARISMATIC KNUTE ROCKNE TURNED NOTRE DAME INTO A
NATIONAL POWERHOUSE.

A BROODING, ECCENTRIC GENIUS, FRANK LEAHY LED THE IRISH
TO FOUR NATIONAL CHAMPIONSHIPS.

IN 1943, ANGELO BERTELLI JOINED THE MARINES AFTER PLAYING SIX GAMES. STILL, BERTELLI WON THE HEISMAN TROPHY.

FRANK TRIPUCKA WAS SO THRILLED TO PLAY FOR THE IRISH, HE DIDN'T MIND THE UNIVERSITY'S STRINGENT RULES.

IN 1953, WAYNE EDMONDS BECAME THE FIRST BLACK NOTRE DAME PLAYER TO MONOGRAM IN FOOTBALL.

JOHNNY LATTNER, A HEISMAN TROPHY WINNER, WAS ONE OF THE PROGRAM'S MOST POPULAR PLAYERS EVER.

PAUL HORNUNG WAS BEST KNOWN FOR HIS TALENT, BUT HE WAS ALSO A GRITTY COMPETITOR.

WHEN A YOUTHFUL TERRY BRENNAN REPLACED FRANK LEAHY,
SOME OF THE VETERAN PLAYERS RESISTED THE CHANGE.

IN THE THRILLING 1964 SEASON, ARA PARSEGHIAN RETURNED
NOTRE DAME TO NATIONAL PROMINENCE.

DURING HIS 35-YEAR REIGN AS PRESIDENT, FATHER HESBURGH RULED THE UNIVERSITY WITH A FIRM HAND.

FATHER JOYCE, THE SCHOOL'S VICE PRESIDENT, WAS LARGELY RESPONSIBLE FOR OVERSEEING ATHLETICS.

JOHN HUARTE DID NOT EARN A LETTER HIS JUNIOR YEAR. AS A SENIOR, HE WON THE HEISMAN TROPHY.

Notre Dame Photographic

JIM LYNCH CALLED THE NOTRE DAME–MICHIGAN STATE GAMES "BONE ON BONE."

Notre Dame Archives

WHEN SKINNY JOE THEISMANN CAME TO NOTRE DAME, HE SURPRISED HIS OWN TEAMMATES WITH HIS TOUGHNESS.

Notre Dame Photographic

TOM CLEMENTS WAS SUCH A GREAT ATHLETE, DEAN SMITH HAD RECRUITED HIM TO PLAY POINT GUARD AT NORTH CAROLINA.

Notre Dame Photographic

Notre Dame Photographic

BOB GOLIC ALWAYS PLAYED BEST DURING BIG GAMES. AGAINST MICHIGAN ONE YEAR, HE MADE 26 TACKLES.

Notre Dame Photographic

DESPITE HIS ENORMOUS TALENT, JOE MONTANA SAT ON THE BENCH FOR THE FIRST TWO GAMES OF HIS JUNIOR YEAR.

EVEN A NATIONAL CHAMPIONSHIP IN 1977 COULD NOT SATISFY
ALL OF DAN DEVINE'S DETRACTORS.

FEISTY LINEBACKER NED BOLCAR LED THE IRISH IN TACKLES IN
TWO DIFFERENT SEASONS.

FRANK STAMS WAS A TERRIFIC LINEBACKER, BUT THE FORMER
FULLBACK ALSO KNEW HOW TO BLOCK.

TAILBACK ALLEN PINKETT IS STILL THE
SCHOOL'S ALL-TIME LEADING RUSHER.

GERRY FAUST GETS A RIDE FROM HIS PLAYERS AFTER ONE OF HIS
MORE STIRRING VICTORIES.

LOU HOLTZ LED THE FIGHTING IRISH FOR 11 SUCCESSFUL AND
CONTROVERSIAL YEARS.

RON POWLUS WAS EXPECTED TO WIN TWO HEISMANS, BUT DID
THAT PRESSURE HINDER HIS PERFORMANCE?

FULLBACK MARC EDWARDS WAS ONE OF THE TEAM'S TOUGHEST
PLAYERS DURING THE 1990S.

THE LEPRECHAUN IS NOTRE DAME'S TEAM MASCOT.

THE BEAUTIFUL GOLDEN DOME CASTS ITS GLINT OVER THE CAMPUS.

NOTRE DAME STADIUM—THE HOUSE THAT ROCKNE BUILT— SITS UNDER THE STRIKING MURAL OF TOUCHDOWN JESUS.

ATHLETIC DIRECTOR MIKE WADSWORTH SAYS LOU HOLTZ LEFT
NOTRE DAME VOLUNTARILY. BUT SOME IRISH FAITHFUL STILL
WONDER.

on the next play. Quarterback Tom Clements was so smart, athletic, and preternaturally poised that Dean Smith had invited him to play point guard at North Carolina. Halfbacks Art Best and Eric Penick had 9.7 and 9.5 speed, respectively.

On defense, the Irish started three blue-chip freshmen: defensive ends Ross Browner and Willie Fry and strong safety Luther Bradley. Free safety Mike Townsend was coming off a school record 10-interception season. Mike Fanning and Steve Niehaus, 540 pounds of defensive tackle, would discourage teams from running inside.

With kicker Bob Thomas and punter Brad Doherty, the Irish had two of the nation's best specialty players. Thomas once hit 62 straight extra points, then the second longest streak in college football history. Doherty was a master at coffin corner punts, and at punting for maximum hang time and not merely distance. Doherty, in fact, personified the 1973 squad. He cared more about team achievements than personal statistics.

By October 27, Notre Dame was 5–0 and had outscored its opponents 168–20. So why were the Irish still mired at No. 8? The pollsters wanted to see how Notre Dame would fare against Southern Cal.

The tension built all week before the South Bend showdown. The No. 6-ranked Trojans were defending national champs. They were 5–0–1, with a 23-game undefeated streak. The Irish had not beaten them since 1966. Parseghian, for all his success, was only 2–5–2 against Notre Dame's most bitter rival.

There was also the Anthony Davis factor. A.D., as he liked to be called, had taken apart the Irish by scoring six touchdowns against them the previous season. He had also rubbed it in, by dancing on his knees on national television.

ART BEST: "Arrogant sons of bitches. That's the way I looked at USC's players. Their fans were not much different. They were arrogant SOBs with swimming pools."

FRANK POMARICO: "I never hated the guys from USC. But they clearly exemplified a different lifestyle. USC was Hollywood, the beach, that star-celebrity thing. Notre Dame was the Midwest. South Bend, Indiana. Shoveling snow. It was the furthest from glitter you could get."

MIKE TOWNSEND: "I'd never seen our student body so riled up. They had pictures of Anthony Davis doing his knee dance, and they taped them all over campus on the sidewalks. You'd be walking to class and all these kids would be stomping on Anthony Davis."

LUTHER BRADLEY: "On Friday afternoon, Southern Cal showed up. They were the only guys all season who walked through our campus. They strolled for an hour or so with their little red blazers on. They looked like they owned the place. That kind of pissed us off."

On Saturday afternoon, as the two teams limbered up before the game, the scene fairly reeked of glamour and tradition. In the longest and most prestigious intersectional rivalry in any collegiate sport, the 45th game would be played in the house that Rockne built. Towering above the northern goalposts, on the side of the 14-story Hesburgh Library, was the 132-foot-high mosaic of Christ. Since the mural, which was completed in 1964, depicted Christ with his arms extended upward, Notre Dame's students had dubbed it Touchdown Jesus. By 1973, it was already college football's most famous image.

After pregame warmups the players returned inside for pep talks and team prayers. When they came back out, Luther Bradley tried taking Lynn Swann's head off.

WILLIE FRY: "On USC's very first play, Pat Haden threw a short pass to Lynn Swann. Luther hit Swann so hard that his helmet flew off. Swann just stared at him, as if to say: 'You're a freshman. What do you think you're doing?' Luther shoved him back toward USC's huddle, as if to say: 'Why are you asking?'"

LUTHER BRADLEY: "Swann scared me more than anyone on their offense. Not Anthony Davis. Davis was pretty quick. He was a good utility back. But he wasn't a real tough guy. He wouldn't stick his nose into too much stuff. On occasion, he'd run out of bounds.

"Lynn Swann could beat you deep. He could catch a short pass and turn it into big yardage. Well, Swann was lined up on my side on USC's first snap. I could tell it was a screen play, and I knew I couldn't let Swann into the open field. So I just attacked the screen. I was going to get to him before the blockers came.

"It was one of those plays where everything worked out. I got a great angle on Swann. I gave him a great shot. I dislodged not just the football, but also his helmet. That got everyone pumped beyond belief."

However, the Irish led just 13–7 at halftime. Then, on their first offensive play of the third quarter, Penick swept left from the Notre Dame 15. As Pomarico and DiNardo wiped out their men, Penick raced for an 85-yard touchdown.

MIKE TOWNSEND: "That was the prettiest play I ever saw. Eric was running straight down our sideline, straight toward Touchdown Jesus, straight toward our student section. After all those years of trying to beat USC—all that time not getting what we wanted—it was like the gods looked down on us. And they said, 'This will be.'"

When it was all over, and the Irish had triumphed 23–14, John McKay left the field humming the Notre Dame Victory March. "There was nothing else to hum," said the white-haired Irishman with the wry sense of humor.

Notre Dame routed Navy, Pittsburgh, and Air Force the next three weeks. When the Irish destroyed Miami 44–0, their 10–0 record gave Parseghian his first perfect regular season. It was also the first in South Bend since Leahy went 10–0 in 1949.

That victory over Miami moved Notre Dame to third place nationally. Although Oklahoma was ranked second, the Sooners were on probation and couldn't appear in bowl games. This cleared the way for a classic Sugar Bowl.

FRANK POMARICO: "The scenario was perfect. Alabama was No. 1 and we were No. 3. So the winner would be the national champion. You also had the North against the South, the Catholics against the Baptists, Ara Parseghian against Bear Bryant. Plus you had these two rich football traditions, and this was the first time they had ever played."

LUTHER BRADLEY: "I was a nervous wreck before that game. I was still a freshman, and Alabama had all these guys I'd read about in high school.

"The afternoon of the game, it was time to go down and catch our bus. I got in the hotel elevator and Tom Clements was in there. I said, 'Tom, I'm really nervous. I've never felt like this before a game.' Tom said real calmly, 'Pressure is self-inflicted. Just go out and have fun and you'll be fine.'

"I just looked at him. I couldn't believe this guy was that relaxed."

In the thriller against Alabama, Clements threw only 12 passes and completed seven. But his seven completions went for 169 yards, and the final pass he threw was one of the biggest in Notre Dame history.

The Irish led 24–23 with 2:12 left. They also had the ball, but it wasn't exactly a comforting situation. Notre Dame had third-and-eight at its own two.

TOM CLEMENTS: "Then Bear Bryant called time-out and I went to the sideline. Ara gave me the play. He wanted a pass to Dave Casper.

"It was a great call in retrospect. We needed to get a first down. If we punted, Alabama had plenty of time to beat us.

"But when Ara first called it, I was surprised. A pass meant I would be dropping back into our end zone. I could slip and fall on the wet grass. Or Alabama could sack me. Either way, they get a safety and we lose. So I said, 'Ara, are you sure you want a pass?' Ara said, 'Yeah, I'm sure.' "

Clements faked a handoff before dropping back. An Alabama safety bit so hard that he ran right past Notre Dame's second tight end Robin Weber. So even though the first option was Casper, Clements showed no hesitation. He hit Weber for 35 yards and a monumental first down.

LUTHER BRADLEY: "See what I was telling you before? Tom Clements was cool as a cucumber. It's the most important pass of his career, and Clements hits his secondary receiver."

WILLIE FRY: "There was this wild roar from our sideline after that play. Then everybody hugged and kissed and embraced, because it had been a long season and we knew it was over."

By upsetting top-ranked Alabama 24–23, Notre Dame earned its sixth national title since the Associated Press began polling in 1936. Two of those championships were won by Parseghian.

In the postgame locker room, senior guard and captain Frank Pomarico huddled with his father, a New York City policeman who had traveled to New Orleans in the hopes and dreams of sharing this very moment.

FRANK POMARICO: "When I grew up in Brooklyn, my father put a weight bench in our basement. We would go down there at night and lift together. Because my father and I were reaching for the stars. We were trying to get me bigger. So I could one day play for Notre Dame.

"That's why it felt so great in our locker room that night at the Sugar Bowl. My father was in there with us. My grandfather was there. So was my little brother, who was only ten years old.

"We were not really doing the yelling and screaming. We were sitting back and watching it all happen. But we were very emotional. We wanted to hold that moment as long as we could."

23

❧

A LEGEND DEPARTS

1 9 7 4

IN JULY 1974, SIX MONTHS AFTER WINNING HIS SECOND national title, Ara Parseghian was vacationing in Florida when he received horrible news from back in South Bend. Six Notre players, while attending summer school, had been accused of having intercourse with the same 18-year-old woman in a third-floor room of the campus dormitory Stanford Hall.

From there the story blurred. The woman never filed a formal complaint, but she did call the police and say she was raped. The six players insisted no rape had taken place. They said the young woman had consented.

Regardless, the school suspended all six for one year. In the instant media frenzy, the New York *Daily News* shouted the headline: "SEX SCANDAL OUSTS SIX NOTRE DAME GRIDDERS." Without the heavy breathing, *Esquire*'s Roger Kahn devoted a part of his column to this shocking development at Notre Dame.

ARA PARSEGHIAN: "That was a very difficult time for me emotionally. I can remember pulling up to my driveway when I first got home from Florida. I already realized how serious this would be. I could see all the players and parents who'd be involved, the girl and her family, the civil authorities, the university administrators, the South Bend media, the national media.

"So I was just sitting there. I couldn't even go into the house. And from that moment forward, everything I saw happening came true. There's no question about it. It became overwhelming."

ROGER VALDISERRI: "Ara was also getting high blood pressure. He was having trouble sleeping at night.

"After eleven years, that's what the Notre Dame job does to you. It's the pressure from the outside and the pressure you put on yourself. Anybody sitting in that chair feels the weight of Notre Dame's past. They know what's been accomplished by Rockne and Leahy. That's a pretty tough assignment, I think."

TOM PAGNA: "At Notre Dame, you can't eke out a win. The public won't accept it. You have to win big. Look good doing it. Don't make it a contest. I mean, the public likes to bet. They like to bet on the spread. You know what I'm saying?"

JOHN UNDERWOOD: "Toward the end of Ara's career, he was just too intense. It was almost like all his nerve endings were exposed. You could walk up behind him and tap his shoulder, and he would jump three feet."

The preseason polls only heightened expectations. Despite the loss of six players to suspension, and Casper, Pomarico, Townsend, and Bob Thomas to graduation, Notre Dame entered the season ranked No. 2. Then, after two opening wins, the Irish got upset at home by unranked Purdue. The final score was 31–20, but the game was never close. Purdue led 24–0 in the first quarter.

On November 2, 6–1 Notre Dame played against Navy in Philadelphia. The year before in South Bend, the Midshipmen had been routed 44–7. This time they led 6–0 in the fourth quarter before finally losing 14–6.

It was late that evening, on the darkened flight back to South Bend, when Parseghian decided he wanted out.

ARA PARSEGHIAN: "It was a series of things. First there was the incident in the summer. Then one of our players got his eye poked out. Then another player lost his leg when his car exploded. Then three close friends of mine died within a short time. So you're going to hospitals. You're going to funerals. You're walking around and asking, 'What's gonna be next?'

"Then you also become a victim of your own success. We were 10–2 in 1974. Well, 10–2 under normal circumstances isn't bad. But when you measure it against the undefeated season in 1973, the national championship, you begin to feel like maybe you failed. And losing never gets any easier for you. The hurt and the agony are going to come.

"There was also this business of always having to win by a large margin. Then it happened again at Navy. We won the ball game, but it went down to the wire. Then, after the game, we were standing outside the stadium by our bus. I saw these two fans coming. I could see they'd had too much to drink. Normally, our managers would grab them. But this one guy ran up and grabbed me. Then he kissed me on the lips.

"Now you can imagine how I felt at that moment. I mean, boy, you could fry an egg on my neck. When I finally got home, my wife was sitting in our family room.

I threw down my overnight bag. I said, 'Who needs this? Enough!' "

At first, he told only two people the pressures he felt: his wife Katie and his brother Jerry. Then one day Parseghian called Father Hesburgh.

FATHER HESBURGH: "Ara said he was taking pills to get to sleep at night, and pills to wake up in the morning.

"I said, 'Ara, that's it. It's all over right now. I'm not interested in just Notre Dame football, I'm interested in you as a human being. I'm not saying this because I don't like you. I love you. I wish you could stay forever. But if that's where you are, and that's what it has brought you to, it's THE END. I'm not firing you. But I am telling you for your own good: Run. Drop it. Get out. You've got a wife and kids.' "

At this point, Parseghian says, he planned on resigning after Notre Dame's bowl game. But he had not ruled out a return to football. He told his wife he would take one full year off. Then he would see if he still had the itch.

The Irish followed the Navy game with routs over Pittsburgh and Air Force. This last victory, in South Bend, was Parseghian's 94th at Notre Dame. Only Rockne had more, with 105, and Rockne coached 13 years to Parseghian's 11.

On November 30, in the regular season finale at USC, the Irish led 24–0 with only 11 seconds before halftime. Then the Trojans scored the game's next 55 points. After USC won 55–24, *Sports Illustrated* called it "one of the most remarkable scoring blitzkreigs in college football history." In Notre Dame's own history, few defeats had ever been more shocking.

Two weeks later, on December 15, 1973, Parseghian

announced his resignation at a Sunday night press conference held in South Bend. "After 25 years as head coach I find myself physically exhausted and emotionally exhausted," he said. "I am not leaving Notre Dame at this time to take any other coaching position either on a college level or in the pro ranks. I just felt that I should get away from coaching for at least a year, after which I will review my coaching future."

Actually, Parseghian had no intention of announcing his plans so soon. He wanted to wait until the season ended, at which time he would inform his players and staff. But the day before his Sunday press conference, Sid Hartman of the *Minneapolis Tribune* gave Parseghian no choice but to go public.

Hartman wrote in his column: "It's a good bet that the Orange Bowl game against Alabama will be the last game Ara Parseghian coaches at Notre Dame." Hartman added that the Baltimore Colts were after Parseghian, and that Ara was also popular in Chicago. But he ended his item with: "It is also possible that Parseghian may quit coaching."

GERRY DiNARDO: "It was all over the news. I heard it on the radio in my car. I was very angry. I was really bitter. I couldn't believe he didn't tell us himself.

"But then Ara called a team meeting. He said, 'I didn't release this. This isn't the way I wanted you to find out.'"

ARA PARSEGHIAN: "Father Joyce and I had wrestled with this, and we had agreed to announce it after the bowl game. Then suddenly one night, I was out socially. When I got back home, my son came running up. He said, 'Dad, it's been on the radio that you're resigning.'

"This is late Saturday night. I'm in a state of shock.

How the hell did this get out? I mean, we had this thing planned.

"So I called Father Joyce on Sunday morning. He said, 'Yeah, it got out. It got out in Minnesota. From a writer by the name of Sid Hartman.'

"Well, Sid Hartman was a friend of Dan Devine's. Dan Devine released it to him. Because Devine was going to replace me at Notre Dame. But at the moment, he was still coaching the Green Bay Packers. Devine was on the hot seat. It looked like he might be dismissed. So he wanted to get this announced before the Packers dismissed him. That was a much better scenario for him obviously.

"So now I'm embarrassed as hell. I hadn't even sat down and told our squad. I hadn't told our assistants.

"It's sad that it happened like that. And so obviously this has rankled me over the years. That's why I don't have a great fondness for Dan Devine. He created more confusion. He made things even more difficult than they were. That was a very self-serving thing to do."

In its December 30 issue, *Time* magazine also reported that when Devine was hired by Notre Dame, "he was about to get his walking papers from the National Football League's Green Bay Packers."

In 1972, the story continued, Devine had taken the Pack to the playoffs, "but since then they have slumped badly, finishing this season with three straight defeats and a sagging 6–8 record."

In the emotional aftermath of Parseghian's resignation, rumors began circulating that he had been treated shabbily by Notre Dame. These rumors intensified when Devine was announced as coach just two days after Parseghian resigned.

The most stubborn rumor was this: Parseghian wanted one year away from coaching. While taking this time off, he wanted one of his assistants to replace him. Then, once his sabbatical ended, he wanted to coach at Notre Dame again.

What happened next, according to the speculation, when Parseghian told Notre Dame of his request?

Two theories dominated. The first was that Father Joyce simply said no. Parseghian then quit Notre Dame in disappointment.

The second was that Father Joyce told Parseghian to give it more thought. Parseghian returned in a week and said he felt the same way. Father Joyce said, "We just hired Dan Devine."

The principals respond.

FATHER JOYCE: "There is no validity to that whatsoever. Ara and I never talked about a leave of absence. But if he had wanted that, I would have loved it. I would've been very happy to make that arrangement."

FATHER HESBURGH: "Never discussed it. Not once."

ARA PARSEGHIAN: "No. Those stories are wrong. How could you possibly step aside for one year? What if Notre Dame won a national championship? What if they went undefeated? Then I walk in and tell the coach to step aside? Doesn't work. It's not the right thing to do. Anyone with common sense would tell you that.

"As for other coaching possibilities, I promised my wife I'd take one decent year off. But if I did come back, the next step would have been professional football. For one thing, I had many offers. And where else you gonna go from Notre Dame? You gonna go to another college? No way. You're gonna go to pro ball.

"Now let me tell you how this story might have got started. I *did* want to be replaced by one of my staff members. We had two or three guys who I felt could replace me. They had served with me for eleven years. They knew the alumni and recruiting. So that much, yes, I wanted. And I tried very hard to influence that decision.

"This is how it happened. When I met with Father Joyce to tell him I was resigning, I told him I wanted a staff member to replace me. Then I brought out this yellow legal pad. It had all my notes on why one of my coaches should replace me. But Father Joyce had some things to do. I had some things to do. So he said, 'Let's meet again in a week.'

"In the meantime, he called my wife Katie. He asked if I was serious about leaving. Katie told him I was. She said we had talked it over.

"So when we met one week later, he saw me taking out my legal pad again. Father Joyce said, 'Don't go any further. I've already got your replacement.'

"I was disappointed. I wanted one of my staff. But what are you gonna do? I didn't have the right to make this decision. So I tried to influence it. But I didn't win that one."

During this hectic December, Notre Dame had to prepare for its clash with Alabama in the Orange Bowl. The top-ranked Crimson Tide was 11–0. They desperately wanted revenge for the 24–23 Sugar Bowl loss to Notre Dame one year before, which killed Alabama's claim to the national title.

The Irish, 9–2 and ranked No. 8, came in seeking redemption for their embarrassing 55–24 loss at Southern Cal. Above all, says Ken MacAfee, they were hell-bent on winning Parseghian's last game.

MacAfee, a three-time All American, entered the College Football Hall of Fame in 1997. He is arguably the best tight end in the history of Notre Dame football.

KEN MACAFEE: "We went down to Florida a few days early. The coaches stayed low-key. They even had some meetings on the beach. But the seniors were getting tense. They kept saying, 'We're winning this one for Ara. We don't care what it takes.'

"The seniors got more emotional all week. The final practice we held, the coaches called off early. Guys hit each other so hard that fights were breaking out. Ara just said, 'That's it. We're ready to play.'"

On a balmy winter night in Miami, before 71,801 at the Orange Bowl, Notre Dame upset Alabama 13–11. The loss deprived the top-ranked Tide of a national championship. The Irish ended their season at 10–2 and ranked fourth, as Parseghian went out with another dramatic victory over a national power.

Parseghian, who made the College Football Hall of Fame in 1980, left Notre Dame with a 95–17–4 record. In 1964, he took over a woebegone program and returned it instantly to national prominence. Parseghian won two national championships. His 1973 team went 11–0, Notre Dame's first perfect year since 1949. There were victories in the Cotton, Sugar, and Orange bowls, all of them over No. 1-ranked teams.

But what would these triumphs mean if they were produced by a man with less integrity? Was winning really the essence of Ara Parseghian?

Tom Pagna, his longtime assistant, says no.

TOM PAGNA: "More important was his impact on his players. Look at the players he coached who are now thriving. Look at the players who learned that you can win without cheating. That's the greatest tribute to Ara Parseghian."

ARA PARSEGHIAN: "It's been a terrific relationship with Notre Dame. Our presence here in South Bend is testimony to that. By 'our,' I mean Tom Pagna, John Ray, Wally Moore, Joe Yonto, George Kelly, and me. We all coached together. We're all still a part of this community. I think that says how much we love Notre Dame, and love this area.

"I mean, here we are sitting in my office. What do you see when you look out that window? The Golden Dome. I really don't know what else there is to say."

24

THE NEW REGIME

1 9 7 5

On December 17, 1974, Dan Devine was introduced as the 23rd football coach of the Fighting Irish. Devine had lived in Green Bay with the legend of Vince Lombardi. Now he would contend with Rockne, Leahy, and most profoundly Parseghian.

Born in Augusta, Wisconsin, Devine played football and basketball at the University of Minnesota–Duluth. He started coaching in college at Michigan State. At age 28, he got his first head coaching job at Arizona State.

In Devine's three years in Tempe, the Sun Devils went 27–3–1 and delivered the school's first undefeated season. Devine moved to Missouri in 1958 and became a statewide icon by building a record of 93–37–7. In 1971, he left behind his fiefdom in Missouri to try to resurrect the ailing Packers. In only his second season, Devine led Green Bay to a 10–4 record and Central Division title. But when his third team slumped to 5–7–2, he became the target of fan abuse. One of Devine's six daughters was spat on.

His family received obscene phone calls. Insults were screamed at his wife in the stands at Lambeau Field.

By December 1974, Devine's NFL record was 25–27–4 and he was reportedly about to be fired when Notre Dame offered him a five-year contract. This was shocking news to some in South Bend. But Father Joyce and Devine had a history.

FATHER JOYCE: "I had talked to him before I hired Ara. In 1964, Devine had a great reputation at Arizona State and Missouri. He was a more outstanding coach, in college football eyes, than Ara was at the time. Devine was also a Catholic.

"So Devine and I had contacts. In fact, I would have hired him before I hired Ara. But Devine wasn't available. And we would not ask him to break his contract with Missouri."

Devine has a slightly different recollection. He says he was offered the job.

DAN DEVINE: "I spent one day at Notre Dame with Father Hesburgh and Father Joyce. They were obviously fantastic administrators, and the campus was beautiful. But my wife and I had a large family, and our kids were settled in school. Missouri had also treated me very well. So I didn't take the job. But when Father Joyce called me again some ten years later, I said, 'Father, this may be the shortest interview you've ever had.' "

FATHER JOYCE: "When Ara said he was leaving, I did move awfully fast to hire Devine. I didn't want the delay, because you start getting besieged by coaches from all over the country.

"But the biggest factor was Devine's record in college. I knew he wasn't successful in Green Bay, but I felt he had been treated very unfairly. So in looking at his outstanding college career, I felt he would fit right in with us at Notre Dame. And by gosh, he did. I'm very proud of what Dan Devine did here."

But as Father Joyce concedes, there were many who felt Devine was an awkward fit at best.

FATHER JOYCE: "Devine was never accepted by the rank-and-file subway alumni, the real alumni, our athletic director Moose Krause. Even his first Notre Dame team didn't like him. At one point, I got word from the chaplain. He said, 'These guys are liable to revolt. They just don't like Devine.'

"I don't understand it. It's one of the big mysteries of my life. Dan Devine's record here was excellent.

"But I suppose it had something to do with Dan's personality. Ara was so charismatic, so forceful. Devine was so laid-back, softspoken. And all of us here hated to lose Ara. So it was probably a reaction to that. They never accepted Devine because they wanted another Ara."

This was especially true in Devine's first year, when his team was mostly comprised of Parseghian holdovers. Parseghian's ex-players saw him as a straight shooter. They saw Devine as calculating. They saw Parseghian as a born public speaker. They saw Devine as a cure for insomnia. They saw Parseghian as a tactical wizard, but secure enough to let assistants do their jobs. They saw Devine as a figurehead, who relied on his assistants to bail him out.

Yet during the tumultuous Devine years, he was also well-respected by several prominent players such as Dave Duerson, Willie Fry, Dave Huffman, Vegas Ferguson, John Scully, and Jerome Heavens. So perhaps Randy Harvey put it best, in a story he wrote on Devine for the *Chicago Sun-Times*. Harvey compared Devine to "Richard Nixon when he was in the White House. It is hard to figure out how one man can evoke such conflicting emotional responses."

Even today, when asked about Devine, his former players seem to agree on only one thing. Dan Devine has guts. How else does a man take jobs in Green Bay and South Bend?

DAN DEVINE: "Well, I suppose I'll take that as a compliment. But to be honest about it, I never saw following Lombardi as a handicap. I never felt added pressure because I followed Ara. I knew there would be some disenchanted players. That's always the case when you follow a popular coach. But I was never aware of anybody giving less than 100 percent effort. That was pretty much the bottom line."

In Devine's first season, he and others have said that Notre Dame lacked talent. But the roster included the following freshman and sophomores: Ken MacAfee, Joe Montana, Dave Huffman, Ernie Hughes, Jim Browner, Ross Browner, Willie Fry, Luther Bradley, and Bob Golic.

What the Irish really lacked was experienced upperclassmen. Ten offensive starters had graduated, including senior quarterback Tom Clements.

The schedule makers didn't smile on Devine either. Notre Dame opened the year with a difficult five-day stint including a Monday night road game followed by a game Saturday in South Bend.

On September 15, the ninth-ranked Irish opened at unranked Boston College. Notre Dame won 17–3, but the offense sputtered and the score was tied 3–3 at halftime.

Even more memorable, according to some players, was what happened in the pregame locker room.

KEN MACAFEE: "It's Dan Devine's first game. We're about to play on national television. It's pretty tense in there. So Devine gathers us around. He says, 'This is the first play we're gonna run tonight.'

"Then he tells us the play and everyone looks at each other. Nobody knew what he meant. Nobody heard of the play. Because we didn't have it in our playbook."

JOE DOYLE: "Actually, that wasn't unusual. Devine's entire first season, he would send in plays from the playbook in Green Bay. The Notre Dame players would say, '*What?*' Then they'd have to call a time-out to find out what the hell he was talking about.

"See, the whole key with Dan was his assistants. As long as they were in charge, the teams played pretty well. But when he'd interfere, things could get strange."

In fairness to Devine, it should be noted that Doyle and MacAfee each had their battles with him. So we should also hear from center Dave Huffman, a two-time All American and well-liked team leader.

DAVE HUFFMAN: "Dan Devine won a national championship at Notre Dame. But he was never one of the boys. He was never considered a 'Notre Dame guy.' But to win one national championship in six seasons? If you look at what's happened at Notre Dame since then, I think that ratio is pretty good.

"Now, is that to say his first team had no divisions? You could try and hide things. You could say no. But absolutely, yes, there were divisions. Part of that was caused by Dan and Joe Montana. Boy, you want to talk about a relationship that to this very day everybody has tried to be calm and quiet about and not fan the flames? That was Joe Montana and Dan Devine."

ROGER VALDISERRI: "Inexplicable. That's how I'd character-ize their relationship. One time during spring practice, Joe came into our sports information office. Joe's wife, Kim, was working there for me. Joe was practically in tears. That's how frustrated he was. Because Joe couldn't even get on the practice field. Devine wouldn't give him any snaps.

"There was something about Joe that Dan didn't like. I don't know what it was. I don't think anyone did. But everyone knew it existed. It was obvious that Devine wasn't playing Montana when everyone else at Notre Dame thought he should be."

KEN MACAFEE: "It was an even bigger issue two years later. By then, Joe was a junior. But he was still on the bench our first two games. In that second game, we lost to Mis-sissippi. That's when things escalated.

"But even in seventy-five, people were talking about it. Joe would come into games and pull them out for us. Then Rick Slager would be starting again next week.

"I think Devine knew how to recognize talent. So I don't think it was that. I think he had something personal against Joe. And if Joe ever really talked about it, he'd say he felt toward Devine about the same way I did. Joe and I used to have our lockers together. Whenever Devine would give his pregame speech, Joe and I would just shake our heads and smile. Anything Devine said just didn't hit home."

Still, Devine wasn't the only coach Montana clashed with. Before his junior year at Ringgold High in Monon-gahela, Pennsylvania, his coach wanted him to join in a summer weight training program. Montana, who was a great all-around athlete, already had his heart set on playing summer basketball and American Legion baseball. So Montana didn't lift weights with the football team. When his junior year began, Montana's coach benched him.

About 15 years later, Montana had a beef with San Francisco 49ers coach Bill Walsh. In 1987, when Walsh pulled Montana for Steve Young in an NFC playoff game, Montana felt disrespected. In 1988, when Walsh gave Young three starts, Montana seethed again. Of course, Montana responded in typical fashion: He led San Francisco on a breathtaking 92-yard drive in the final moments of Super Bowl XXIII to beat the Cincinnati Bengals 20–16. In his NFL career, Montana ended up with four Super Bowl rings. Some experts consider him the greatest quarterback ever to play the game.

This brings us back to South Bend, Indiana. In 1974, Parseghian's last year, a still-skinny Montana spent his freshman year on the scout team. In 1975, Devine's inaugural season, Montana backed up Rick Slager as Notre Dame defeated Boston College and Purdue. The next week against Northwestern, Montana entered the game when Slager got injured in the first quarter. The Irish trailed 7–0 and ended up winning 31–7. Montana completed six of 11 passes for 80 yards, passed for one touchdown and ran for another.

Montana started the next week against Michigan State, but only threw five passes in a 10–3 defeat. Then, back on the bench against unranked North Carolina, he relieved a struggling Slager with Notre Dame down 14–6 and 5:11 to play. Montana threw for 129 yards and the Irish pulled out a 21–14 win.

The next week at practice, Montana was back taking snaps with the second team. When reporters demanded to know why he wasn't starting, Devine didn't want to promote a quarterback controversy. His spin was that Notre Dame was fortunate: It had two fine quarterbacks.

Today he's a bit more blunt.

DAN DEVINE: "The first time you ever looked at Joe Montana—I mean physically—you would have some questions. You would ask: 'Can this guy play?' Because until Joe Montana started lifting weights, he never really impressed you physically.

"I also had great professional respect for the coaching staff that preceded us. Well, if you look at what happened to him in 1974, he was last on the depth chart. He just apparently wasn't good enough to play.

"In 1975, Joe was listed fourth on the depth chart going into our game against Northwestern. But when Rick Slager got hurt, I didn't go with our number two or number three guy. I went with our number four guy. It was more a hunch than anything else. I just felt Joe gave us the best chance to win that game.

"I hope this doesn't sound egotistical, but I think I did a heck of a job coaching Joe. Early in his career, I handled him with a certain amount of discipline. Because Joe, as a sophomore, was not a very well-disciplined football player. Then, as time went on, I put more of my trust in him. And he was able to accept more responsibility."

KEN MACAFEE: "After Joe pulled out the North Carolina game, Devine went back to Rick Slager. There was a lot of unrest by then. So the night before we played at Air Force, I spoke with Moose Krause and Colonel Stephens at our hotel.

"I said some of our players weren't too enthusiastic about Dan Devine's presence at Notre Dame. They said I should tell this to some of the people above them. I said, 'Well, like who?' They said Father Joyce.

"I said, 'What exactly am I gonna tell him?' Colonel Stephens said, 'Just come with me.'

"The Colonel took me to Father Joyce's suite. He knocked on the door and said, 'Excuse me, Father. Kenny wants to say something to you.' Then the Colonel walked away.

"Here I am, a sophomore, standing in front of the vice president of Notre Dame. But we sat down and talked in his suite. I said, 'A lot of the players here are less than enthusiastic about Dan Devine. I don't think he's the type of coach that Notre Dame is looking for.'

"Father Joyce said, 'I was the one who chose him. Eleven years ago, it was between him and Ara Parseghian and we hired Ara. Now we have Devine, and I think we are fortunate to have him.'

"I said, 'Well, frankly, Father, I think you were wrong in your decision.'

"The next day we played Air Force. We were losing 30–10 in the fourth quarter. I said to myself: This is actually a good thing. We're getting killed by a terrible team. Everything I told Father Joyce yesterday is coming true.

"Now, to have those thoughts during a game just isn't right. But then Montana replaced Slager. We scored 21 points in the fourth quarter. I caught the TD pass that tied the game. We won 31–30. It was one of the better comebacks in Notre Dame history. But before Montana came in, we were being humiliated by Air Force."

Montana finally started the next two weeks. He struggled against USC and Notre Dame lost 24–17. He looked sharp in a 31–0 win over Navy, but a broken finger ended Montana's season.

Devine's own season ended in yet another squabble. With their record 7–3, the Irish players rejected a Cotton Bowl invitation. Since that 7–3 could easily have been 5–5 if not for Montana's heroics against Air Force and North Carolina, some players felt undeserving of a bowl game. Others had simply overdosed on Devine.

DAVE HUFFMAN: "By the time the news came out that Notre Dame wasn't going, we had beaten Miami to end the regular season. So then the official line was, at 8–3, we really aren't a bowl team.

"But before the Miami game, our players had held a meeting without the coaches. Our seniors basically said: 'We ain't playing no bowl game under this regime. Any questions or comments?' "

KEN MACAFEE: "We met in this little room in the ACC. Our captains Ed Bauer and Jim Stock wanted to go. They said the Cotton Bowl was a major bowl. They went through all the plusses. Then some of the seniors started saying, 'Bullshit. We're not playing another game for him.'

"Bauer wouldn't let up. He wanted to end his career by playing in a bowl game. But there were too many seniors saying no. So then a few guys stood up and things got heated.

"There were also a million rumors going around. One of them was that Ara would come back. So by turning down a bowl game, we felt by some magic dust that Ara might reappear and coach us again."

DAN DEVINE: "It was a long and demanding season on everyone. We played a tough schedule. We didn't have many good players. I mean, pro-caliber players. So that was my toughest year at Notre Dame. And that's why I didn't try to change their minds. If this team didn't want to play in a bowl game, then I didn't want to take them."

DAVE HUFFMAN: "Dan honored his team's decision. But in a private meeting somewhere, he was livid with rage. He said, 'No team will ever have this choice again! We will make these decisions from now on!'

"It was a traumatic season at Notre Dame. This was sort of an ugly ending to it."

25

❧

TURMOIL AND A TITLE
1 9 7 6 — 1 9 7 7

IN 1976, WITH MONTANA SIDELINED ALL YEAR WITH A SHOUL-
der separation, the Irish finished 8–3 for the second
straight regular season. This time around, though, Notre
Dame accepted a bowl bid without soliciting input from
its players. Not that it made any difference. A majority of
the Irish would have voted yes.

Why the change of heart? The players respected Penn
State, their Gator Bowl opponents, and felt a convincing
win could establish them as contenders for 1977. MacAfee
says they were also getting used to, if not exactly embrac-
ing, Dan Devine.

In the December 27 Gator Bowl, Notre Dame domi-
nated Penn State in the first half and built a 20–3 lead.
The Irish ended up winning 20–9, and Devine was 1–0 in
Notre Dame bowl games.

In September 1977, *Sports Illustrated* put "NOTRE
DAME'S PEERLESS ROSS BROWNER" on the cover of its college
football preview. The story inside picked the Irish as

No. 1, based on the return of 18 starters and four All-Americans (Browner, MacAfee, Fry, and Bradley.)

"Notre Dame should go undefeated," *SI* predicted. "Particularly since the Irish play a schedule that includes only two nationally ranked teams: Pittsburgh in the opener and USC on October 22."

Who would be throwing the ball for this powerhouse? "Junior Rusty Lisch steps in at quarterback for Rick Slager, who graduated."

Joe Montana wasn't even mentioned. Which actually made sense, since he began the season behind not only Lisch, but also Gary Forystek.

Lisch was a humdrum leader, an average passer, and one of the team's best athletes. Forystek had size and strength and a powerful arm. But he wasn't Joe Montana. So what was going on at Notre Dame?

Devine cites medical reasons, saying Montana wasn't given clearance to play until after the season was two games old.

KEN MACAFEE: "That was an excuse. Devine said Joe wasn't throwing well yet because his shoulder was bothering him. Devine used that for a while. Then Joe came out and said, 'No, my shoulder is fine.'

"Devine just wanted to play Rusty Lisch. That's all it really was."

In Montana's 1995 autobiography, *Montana*, he explains himself how he felt about being third-string. "At that point," Montana writes, "Coach Devine and I had the kind of relationship you would expect between a player who thought he should be playing and a coach who thought he shouldn't. An antagonistic relationship."

Devine today is an avid Montana supporter. But when

pressed to explain why Montana was third on the depth chart, he eventually gives some unvarnished insight.

DAN DEVINE: "Joe was not a good recuperative-type athlete. He sat out an entire season because of a separated shoulder. But he still played Bookstore Basketball the following spring. Now, he didn't reinjure his shoulder. But if you sit out a year, you normally don't play Bookstore Basketball. That tournament was like football. It was very rough and tough."

Now we're getting somewhere. The football coach was irked when his quarterback played intramural hoops.

In any case, Montana warmed the bench as Notre Dame beat Pittsburgh 19–9 in the season opener. The Irish then played at feeble Mississippi, a team it figured to rout even if Digger Phelps played quarterback. So after a stunning 20–13 upset, the pro-Joe/anti-Dan crowd started howling.

KEN MACAFEE: "We were heavily favored against Mississippi. We were favored to win the national championship. But now we're 1–1. And we could have been 0–2. In our first game against Pittsburgh, their quarterback Matt Cavanaugh broke his wrist. Pittsburgh was beating us when that happened.

"So here we go again with the quarterback controversy. Here is Joe Montana, who doesn't have a grass stain on his uniform. Here's Gary Forystek, who has a great arm. But Rusty Lisch is still starting."

Middle linebacker Bob Golic says it wasn't just offensive players like MacAfee who couldn't figure out why the team's best quarterback could not get on the field. Golic, who was a junior, set a Notre Dame record that year with 146 tackles. He somehow played even better as a senior. Then Golic made 152 tackles, including 26 in one astounding performance against Michigan.

BOB GOLIC: "Our whole team wanted Montana. The fans wanted Montana. Obviously, they did. Because they were always yelling, 'WE WANT JOE!'

"With the players, it had nothing to do with us not liking Rusty. But a lot of the guys just said, 'You know, why not? Why *not* Joe?'

"But then let's face it. Everybody knows what Joe's lot in life at Notre Dame was. For whatever reason, Dan Devine did not believe in him."

LUTHER BRADLEY: "Joe would make it hard on our defense at practice. And the seventy-seven defense was pretty awesome. So naturally we said, 'Damn. Maybe this guy should be in there.'

"But they had their guy in there, and he was just adequate. But there was a reason for that. Parseghian recruited Montana. Devine recruited Lisch. So Devine favored the guy he recruited.

"I think Joe would have stayed stuck on that bench forever. But then Devine needed him against Purdue, and Joe saved the day. But it wasn't like they were buddies after that. It was more like Devine said: Okay, you're my guy. But we don't have to hug and kiss. I'll just bear being with you. Because you're taking us to the promised land."

Notre Dame played at Purdue in the season's third game. Lisch started again before getting lifted for Forystek. Briefly, Forystek looked sharp. Then, as he rolled out on one play, he took a savage blow from Purdue linebacker Fred Arrington. Forystek collapsed with a broken collarbone and a serious concussion. Some players recall

Forystek turning blue. Some feared their teammate was dying.

KEN MACAFEE: "After Forystek went down, Devine went back to Lisch! But Lisch was his usual self. He just wasn't getting the job done. At that point, Devine was forced into doing something. We clearly were going to lose and be 1–2. So he finally sent in Joe."

ROGER VALDISERRI: "It was already the fourth quarter. Lisch couldn't move the offense. Then our assistant coaches got involved. They told Devine, 'You gotta put in Montana.'

"When Joe went in, our players on the field started jumping up and down. I was sitting in the press box with the SID from Purdue. He said, 'Why are they doing that?' I said, 'Because you guys are in trouble now.' He said, 'What do you mean?' I said, 'Wait and see.' "

Montana entered the game with 11 minutes left and Purdue winning 24–14. He drove the Irish to 17 straight points and a heart-stopping 31–24 victory.

Quarterback controversy? Not anymore. Yet even with that fiasco behind them, the Irish (4–1) were favored to lose in South Bend against USC (5–1). It wasn't just Southern Cal being ranked fifth and Notre Dame 11th. Over the past ten years, the Trojans had lost to the Irish only once.

WILLIE FRY: "At the top of the practice week, Devine called our captains into a private meeting. It was Ross Browner, Terry Eurick, and me. Devine left the room, then came back holding green jerseys.

"The three of us went nuts. We wanted to play USC right there in his office. Then Devine said not to tell the other players."

DAN DEVINE: "The color green has always been associated with the Irish. So Notre Dame teams had worn it from time to time. But they hadn't worn it since 1963. The last coach who was very successful wearing green was Frank Leahy. I can still remember this one old football magazine. On the cover was Johnny Lujack in green.

"So I had toyed with this since my first year there. But I saved it for USC. Because I felt they were the turning point for us. If we could beat USC, we had the backbone and talent to make a run for it all."

DAVE HUFFMAN: "They were setting us up all week. But we had no idea what they were doing. We just thought our coaches had gone insane.

"On Friday, Tom Fallon came into our dressing room. He was the tennis coach. He sang us a song called '*The Wearin' of the Green.*' In his Irish tenor voice, he's singing these dramatic words to us. 'They're hanging men and women for the wearin' of the green.'

"This went on all week. Stories about Notre Dame and the Fighting Irish and the history and the mystique and what this game will mean to us forty years from now. The players were like: Are all these people senile?"

BOB GOLIC: "Digger Phelps spoke at the pep rally Friday night. Digger kept yelling, 'GO GREEN! THE GREEN MACHINE!' Real weird stuff like this. And we have no clue.

"Saturday morning we go to our locker room. We see our blue jerseys hanging. Everything is normal except for our game socks. They've got green stripes on top instead of blue.

"So then I'm thinking: Oh. That's why Digger kept talking about green. That's why Coach Fallon was singing about the Irish. Cool. We're wearing green socks.

"Then we go outside and warm up in our blue jerseys. We come back inside before the game, and I see this green thing hanging there. Now I'm thinking: Great. Souvenir tee-shirts. They probably say: NOTRE DAME BEATS USC.

"Then everyone realizes these are green *jerseys*. I hear one of our captains yell, 'PUT 'EM ON!'

"Guys go absolutely wild. Guys smash into each other. Guys start laughing. Guys are ripping off their blue jerseys and putting on the green. There's only a couple mirrors in this locker room. These tiny mirrors, hanging on these support posts. Guys are killing each other to see themselves in these green jerseys."

DAN DEVINE: "I didn't even go in there. I had nothing to say. Everything had been said."

BOB GOLIC: "Then we go from our locker room to our tunnel. We run onto the field and this burst of green pours out. Our stadium goes dead silent for two seconds. Our fans are grasping this. Then the stadium erupts."

WILLIE FRY: "Dennis Thurman played cornerback for USC. We talked about that game when we both played in the Senior Bowl after the season.

"Dennis said USC's players were loosening up on their sideline. Then they saw a few guys in the tunnel with green and gold jerseys. They thought it was Notre Dame students, about to lead the players out on the field. USC looked closer and saw number 94. That was Ross Browner. A USC player said, 'Wait a minute, man. This is not the fans. This is Notre Dame.' "

MacAfee caught eight passes and scored two touchdowns. Montana threw those two touchdowns and ran for two more. Golic blocked a punt and Bradley tied a school record with his 15th career interception. The DUMP

DEVINE bumper stickers being sold outside the stadium for $1 went back into storage. Notre Dame crushed USC 49–19.

Five victories later, the regular season ended with the Irish 10–1 and ranked No. 5. Their Cotton Bowl opponent was No. 1-ranked Texas. So with a commanding win, Notre Dame had a shot at the national championship.

Tough assignment, though. The 11–0 Longhorns had Heisman Trophy winner Earl Campbell, Outland Trophy winner Brad Shearer, and Olympic gold medal winner Johnny (Lam) Jones, who came billed as the world's fastest football player.

The oddsmakers made Texas seven-point favorites. *Newsweek*'s Pete Axthelm, citing the Longhorns' speed, said Notre Dame couldn't beat what it couldn't catch. A reporter in Dallas asked Golic, "Do you think this game will be a rout?"

Golic was having a monstrous senior year. He was bigger than a barn. Why should he toady for Texas? Golic answered, "Yeah. A rout for Notre Dame."

BOB GOLIC: "Boom. It went in the papers. Then it went up on the Texas bulletin board. Then I got chewed out by our coaching staff."

KEN MACAFEE: "Devine gathered us around him at the next practice. He said, 'You think this game will be a blowout? Texas is number one and we are number five. They have everything to lose. We're playing in their backyard. Texas will come out fighting.'

"Devine actually seemed quite irritated. Then he cut practice short by a good hour. He said, 'Get the hell off this football field. I don't even want to see you.'

"I thought: All right. This guy is finally getting riled up."

Then Brad Shearer pitched in and did his part. A 250-pound defensive tackle, he had already been named the country's outstanding lineman. Shearer came into the Cotton Bowl talking a blue streak, and most of it was directed at Ernie Hughes, the Irish guard who'd be lined up across from him.

KEN MACAFEE: "Ernie Hughes was a wild man. He had this red hair. When Ernie would get mad, his neck would turn red. Then his face. Then his whole head. So all week we said, 'Hey, Ernie. Brad Shearer says he's gonna kick your ass.' "

DAVE HUFFMAN: "Ernie Hughes ate him alive. Ernie Hughes destroyed him. There are still offensive linemen talking about it."

If Shearer was mostly mouth, Earl Campbell was all neck and thighs. But as Golic came up huge with 18 tackles, most of them on Campbell, it took the bruising fullback 29 carries to gain his 116 yards.

On offense, Vegas Ferguson ran for 100 yards and caught a 17-yard TD pass from Montana. MacAfee ended a dazzling career with four receptions for 45 yards.

After Texas had gone down 38–10, some Notre Dame players campaigned for No. 1. They didn't need to, though, after beating the country's top team by 28 points.

The AP national championship was Notre Dame's seventh, more than any college football team in the country. Dan Devine had weathered the loss to Mississippi, the Montana controversy, the disgruntled alumni. He had won a national title in his third season—just as Rockne, Leahy and Parseghian had done.

26

THE WHEELS FALL OFF

1978 – 1979

IN SPRING 1978, MACAFEE, BROWNER, AND BRADLEY WERE ALL first-round draft picks. Fry and Hughes were selected in rounds two and three. A total of nine Fighting Irish began drawing NFL paychecks.

With this kind of attrition, there were few who expected Notre Dame to repeat as national champions. But with Montana, Golic, Ferguson, and Jerome Heavens all returning, not a soul thought the Irish would lose their first two games.

It happened anyway. And if that wasn't shocking enough, both defeats came at Notre Dame Stadium, where the Irish hadn't started 0–2 in 82 years.

In the 1895 home opener, Notre Dame lost 32–0 to Chicago Physicians and Surgeons. In 1978, the Irish fell 3–0 to Missouri. Neither foe was exactly the neighborhood bully.

On November 23, in the second home defeat of 1978, Notre Dame lost 28–14 to Michigan. This series had not been played since 1943, when it was abruptly severed by Michigan. The official reason was scheduling conflicts. The reason Fritz Crisler gave Leahy was Notre Dame's "dirty play." But many in South Bend charged Crisler with anti-Catholicism.

By late 1968, Crisler had retired as Michigan's athletic director. His successor Don Canham desperately wanted to fill up Michigan Stadium, which held up to 101,000 fans, but had averaged just 67,000 per game in 1968. Shortly after that season, Canham ran into Moose Krause at a football banquet.

"I know how you can fill that place up," Krause said.

"By playing Notre Dame," Canham replied. The athletic directors shook hands and a contract was signed in 1970. But since both teams scheduled so far in advance, it was 1978 before the rivalry resumed.

As this historic game approached, Michigan coach Bo Schembechler was his usual contrary self. Beating Notre Dame, Schembechler said, was not as important to him as beating Michigan State, Ohio State, or anyone else in the Big Ten for that matter.

Sure it wasn't. That's why Schembechler started quarterback Rick Leach, even though he'd been hobbling all week on a badly sprained ankle.

Leach ended up throwing for three touchdowns, while his counterpart Montana threw two interceptions and got tackled in the end zone for a safety. Afterward, Notre Dame was 0–2 and out of national championship contention. That's when the anti-Devine movement smelled blood.

DAVE HUFFMAN: "Nobody dreamed the wheels would fall off that quickly. Naturally, Devine took the hardest shots. He was getting tagged from every direction.

"But what are you gonna do? Quit because you can't win the national championship? Say the season is over, the way Ron Powlus once did? That may be fine for the younger generation. We just picked up our jocks and went back to work."

Their tenacity paid off. After their shocking 0–2 start, the Irish won nine of ten and finished ranked No. 7 by the AP.

Their last and most bizarre win came against Houston in the coldest Cotton Bowl in history. Huffman, a Dallas native, recalls the famous Chicken Soup game.

DAVE HUFFMAN: "It was the worst ice storm to hit Dallas in thirty years. It was brutal, and biting, and the fans stayed home in droves. There were like 30,000 people there. But a lot of them were already gone by halftime.

"Of course, you already know about Montana. It was just flat-out freezing in the first half, and Joe was this skinny college kid to begin with. Quarterbacks also don't wear a lot of clothes or pads. They need to stay fluid and mobile. Not like us offensive linemen. We can just huddle together like big fat cows.

"Anyway, Houston was beating us at halftime. Then we start the third quarter, and now there's this new set of hands stuck up my butt. Because Joe never came back out. He was still in our locker room, eating hot chicken soup, in the beginning stages of hypothermia."

What happened next is Irish folklore. Notre Dame trailed 34–12 with 7:37 to go. The thawed-out Comeback Kid, who had missed most of the third quarter, hit Kris Haines for the winning TD pass on the game's final play. Final score: 35–34.

By the fall of 1979, Montana was a rookie in San Francisco, Notre Dame's offense was all Vegas Ferguson, and its defense was small and inexperienced. The Irish went 7–4, their worst showing since pre-Parseghian 1963.

Again, the flak popped loudest near Devine. Since winning his national title, his record was 16–7, including home losses to Missouri, Michigan, USC, and Clemson. Thus with his five-year contract now expired, it was widely believed that Devine would be sacked.

The rumor mill was wrong. After the 1979 season finale, Father Joyce told Devine that he would be coming back in 1980.

JOE DOYLE: "But Devine did not receive a new contract. Everything was verbal. Notre Dame did the same thing with Ara. The day that he retired—after eleven seasons—his original contract was still in his desk.

"That was just Notre Dame's policy at the time. But I think Devine wanted something more solid than that. And I think this became an issue in 1980."

In 1979, Devine's best player was linebacker Bob Crable, whose 187 tackles set a single-season school record that's never been broken. Crable is also Notre Dame's all-time leading tackler (521).

Here he gives his perspective on Devine, and his status at Notre Dame after five seasons.

BOB CRABLE: "He still wasn't getting accepted by the alumni. But not just because he had a few subpar seasons. Devine had some idiosyncrasies, you know. He would wear a nice suit to the monogram luncheon, but he would also wear gym shoes. Well, that would raise a few alumni eyebrows."

Other players say Devine was so concerned about germs that sometimes at practice he covered his mouth with tissues. They say he drifted and rambled during team speeches. They say he constantly wore a towel around his neck.

Of course, his quirkiness wasn't his real crime.

BOB CRABLE: "Devine's biggest problem was that he wasn't Ara. That's really who the alumni wanted back."

Crable is right. The Parseghian legend had grown, rather than faded, since his resignation in 1974. So the truth be told, Devine never had a chance.

But as this decade closed, there was another dramatic coaching change coming. Then, finally, Dan Devine would be viewed quite differently. His successor Gerry Faust would see to that.

PART V

THE EIGHTIES

27

✤

THE DEVINE ERA ENDS
1 9 8 0

ON AUGUST 15, 1980, DAN DEVINE ANNOUNCED THAT THE impending season would be his last at Notre Dame. Coming at such an odd time—three weeks before the opener against Purdue—the news prompted questions from writers across the country, exemplified by the *Chicago Tribune*'s Dave Condon.

"The pressures at Notre Dame finally got to Dan Devine," the veteran columnist wrote. "There was pressure on Devine, all right. But did he jump or was he pushed?"

Devine says now what he said then. He wasn't even nudged, let alone pushed. He left for personal reasons.

DAN DEVINE: "My wife had been having trouble with one eye. Then she had cataract surgery on her other eye. After that she was virtually blind. Then one day it hit me while I was driving to work. What if something happens when she's alone?

"I was also getting fatigued by this time. Coaching

does that to you after a while. But the main reason by far was my wife's health. If she had been perfectly healthy, I wouldn't even have considered resigning. And Father Joyce was wonderful about it. He said, 'Danny, this is your decision. But this job is yours as long as you want it.' "

JOE DOYLE: "I think his resignation was a ploy. That's why he announced it before the season. He wanted Notre Dame to tell him later: 'Dan, we really need you.'

"Strangely enough, he had a very good season that year. But he never got asked to come back."

It should be noted again that Doyle and Devine were never friendly. But even two prominent freshmen who liked Devine, quarterback Blair Kiel and halfback Greg Bell, feel this story may have other layers.

BLAIR KIEL: "Dan wanted another five years. But Notre Dame wanted to keep it year-by-year. That was my understanding of it. But maybe there's even more hidden stuff behind that."

GREG BELL: "I think most of it had to do with his wife's illness. I got to know Jo Devine very well. She was one of the reasons I came to Notre Dame. And when Jo told me herself—'Please don't blame Dan, he's doing this for me'—that was all I had to hear.

"But I do think other things were going on. If eighty percent of it was based on Jo's health, then twenty percent was pressure from the university. Dan wasn't loved by Ara Parseghian. Dan wasn't loved by all the administrators. Whether or not they say so, he didn't fill the role of the stereotypical Notre Dame football coach. He couldn't woo a whole crowd like a Lou Holtz. He wasn't flamboyant like Ara. He wasn't a Gerry Faust, whose excitement was always boiling over. Meanwhile, Faust was still down at Moeller High in Cincinnati. He was wooing Notre Dame like crazy, with all the Hail Marys and rosary beads."

Whatever the factors were, Devine shocked his players when he announced his resignation. Especially confounded were highly recruited freshmen like Kiel and Bell, who had chosen Notre Dame over dozens of major programs.

BLAIR KIEL: "We'd only been on campus two or three days. So my gut reaction was, Should I stay here or what?

"Then I talked to an older player named John Scully. He was a senior and a captain. He said you go to a school for the school and not the coach. He said Notre Dame is a great university. So why throw that away?

"John Scully did that with a lot of freshmen. He was really one of the heroes in the whole thing."

GREG BELL: "Dan Devine's resignation came out of the blue. We were *three weeks* away from our first game.

"Now I suppose you can say it was written in the stars. Because every other recruiter was telling me, 'Devine's not going to stay.' But I took Dan at his word. He told me himself, 'Greg, I'll be here for you the whole four years.'

"Then we had this team meeting before the season. It was in the ACC. Devine walked in and said, 'I made some promises to you guys. But due to Jo's health, this will be my last year.'

"You should have seen the reaction in the back row. Generally, there's where all the brothers sat. And there were a lot of upset brothers sitting back there. We were like: 'Ain't this a trip. He said he'd be our coach the next four years.'

"Do I blame Dan for that? Yes and no. No, because I feel he mostly left because of Jo. Yes, because I know if he'd stayed there four years, our team would have won a national championship. We might have won two national championships. That's how much talent we had on those next few squads."

Dave Duerson agrees with Bell. A sophomore defensive back in 1980, Duerson was All-American his last two seasons. He later made All-Pro and won Super Bowl rings with the Chicago Bears and New York Giants.

DAVE DUERSON: "I can't speak for my teammates, but I wanted to win that season for Dan Devine. This was a guy who lived and died and breathed Notre Dame football, and still does to this day. I loved Dan Devine. I wanted to see him go out with a national championship."

The Irish opened the season ranked No. 12. Yet even with freshman quarterback Kiel starting, they were 7–0 and ranked No. 1 in early November. Next up came 1–7 Georgia Tech. But instead of an easy win, Notre Dame left Atlanta with a shocking 3–3 tie.

DAVE DUERSON: "We were heartbroken. We lost our No. 1 ranking. Now we gotta go to Alabama.

"It got pretty tense down there. They didn't like Notre Dame, they didn't like Catholics, and they weren't too fond of blacks. Then our hotel had a bomb threat. So we were thinking all these crazy thoughts. We were thinking Klan.

"Devine called a team meeting before we left for the stadium. Then suddenly he kicked out his assistants. Nobody knew what the hell was going on.

"Devine just started telling all these jokes. Corny jokes, nasty jokes, we were laughing up a storm. It was exactly what we needed to loosen up. Then we kicked the dog out of Alabama."

The Bear didn't fare well either. As the Irish won 7–0, Bryant's record against Notre Dame dropped to 0–4. Three of those losses came via Devine.

The quelling of the Tide kept the Irish undefeated, earned them a No. 2 ranking, secured a Sugar Bowl bid against top-ranked Georgia, and kept them in national championship contention.

Before meeting Georgia, though, Notre Dame had a key game at USC on December 6. Fortunately for the Irish, they had two weeks to prepare because of a bye week. Unfortunately, school officials chose this time to make a stunning announcement. They were hiring Gerry Faust straight from high school. Faust had no college coaching experience.

The Irish lost 20–3 in Los Angeles, which probably ended their quest for a national title. But how much effect had this announcement had?

On the one hand, USC had gone 8–2 in its last ten Notre Dame games. This year the Trojans were ranked only 17th, but they still had terrific players like Ronnie Lott, Dennis Smith, Chip Banks, and Keith Van Horne. On the other hand:

DAVE DUERSON: "I don't know if it was *the* deciding factor. But we'd all be kidding ourselves if we said it played no part. Because it instantly caused division on our team.

"We had a number of Notre Dame guys who'd come from Moeller. They were getting excited. Their high school coach was gonna be the man. But a lot of us were feeling, Wait a minute. This is Dan Devine's football team.

We still have a shot at the national championship. We can't even think about next year.

"So now the focus was changed. Now there were guys concerned about different things. That was true all the way through the Georgia game. Take the quarterback position, for example. You had Blair Kiel starting that whole season. But now you have Tim Koegel, our reserve quarterback, who played for Faust at Moeller. Now Koegel figures the job is gonna be his. Now Kiel has to wonder if Faust will play favorites.

"So the timing was very poor. It was literally the most crucial part of our season."

BLAIR KIEL: "I thought they should have waited. Then again, I was also shocked at who they hired. I never thought Notre Dame would hire a high school coach."

BOB CRABLE: "I was real excited. I played for Gerry at Moeller and we had tremendous success. But they should have named him after the Southern Cal game. Up until then, our team was very focused. Then we went to Southern Cal and crapped in our hats."

John Mosley was a freshman halfback that season. Versatile, athletic, and unselfish, Mosley would later play flanker, cornerback, and specialty teams. He was a well-respected captain his senior year.

Mosley recalls what happened after the USC game, as the media buzzed around Notre Dame's next coach.

JOHN MOSLEY: "Gerry came on campus for this big press conference. Gerry, as you know, is not a quiet man. He was surrounded by family and friends. He was walking around excited and talking to our players.

"We had a major bowl game coming up. It was Dan

Devine's last game at Notre Dame. But suddenly it's Faust who's in the spotlight."

GREG BELL: "That whole situation wasn't right. Devine probably won't say it, but he never liked the way Gerry appeared on campus before the bowl game.

"Part of that time was during our Christmas break. The student dorms were closed. So we stayed at the Morris Inn before we left for New Orleans. One day Gerry showed up. He came in and talked to all the Moeller guys. He sat down and talked with me. He said, 'Hey, I need a fast back. You're gonna get an equal opportunity to win a spot.'

"It was kind of strange. Gerry was right there with us at the Morris Inn, and we still had a shot at the national championship. Devine was pissed off about that."

Devine, who is exceedingly cautious in interviews, initially sidesteps the subject. But then it becomes apparent: This was not the farewell he envisioned.

DAN DEVINE: "I want to emphasize something: I was not surprised by the timing of the announcement. I knew all about it. Father Joyce and I met with a few games left in our season. There were all these rumors on who would replace me. Father Joyce said it was starting to leak out. He just wanted to end all the speculation. So he said, 'Do you think we can announce this before the end of your season? The call is up to you.'

"I told Father Joyce yes. Because I thought I could handle anything. But I overestimated myself. I wasn't capable of handling that. Because Gerry virtually moved right in. We were in a situation with two head coaches.

"Well, it didn't work out. You can't have two coaches on campus when one coach is trying to prepare a team for Southern Cal and the Sugar Bowl. And particularly since Gerry was a high school coach, I don't think he realized how important the mental preparation for a big game is.

"Fortunately, things improved as the Sugar Bowl got closer. Gerry was less in our hair then. Actually, that's not fair. He was a less visible presence during our preparation."

In his last game, the Sugar Bowl, Devine admits he was too emotional. He spent too much time cheerleading, he says, and not enough time coaching. *Sports Illustrated* agreed, calling some of the Notre Dame play-calling "misguided."

Still, the seventh-ranked Irish gained 328 total yards to top-ranked Georgia's 127. The main reason Notre Dame lost was its generosity. The Bulldogs recovered one fumble at the Irish one, and another at the Irish 22. Georgia scored touchdowns each time in a 17–10 win.

The Bulldogs, 12–0, nailed down their first national title in 46 years. The Irish wound up ranked ninth with a record of 9–2–1.

Despite the downbeat finale, Devine left Notre Dame with a six-year winning percentage of .764 (53–16–1), three bowl victories, a 17–10 record against ranked opponents, and a national championship in 1977. He inherited the program when it was strong, kept it near the top, and left Gerry Faust a team loaded with talent. In 1985, with a career record of 126–42–7, Devine was elected to the College Football Hall of Fame.

Today the Hall of Fame is located in downtown South Bend. Which is a bit ironic, since South Bend is the one place where Devine has always been held to the harshest standard.

DAVE DUERSON: "I admired Dan Devine. He reminded me of my father, a man who only spoke when something needed saying.

"I also had great respect for his coaching skills. Having played for Mike Ditka and Bill Parcells, I saw my share of great coaches. Dan Devine was right there at the top.

"I think people came to realize that later. Dan didn't get the full respect he deserved until after the Faust years. It was sad that it came down that way, but the demise of Gerry Faust was the rise of Dan Devine."

28

❦

FAUST FEVER

1 9 8 1

WATCHING NOTRE DAME WALK THROUGH THE FAUST YEARS boggled the mind. So how did it come about? Why did the nation's most lustrous football program install a coach directly out of high school?

FATHER HESBURGH: "What was attractive about him then is what's still attractive now. Gerry's a great gentleman. He's a wonderful Christian. He's generous to a fault. There isn't a nicer guy walking around. We felt he was someone to take a chance on."

FATHER JOYCE: "He was a marvelous human being. He was obviously the most successful high school coach in the country. He had built this powerhouse, at this small Catholic school in Cincinnati.

"But more than that, I was impressed with the kids he'd sent to us from Moeller. I don't recall them all, but there was Bob Crable and Steve Sylvester and more than a dozen others. They seemed to be really fine men. They seemed well-trained. They played good football for us.

"So that was what impressed me. And even though he had no college experience, everything else about him seemed too good to be true. So I was willing to take a gamble. And it turned out to be a mistake. We'd been burned once before with Terry Brennan. I should have known better."

In retrospect, this may be the biggest understatement in Notre Dame history. But Father Joyce wasn't alone. Faust had millions of true believers when he first entered the picture.

For starters, there was his staggering 18-year record at Moeller: 174–17–2, victories in 90 of his last 93 games, nine undefeated seasons, 12 city championships, five state championships, and four mythical national championships.

Faust was also so bubbly and energetic, it was felt he could jump-start the alumni who either slept or fumed through the Devine years. Faust had nice details, too. Growing up Catholic in Dayton, Ohio, he sang the Irish fight song while bicycling home from football practice. He kept a statue of the Virgin Mary and a drawing of Knute Rockne in his office at Moeller. He once nixed a top recruit for talking back to his mother.

Dick Schaap has known Faust since his Moeller days. Schaap is the author of several classic sports books, including *Instant Replay* with Jerry Kramer and *I Can't Wait Until Tomorrow . . . Because I Get Better Looking Every Day* with Joe Namath. He is also the host of the *Sports Reporters* on ESPN.

DICK SCHAAP: "I made a few trips out to Moeller when Gerry was there. It was a factory. They had this magnificent weight facility. Gerry had a large staff of assistant coaches. He had hundreds of kids out there playing football on different levels. It was an awesome sight.

"Whenever I went out there, they were always in the midst of some incredibly long winning streak. On one trip I took my wife, who was not yet my wife. Gerry invited her into the locker room to hear his pregame speech. Besides her getting to look at all these nubile seventeen-year-olds running around in various states of dress, I think my wife was ready to suit up and go out there. That's how charging and emotional Gerry's speech was.

"When Notre Dame hired him, I went there right away for ABC. I remember going to the gym with Gerry and Digger Phelps. We had the camera rolling and Gerry picked up a basketball. He threw it overhand from 30 feet and got nothing but net. Well, you know, it looked like a great omen. And Digger was very excited to have him there. He said, 'This will be great. He can teach me how to pray, and I can teach him how to curse.'

"So that was the attitude when Gerry took the job. Here was a decent guy, whose dream it was to coach at Notre Dame. There were a lot of excited people, and I was among them."

Faust Fever started in earnest during spring 1981. Reporting from the first day of spring practice, Ray Kennedy of *Sports Illustrated* wrote: "If enthusiasm is what it takes to shake down the thunder, then Faust is Thor himself." One Chicago headline read: "NEW PROBLEM: WILL IRISH BE TOO GOOD?" Faust's biographer Danny Dressman predicted: "He will be the greatest success since Rockne." Even those on planet earth called Faust's first recruiting class—including 26 total prospects and 13 *Parade* All-Americans—one of the most talented in school history.

GERRY FAUST: "I sort of took that stuff in stride. We were very successful at Moeller. We were basically America's High School Football Team. So I was used to a lot of media coverage, and I didn't pay much attention to it. I just kept working hard, and I figured everything would turn out fine."

Defensive lineman Mike Golic was one of those 13 prep players honored by *Parade.* In 1983, Golic was voted defensive MVP. He was a senior tri-captain in 1984.

MIKE GOLIC: "Notre Dame had no clue if Faust could really coach at the college level. But coming off the Devine years, they wanted a great PR man for the school. Faust was incredible. He was always rah-rah. He hung out with Notre Dame's students on the lawn. He brought pizzas to their dorms. He played Frisbee with them. The feeling on campus was, We just had a football coach we never saw. Now, by God, we have a man of the people!"

GREG BELL: "His biggest supporters were all the Moeller kids. And personally, as a kid who grew up playing foot-ball in Ohio, I had to respect Moeller's program. It was legendary.

"So that spring was exciting. You had praise for Faust coming in from people like Don Shula and Tom Landry. Naturally, our players had huge expectations."

DAVE DUERSON: "Gerry was running around the practice field, slapping guys on the back. It was new. It was fresh. He was getting us gigged up."

According to Jay Underwood, a freshman offensive tackle who experienced the entire Faust regime, the first hint of trouble came when Faust switched the team's jer-seys from green to blue.

JAY UNDERWOOD: "Notre Dame, under Devine, had started out by wearing navy blue. But then they put on the greens and won an important game against Southern Cal. So at some point they switched to green full time.

"So I expected to wear green when I showed up. But Gerry broke out these royal blue jerseys with gold stripes. It wasn't a bad-looking shirt. But some of the Notre Dame purists weren't too thrilled. Neither were the guys who played for Devine. They thought the new shirt looked a whole lot like Moeller's."

Faust explained when questioned by the press: "Blue is the color of the Blessed Virgin Mother. She's gotten me this far, so I'm going to stick with her." Still, Underwood seems to be right. The Devine holdovers saw Moeller instead of Mary.

BLAIR KIEL: "Some of us got wary when Gerry went to that royal-blue Moeller bullshit. We said, 'Uh-oh, he's bringing that high school uniform in, too.' Because Gerry had already brought in some high school coaches."

DAVE DUERSON: "That was disturbing to me. By then, I was well-entrenched at Notre Dame. I was a junior who had started since I was a freshman. I mean, I'm bleeding green.

"Then Gerry comes in from high school. He brings a handful of high school coaches with him. From high school to Notre Dame? Man, that's too big a leap."

MIKE GOLIC: "My upbringing was old-fashioned. I liked my Notre Dame coaches rough and tough. Because those were the coaches I met when my brother Bob played there.

"That's why my freshman year was so ridiculous. We had one new coach who cried at every pregame meal.

He'd get up to speak, and the tears would come. We were like: Where are the balls here? Where is somebody who has some attitude? Quit your crying, man. We're going into battle. We don't want to see that crap."

GERRY FAUST: "I made some mistakes in hiring the staff. It wasn't that they weren't good coaches, and it wasn't that they weren't good people. It's just that I didn't get the right chemistry together. Some of the guys didn't believe in my philosophy, and some didn't believe in each other. I should have checked that out before I hired them."

DAVE DUERSON: "One of the other big things that cost Gerry respect is that he never separated his family from the team. They would cry in our locker room after losses. Gerry's kid would be in our football meetings. We'd be preparing for games, and his kid would be shooting paper balls through a straw.

"His son was even with us at Friday night movies. Well, because his son was in there, Gerry had us watching stuff like *Bambi Comes Home.* I mean, Disney movies the night before a game?

"The first Friday night of the season, I guess somebody else picked the movie. It was violent, and there were a couple of bra scenes. There was maybe even a tit scene. Gerry had his eyes closed. Then he covered his son's eyes. This is in a roomful of football players."

MIKE GOLIC: "My God! We saw this one . . . I forgot the name. It was about some family escaping somewhere in a hot air balloon. I was like: What the hell are we watching here? I wanna get jacked up!"

More significant than jerseys and movies was Faust installing a radically new offense. He replaced Devine's power-I with a multiple-formation offense based on Moeller's. The spin was that Notre Dame would now play "wide-open football." The truth was that Faust's new offense was mostly whistles, bells, and gadget plays.

Still, Faust inherited 16 of the 22 starters from a Sugar Bowl team which finished 9–2–1. Between this hard fact and Faust mania, Notre Dame entered the season ranked No. 4.

The Faust era began on September 12, before a rapturous 59,075 at Notre Dame Stadium. When the Irish slapped LSU 27–9, they spent one delicious week as the country's No. 1 team.

JOHN MOSLEY: "It got pretty crazy on campus. There was this giant media blitz. Then we went to Michigan and got our ass kicked."

GREG BELL: "Against LSU, I had my first 100-yard game at Notre Dame. I left the Michigan game with my whole torso bruised. Even my butt was swollen.

"Michigan came after us with a passion. They were probably sick of hearing about how great Notre Dame would be with Faust. Schembechler was also a great defensive coach, and we were running this high school looking offense. Michigan beat us 25–7. It wasn't even close."

No, it wasn't. Notre Dame's flashy new offense gained only 207 total yards and went almost two full quarters without a first down.

The Irish, 1–1, then lost 15–14 at unranked Purdue. Late in the game, with Notre Dame ahead 14–7, linebacker Mark Zavagnin dropped an interception that could have ended Purdue's last touchdown drive. Afterward, Faust made a mistake he would regret. He told

Zavagnin in front of other players, "If you intercept the ball, we win the game. You dropped it, so we come home losers."

GERRY FAUST: "I was dead wrong on that. My words came out the wrong way. I felt bad afterward, and I can understand how he felt, and still feels to this day. I have no problem with that."

But Faust's words had an impact on his team. Was he the stand-up guy the public saw, or the commander who blamed his troops when there was heat to be taken?

JOHN MOSLEY: "Morale started dropping after the Purdue game. Gerry started pointing fingers at his own assistants. He thought the Devine guys all had attitudes. In a way, we did. We didn't give a fuck what Gerry was saying. Because he was blaming everyone but himself."

DAVE DUERSON: "There were obvious divisions. You had the Gerry guys and the Dan guys. You had Gerry's coaches and Dan's coaches also. There was no unity. Notre Dame fell apart as a football team."

On November 27, in the last game at Miami, Bell ran back a kickoff for a 98-yard touchdown. Duerson intercepted a Jim Kelly pass and raced 88 yards for another score. Otherwise the Hurricanes dominated, routing the Irish 37–15 and foreshadowing a shift in the two teams' fortunes.

GREG BELL: "We beat Miami 32–14 the season before that. We *killed* Miami that game. They limped off the field.

"In 1981, we had the same group of guys. Miami had the same guys. And Miami beat Notre Dame like a wet potato."

DAVE DUERSON: "That made it official. We were a joke. We were the Notre Dame team that was supposed to win the national championship and never got close."

JOHN MOSLEY: "That season was like the Battle of Waterloo. You had the soldiers. It was just poor planning strategically."

After Notre Dame finished 5–6, its first losing season in 18 years, Faust fired offensive line coach Tom Backhus and defensive line coach Bill Myers. Backhus was a longtime friend who had starred for Faust at Moeller. His firing tarnished Faust's nice-guy image.

GERRY FAUST: "I made the wrong decision there. Backhus didn't get along with some of the other coaches, and I let Backhus go. Well, I shouldn't haven't listened to those other guys. I should have let them go and kept him."

JAY UNDERWOOD: "The Backhus thing shocked the public. But for a lot of players, it just confirmed that Gerry was kind of ruthless. Now I realize when people talk about him, you don't hear the adjective 'ruthless' very often. But he was to a degree. If you look back at his tenure, he went through a lot of assistant coaches.

"Yet, at the same time, the university stood by their commitment to him. I mean, Faust lasted five years for only one reason: he had a five-year contract. So that was the irony of it. Faust had no trouble giving people their walking papers when he was only there by the grace of Notre Dame not doing the same thing to him."

29

LIFE WITH GERRY

1 9 8 2 - 1 9 8 3

ACCORDING TO FAUST'S BIOGRAPHER DANNY DRESSMAN, "Gerry unquestionably is the most prayer-oriented football coach in the world. 'Say a Hail Mary' was an order given to everyone on the Moeller sideline on every play of importance for 20 years."

Faust brought this practice with him to Notre Dame. But his players were older now, and more apt to question their coaches. It also didn't help that the losses were mounting.

JAY UNDERWOOD: "At times I thought he lost his ability to reason. He'd be screaming and flailing and shouting at everyone to say a Hail Mary. I remember thinking: Boy, that's fine if we all pray. But we should definitely start converting some third downs."

DAVE DUERSON: "Most of the older guys would just roll their eyes. But the younger guys were still scared to death of Faust. When he'd tell them to 'Say a Hail Mary,' they'd say it loud enough so Faust could hear them. I thought that was pretty strange."

GREG BELL: "I'm a religious person, but I felt it was inappropriate. I even said to Gerry once during a game: 'Should God help Notre Dame win? Purdue has religious players on their team, too.' "

"This country has millions of people who love Notre Dame," says ex-Parseghian player Pete Schivarelli. "There are also millions who hate Notre Dame. Those people were starting to laugh at us. Because that stuff played into all the stereotypes: Look at the Catholics praying for a touchdown."

Faust says he was surprised by the criticism. He thought midgame prayers would be accepted at a deeply religious school where mass is conducted hourly. In his second season, Faust adds, he cut back on his Hail Marys after conferring with athletic director Gene Corrigan.

In 1982, a more pressing concern was Notre Dame's offense. In 1981, Faust had taken the starting quarterback job from incumbent Blair Kiel and alternated him with ex-Moellerite Tom Koegel. This splintered the team and gave the press a quarterback controversy. About the only positive was that Kiel and Koegel remained friends.

In 1982, Faust made Kiel the undisputed starter. Faust hired quarterback coach Ron Hudson from UCLA and allowed him to install a more collegiate offense. Notre Dame even developed an audible system, which it amazingly didn't have in Faust's first season.

The Irish, ranked No. 20, opened on national television in the first night game ever played at Notre Dame Stadium. Their opponent was tenth-ranked Michigan, which had whipped them 25–7 the year before.

JAY UNDERWOOD: "Shortly before we played them, Faust assembled our team in the auditorium. Then someone turned off the lights and we saw the premier of *Wake Up the Echoes*. That movie gave you the chills. It made you feel great to be at Notre Dame.

"But you know what's kind of ironic? In the original version of *Wake Up the Echoes*, our team from the year before was all over it. Faust was all over it. It showed his locker room speeches. It showed us sitting around with our game faces on.

"Then, after the Faust years, they did a major reediting job. The Gipper was still the Gipper and the Speech was still the Speech and Rockne still died in a plane crash. But they glossed right over Faust. They glossed over our first team. They should have called it *Wake Up the Echoes II*. It was like some wartime propaganda. They tried convincing people it never happened."

Funny how that works. When Notre Dame first hired Faust, you could visit the football department and never know that Dan Devine had existed.

Nevertheless, after previewing *Wake Up the Echoes*, the fired-up Irish delivered the first big win of the Faust years. Greg Bell gained 95 yards and scored one dazzling touchdown. Kiel completed 15 of 22 passes for 141 yards. Duerson made a crucial fourth-quarter interception. The final score was 23–17, but that was misleading. Notre Dame led 23–10 before the Wolverines scored on a fluky touchdown pass.

Afterward, Schembechler stormed off the field without shaking Faust's hand. Then Schembechler blasted his players for 30 minutes while the press eavesdropped outside. In the winning locker room, Faust actually told reporters: "I'm so happy for the kids, the players, the alumni, all the fans, and the University of Notre Dame!"

For the next three weeks, as the Irish defeated Purdue, Michigan State, and Miami, the "Oust Faust" bumper stickers saw reduced sales. Then, with Notre Dame 4–0 and ranked No. 9, two lightweights looked ripe for savage beatings. But the Irish lost at home to Arizona, and tied at Oregon. Neither opponent was ranked nor even respected. Oregon, in fact, had been 0–6.

MIKE GOLIC: "Those were the Gerry Faust years in a nutshell. Our teams ran hot and cold. Look what happened two games after Oregon tied us. We go into Pittsburgh. Dan Marino is a senior. Their offensive line has Bill Fralic and Jimbo Covert. Pittsburgh is ranked No. 1. We're not ranked at all. We don't just beat them. We crush them on their home field."

As the 10-point underdog Irish shocked top-ranked Pittsburgh 31–16, freshman Allen Pinkett broke loose for a 76-yard touchdown run. Four years later, the powerful little tailback would graduate with 4,131 yards rushing, 53 touchdowns, 96.1 yards rushing per game and 899 carries. All are still Notre Dame records.

ALLEN PINKETT: "The Pittsburgh game was exciting. But the best part was what happened back in South Bend. We turned down Notre Dame Avenue in our buses, and there were thousands of students lined up to greet us."

MIKE GOLIC: "It was a wild scene. We opened up the windows and the students were trying to jump inside the bus. I remember thinking: This is why I came here. This is the Notre Dame synonymous with big wins."

After their glorious upset, the Irish were 6–1–1 and ranked No. 13. But when Kiel missed two games with an injured right shoulder, Notre Dame lost to Penn State and Air Force.

JOHN MOSLEY: "I thought Blair's injury was the turning point. We just beat Marino and Pittsburgh. We were on a little roll. Then we played another big game against Penn State. Blair couldn't throw, so Ken Karcher replaced him. Karcher was bellyaching all year long. He thought he should be playing instead of Blair. Then Karcher played and laid a fucking egg."

MIKE GOLIC: "Then we played at Air Force. Those military guys were always tough. You'd knock the snot out of them and they'd bounce right back up.

"But our players were bigger and stronger and faster. Plus, Notre Dame had never lost to Air Force. We were 11–0 against them lifetime.

"Obviously, we knew they'd run the option. But we had this problem on Thursday. We couldn't stop our *prep* team from running the option. I'm not kidding you. Our prep team was scoring touchdowns against our No. 1 defense. I'm not saying it was only the coaching. The players have to execute, too. But if a defense isn't working against the prep team, why would you think it would work on Saturday?

"It was an absolute bloodletting. Air Force whipped us 30–17. They gained almost 300 yards rushing. So there were some serious eyebrows being raised. Does this guy know how to put together a game plan?"

The Irish lost their third straight in the season finale at USC. Their 6–4–1 record left them without a bowl game and outside the Top 20 for the second consecutive year. Still, Notre Dame looked sharp in upsets over Pittsburgh, Miami, and Michigan.

Based on those three big wins, the team's easiest schedule of the decade, and the return of talented players such as Pinkett, Bell, Kiel, Golic, Mark Bavaro, and Stacy Toran, Notre Dame entered the 1983 season ranked No. 5. Kiel says he felt especially optimistic. His shoulder had fully mended and he was a senior captain. The Irish press guide described him as "the first four-year starter at quarterback in Notre Dame history."

In the opener at Purdue, Kiel completed nine of 14 passes for 166 yards and two touchdowns in a 52–6 rout. Kiel threw two more TDs, but also three interceptions, in a 28–23 loss to Michigan State. Then, on national television, the entire offense struggled in a 20–0 defeat at Miami.

BLAIR KIEL: "First, I threw an early interception. Then later I threw a ball to Mark Bavaro. Mark was supposed to turn in and he turned out. I threw it where I thought Mark was gonna be. It ended up getting picked off by Miami.

"Mark walked up as I came toward the sideline. He said he turned the wrong way. I said no big deal. Then Faust laid into me. He said I was terrible. He kept making these gestures, and this game was on national TV. Well, I lost it then. I really laid into him. I was venting three years of frustration. It was an ugly scene."

This sideline altercation—which several players witnessed, but which Faust says he does not remember—led to a quarterback change. As the veteran Kiel got benched, freshman Steve Beverlein started the next eight games.

BLAIR KIEL: "Faust pulled me against Miami after I yelled at him. I knew when we got home I'd probably be reprimanded. Then, on Sunday night, Faust got on me in front of everybody. He said I couldn't talk to him that way. He was yelling, and I ignored him.

"Ron Hudson informed me before our Monday practice. He said, 'You're benched. We're starting Beverlein against Colorado.' I said I didn't agree. Ron said, 'You didn't play that well against Michigan State.' I said, 'I think you're right. But that doesn't warrant this.'

"Beverlein was a good kid. I met his parents and they were very gracious. But it was a tough situation. That was my senior year, and I always dreamed of playing professional football. I remember telling myself: You're still attending a great university. Try and appreciate that. But right now you got shit as far as football."

The 20–0 loss at Miami dropped Notre Dame to 1–2 and out of the Top 20. The prime-time telecast, featuring Hurricane players taunting and cursing the Irish, also served as prologue for college football's most heated rivalry of the 1980s.

JAY UNDERWOOD: "Howard Schnellenberger built up Miami. Then Jimmy Johnson came in and built on that. Other than those two guys, no one did more for Miami than Notre Dame did during the Gerry Faust years. Had Notre Dame been able to keep its thumb on Miami, who knows what would have happened to their program? But for Miami to keep whipping up on us, it gave them tremendous credibility."

Embarrassed by Miami and angry at themselves, the Irish won five in a row. This improved their record to 6–2, and drew the interest of Cotton Bowl officials. But when they collapsed with three straight losses, they tumbled down the food chain to a Liberty Bowl encounter against Boston College.

Even that created controversy. Notre Dame was 6–5 and unranked. It had just gone 0–3 for the second straight November. The Liberty Bowl's executive director was a Notre Dame alum. And when the bowl invitation first arrived, the Irish seniors opposed it.

JOHN MOSLEY: "It was the twenty-fifth anniversary of the Liberty Bowl. So they really wanted Notre Dame in there. The guy running the bowl was this big Notre Dame graduate. Boston College also had Doug Flutie, and they were a Catholic school. So they wanted to sell the game as the Catholic Bowl."

"Notre Dame wanted in, too. It was Faust's third year, and he still hadn't been to a bowl game. But the seniors said no. They didn't want to go."

GREG BELL: "Here's the real story, no B.S. I had injured my ankle earlier that season. Then Faust and I had this screaming match one day at practice. So we didn't talk for a month. Then Faust called me and said, 'I need to talk with you.' I said, 'What do you want?' He said, 'The seniors want you to be at this dinner tonight. Toran and Mosley called and said they want you there.'

"So our whole senior class went to the Morris Inn. Faust got all of us a nice steak dinner. Then it was time to discuss the Liberty Bowl. Rick Naylor, one of our classmates, was from Moeller. Rick said, 'I don't care what anyone says. This team is 6–5. We aren't worth a shit. We don't deserve a bowl game. It's ridiculous that we're even talking about it.'

"Faust felt terrible. He thought Rick was one of his guys. But then Faust made his own pitch. He said the seniors had all been to a Sugar Bowl. He said the younger guys deserved an opportunity. But Faust said we wouldn't play unless the seniors felt it was appropriate. So we said the senior class would take a vote.

"Most of the walk-on seniors voted yes. But almost all the scholarship seniors voted no. So the majority vote was no. Then Mosley tried changing our minds. One of our own guys! Man, did we jump on his back."

JOHN MOSLEY: "I wasn't there for that vote. I was at my old high school in Culver, Indiana. I was the keynote speaker at their banquet. Then our athletic director Gene Corrigan called me. Gene said the seniors had voted not to go. He told me I'd better get right back there.

"So I went to the Morris Inn, where all the seniors were having a team gathering. Rick Naylor, Greg Bell, Stacy Toran—none of them wanted to go. I said, 'Listen, man, we're going. We're the last class here that's ever been to a bowl game. These younger guys don't know the beat. We're the only guys who can show them how to prepare for a bowl game.'

"Everybody got all pissed off at me. They were embarrassed that we were 6–5. They wanted Faust to resign. So they started yelling at me. Stacy Toran and I almost started fighting. Greg Bell had to come and break us up.

"Nothing was resolved, so a meeting was set up for the following day. Just the senior class and Father Joyce. It was a good meeting. He never said, 'You're going.' It was more like a question and answer with Father Joyce. One thing he did say was: 'I'm sorry you guys didn't get to play for Knute Rockne. But this is what you've got.'

"After that we took another vote. This time a majority approved it. But then the word got out. The press found out we didn't jump on it. They knew it took three votes. Then Boston College got wind and started getting cocky. They said: 'Notre Dame doesn't want to play us. They've always been *the* Catholic university. Now they're afraid we'll beat them.'

"That was ridiculous, but that was how Boston College was starting to get. Remember when they beat Miami? When Doug Flutie threw that long miracle pass? Ever since that, they'd started talking shit."

On December 18, before the Liberty Bowl, the *Chicago Sun-Times* printed a long article headlined "WHY FAUST ISN'T WINNING." The story included criticism from prominent former players such as Duerson, Zavagnin, Tony Hunter, and Tom Thayer. Kiel and Mark Bavaro, both still active, also expressed some hard feelings toward Faust.

Kiel later apologized for his statements. But the article got wide play and sparked the season's biggest controversy.

GERRY FAUST: "It was the most devastating thing that could ever happen to a coach. And a lot of it was half-truths. Three of the kids came to me. They all said they felt betrayed by the writer. They felt they were really misrepresented.

"I just said, 'Forget about it. Just be careful the next time you talk to the press.'

"That was all I said to them. Then I started Blair Kiel in the Liberty Bowl. Blair was a senior. He had done a lot for Notre Dame. So I told the coaches: 'We're gonna start this kid.'

"And this was after Blair had said some things."

At the Liberty Bowl in Memphis, Kiel got his first start after eight games on the bench. He completed 11 of 19 passes for 151 yards and one TD despite throwing frozen footballs in 11-degree weather. Pinkett gained 111 yards and scored two touchdowns. After unranked Notre Dame defeated 13th-ranked Boston College 19–18, Faust got a ride off the field by some of his players. The irrepressible coach then told reporters, "This is the beginning of something great."

Some found that a stretch, though. The 7–5 Irish had just beaten their first team with a winning record. They finished unranked for the third consecutive year and lost three games in South Bend for the first time since 1963.

JAY UNDERWOOD: "There were a lot of rumors flying before that bowl game. Some players thought if we lost, then Gerry would be out. He had a five-year contract, so nobody really saw him getting fired. But if Notre Dame indicated that it wanted him to leave—and if Gerry saw the writing on the wall—we thought he might resign.

"So after our last game, I recall a lot of mixed emotions. You always play to win. And Boston College had a pretty good team. But by the end of Faust's third year, a lot of guys had paid a lot of dues. A lot of college careers had been sacrificed. A lot of NFL careers as well. So there was still this underlying feeling: Yeah, we're happy we won. But did we just seal our doom?"

30

✤

KEYSTONE COPS

1 9 8 4 – 1 9 8 5

BEFORE THE 1984 SEASON OPENER, TIM BROWN RAN OUT ON the field without his helmet. The nervous freshman retrieved it when teammates started yelling. Then Brown promptly fumbled away the opening kickoff. Purdue kicked a field goal and ended up winning 23–21.

Of course, Brown felt wretched. But he would later win a Heisman Trophy. In the meantime, the football world was astounded that 8th-ranked Notre Dame could lose to unranked Purdue after routing it 52–6 the year before.

Then, after improving to 3–1, the 1984 Irish made history of sorts. They lost three straight at Notre Dame Stadium for the first time since 1956.

Following the first defeat (31–13 to Miami), the crowd booed Faust and the players as they left the field. During the second defeat (21–7 to Air Force), a national TV audience saw disgruntled fans wearing grocery bags on their heads. In the media coverage of the third defeat (36–32 to South Carolina), *Sports Illustrated* referred to "Notre Dame's Dying Irish."

Severe, but not irrational. Notre Dame was 3–4 and about to play undefeated and No. 6-ranked LSU before 78,033 liquored-up fans in Baton Rouge's Death Valley.

ALLEN PINKETT: "We just lost three games in South Bend. Faust was under fire. This one guy on ESPN said: 'These folks at LSU can't wait for Notre Dame to show up!'

"We were supposed to go down and get our butts kicked. It was going to be the demise of Notre Dame."

MIKE GOLIC: "LSU had their dorms right in the stadium. So as our bus pulled up, they had students hanging out the windows. There were also tons of LSU fans on the sidewalk.

"Right when I got off the bus, I bought an LSU hat. Then as our guys walked to the locker room, there was this gauntlet of LSU fans screaming, 'TIGER BAIT!' I just stopped in my tracks, took off the LSU hat, spit on it, threw it down, and stomped all over it.

"It was hysterical. It almost caused a riot. But I liked it when things got jacked up."

So did Golic's teammates evidently: the Irish stunned LSU 30–22. Afterward, Faust wept openly and hugged his players. He later told reporters: "Our boys would have quit a long time before the first quarter if they'd believed everything that had been said about 'em. But they were strong. And I'll tell you what else. I'm a strong guy, too. I'm gonna make it."

"I'm Gonna Make It" exclaimed the cover of the next *Sports Illustrated*. But even with this major upset, Faust was still 22–19–1. He had already been hung in effigy and criticized even by Parseghian. *USA Today* columnist Tom

Weir, who once called Faust's hiring the "biggest promotion in the history of football," had flatly called for Notre Dame to fire him. However, it didn't seem likely. Faust had one year left on his five-year contract, and as Father Joyce repeatedly told the press: "We honor our contracts here."

What about Faust resigning? Well, that was a different matter. Privately, in fact, Father Joyce and Gene Corrigan tried persuading Faust to quit after the 1984 season ended. Notre Dame by then was 7–5, and had finished outside the Top 20 a fourth straight season.

Faust didn't want to resign, but he also didn't want to "hurt Notre Dame." Therefore, he sought the counsel of Father Hesburgh, who says he told Faust: "You don't even have to ask. I said you had five years the day I hired you."

When it became apparent that Faust would not be fired, some alumni were enraged that the football program would still be allowed to suffer. Other alumni admired a university president who ignored the grumbling of millions and honored one man's contract.

In the 1985 season, the outcome of games seemed meaningful only in their larger context: Could Gerry Faust save himself in the final round? As the scrutiny and speculation mounted, *Newsweek* described it as "perversely riveting." But the pressure took a toll, Faust's players say.

JAY UNDERWOOD: "Remember the photographs they took of Abe Lincoln? He looked pretty good when he moved into the White House. Four years later, he aged thirty years.

"You could see that happening to Faust. The Notre Dame job almost beat that man to death."

ALLEN PINKETT: "It wasn't only the media and the fans. There was tremendous pressure on him from within the organization. I mean, let's face it. There's a lot of money that comes to that school when you win. They get flooded with donations, and playing in those bowl games is big business. So it *is* imperative that you win at Notre Dame. Because the school depends on the money that the football program brings in."

Chuck Lanza agrees with Pinkett. A second-string center in 1985, Lanza was All-American two years later.

CHUCK LANZA: "By 1985, from a marketing standpoint, Notre Dame was not what it used to be. That's why most of us felt that it would be Gerry's last year. Once you start having a negative financial impact, something has to be done."

FATHER JOYCE: "Lord no. The Faust years never became a financial burden. But let's take it one at a time.

"Alumni donations. We discussed that before when Kuharich was coach. Well, the same held true for Faust. The donations never went down. In fact, we were having campaigns during the Faust years. We were raising millions and millions of dollars. I mean, really big money.

"As for bowl game proceeds, they were totally insignificant. Bowl games during that time weren't money makers. By the time you took your team, your band members, and your official party, there was maybe a net of a few hundred thousand. Which is peanuts."

The 1985 season began with a loss at Michigan. Three weeks later, Notre Dame fell to Air Force for the fourth straight year. This dropped the Irish's record to 1–3.

Ned Bolcar was still a promising freshman at the time. In 1987 and 1989, he would lead the team in tackles with 106 and 109. He was also voted twice to be a captain, which has only happened 12 times in 110 years of Notre Dame football.

Bolcar recalls the road trip to play Air Force.

NED BOLCAR: "We walked into the locker room and Air Force had painted it mauve. I guess it was one of their tactics. They painted the locker room a feminine color, to make the visiting team feel less aggressive.

"Well, apparently someone had already told Gerry. He started yelling, 'Hey! Don't look at the walls! Don't look at the walls! It's a mental ploy! It's a mental ploy! They're trying to weaken us! Don't look at the walls!'

"So right away, of course, you got seventy-five guys staring right at the freaking walls. It was hilarious. The players were cracking up inside their lockers.

"Then during Gerry's pregame speech, one of our team captains is lying on the floor laughing his ass off. I mean, he's got tears coming out of his eyes.

"I was only a freshman. I was thinking: You gotta be kidding me. This is Notre Dame?"

The comedy was just starting. At one point against Air Force, Notre Dame had 14 men on the field. Later in the game, the Irish led 15–13 with six minutes left. They also had first-and-goal at the Air Force two. But when they lost 18 yards the next three plays, John Carney attempted a 37-yard field goal. The Cadets blocked the kick and ran it back 77 yards for a touchdown.

Final score: Air Force 21, Bad News Bears 15.

ALLEN PINKETT: "I was totally shocked. We thought we had finally beaten those dudes. Then we found a way to lose to them again."

JAY UNDERWOOD: "There was a lot of anger after that game. Players were throwing their helmets. Faust was running around, trying to console people, and they were muttering at him under their breath. The gloves were off by then. It was every man for himself."

Notre Dame responded by routing USC 35–3. Yet even this sparked bad press after Faust had his players put on green jerseys at halftime. Talk about beating a dead Trojan horse: The Irish were leading 27–0.

CHUCK LANZA: "That was very odd. I don't know what happened there. Maybe the jerseys weren't ready until halftime?"

JAY UNDERWOOD: "I remember thinking: This is horseshit. This will make the news. Notre Dame came out in green when it was already up by 27 points.

"It was ridiculous. I mean, breaking out the green is not done lightly. And Southern Cal was not even good that year. We were killing them wearing blue. Why the hell would you switch to green jerseys? Put them back in the box."

GERRY FAUST: "I got a little criticized after that game. But I told people: 'Hey, I've seen a lot of teams lose being up 27 points.'

"I never had any regrets about it, either. I would have done it again the same exact way."

This is interesting, since the second-half score was only 8–3 in favor of the green-clad Irish. The next week against Navy, Notre Dame again had too many men on the field. But this time it was 16 players, not 14.

Notre Dame then beat Mississippi for its fourth straight win. That's when rumors began that Faust could salvage his job with a victory at No. 1-ranked Penn State.

The Irish didn't exactly win one for Gerry. They trailed

36–0 before scoring, turned the ball over five times, and allowed Penn State to score on seven straight possessions. Even ABC got bored and switched telecasts.

After this 36–6 disaster, Faust had more defeats (24) than any coach in Notre Dame history. That left only two questions. Would Faust resign or make the school fire him? Would Notre Dame hire Lou Holtz or one of the dark horses: George Welsh, Bobby Ross, or Terry Donahue?

On November 26, when Faust announced his resignation at his Tuesday press conference, the only surprise was the timing. Notre Dame would play Saturday at powerful Miami.

GERRY FAUST: "I wanted to take the pressure off the players. They were under so much stress, they weren't performing up to their capabilities. I also wanted Notre Dame to get a new coach quickly. I knew it would help their recruiting, because it was about to start the following week."

NED BOLCAR: "Why before the Miami game? I don't know. The timing was terrible. Even before that happened, Faust had lost control of his coaching staff. He'd lost control of his players. Then things just got more chaotic with Faust's announcement."

ALLEN PINKETT: "Gerry spent a lot of that time crying. He was crying all damn week. I mean, he always dreamed of coaching at Notre Dame. Now he was gonna leave that school a failure."

JAY UNDERWOOD: "Holtz was named coach the day after Faust resigned. Well, we had a senior that season named Mike Perrino. He said to me on Friday: 'It doesn't look good. We're already yesterday's news.'

"Perrino was right. Everyone was looking to the future. So what happened on that Saturday didn't matter—except to Jimmy Johnson and Miami."

ALLEN PINKETT: "Aw, hell, it was party time down in Miami. We were about to play a powerhouse, and we had guys who didn't give a damn. I knew we'd get our butts kicked."

JAY UNDERWOOD: "That was the cherry on top. The final drubbing."

On November 30, the Gerry Faust era crashed and burned in the Orange Bowl. Miami not only won 58–7, the worst Notre Dame defeat since 1944, but Jimmy Johnson rudely ran up the score.

ALLEN PINKETT: "Hell, yeah, he ran it up. But I don't have any hard feelings toward him about that. That wasn't just a football game for them. That was Miami saying: Forget about Notre Dame. Forget about the most national championships, most All-Americans, most Heisman Trophy winners. Miami is the new power in college football."

TIM BROWN: "It did bother me, yeah. It bothered me a great deal. That's not the way the game should be played. But when you're the head coach of the University of Miami, what do you expect?"

What happened next was possibly even grimmer. As weather-related delays kept Notre Dame stranded for hours at the airport, tempers grew short and there was nearly a fight. Several players felt it was race-related.

ALLEN PINKETT: "I won't lie to you. We had some racial tensions on those teams. And guys were tired and pissed, and some of it spilled out."

CHUCK LANZA: "Yes. There was some racial tension in Gerry's last few years. It didn't involve many guys, but it did exist. I'm sure you've heard that already.

"The biggest example was probably at Miami airport. There were some guys pitching pennies. Some other guys thought that was inappropriate. There were some heated arguments that resulted. It was basically white guys versus black guys."

JAY UNDERWOOD: "No. Not at all. I never felt we had any racial tension. But I can tell you what happened, and you decide for yourself what you think it means. I only think it meant we got killed by Miami.

"Bishop Harris is a black coach. Bishop was sitting around with a bunch of black players. The players were being rambunctious and making noise. And Bishop Harris was being loose with them. He was acting like a friend, and that was uncharacteristic. I mean, everyone liked Bishop. But he was still a coach. I never remember him being one of the guys.

"Rick Lance was a white coach. Rick was usually real quiet and stoic. But like everybody else, Rick felt like total crap. He told Bishop, 'Why don't you guys keep it down? Remember, we just got drilled.' Bishop told Rick to butt out. They stood chest to chest and had some hard words. It was absolutely not racial. It was basically, 'I'll kill you! I'll knock your head off!'

"A few players stepped in and told everyone to cool out. The party was over then. Everything calmed down. But I was actually thinking until then: Let's see a fight. We're as low as we can get, but maybe we can go lower. Maybe we can watch two coaches try to kill each other at Miami International Airport."

Amazingly, the trauma wasn't over. Andy Heck, an All-American tackle in 1988, recalls the terrorizing flight back to South Bend.

ANDY HECK: "It was late at night. We hit massive turbulence. I remember Wally Kleine. Wally is six feet nine inches and 300 pounds. He was shaking like a leaf and looked like he might cry. I myself thought the plane was going down.

"Then we couldn't land. The plane was getting thrown as we came into South Bend. Finally, the pilot took one approach. Just seconds before the wheels hit the runway, the pilot hit the throttle and pulled the nose up. He aborted the landing."

ALLEN PINKETT: "I thought we would crash into the runway. And that seemed fitting to me. A 58–7 loss can do that to you. You don't give a damn about anything. Just go ahead and kill our ass."

JAY UNDERWOOD: "The pilot decided we couldn't land in South Bend. So we flew to Chicago. Then we took a bus trip to South Bend. It's only 90 miles, but it took us five hours in all that ice and snow. Because this was the season that wouldn't die gracefully. It had to be prolonged with misery."

ANDY HECK: "We pulled into South Bend at five in the morning. The only thing we had was a meeting that afternoon. Gerry Faust was going to say his good-byes. Then we were meeting Lou Holtz, our new head coach.

"So that afternoon we're all in our meeting room. You can imagine how tired the guys are. Their eyes are all half-closed from the night before. We have this one lineman named Chuck Lanza. He's a big, imposing, intimidating player. Lanza is in the front row with some other guys who will be seniors. Lanza's got one foot propped up on the stage.

"Gerry Faust says a few words and then he exits. Lou Holtz walks through the back door and up the left aisle. He's walking with a purpose. He hops on the stage and he sees Lanza."

CHUCK LANZA: "He asked me what my name was. So I told him. Then he asked how long I'd been playing football. I said, 'About ten years.' He said, 'If you want to play one more, you better move your foot. You better sit up in your chair. And you better pay attention.'

"That was my introduction to Lou Holtz."

31

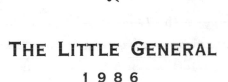

THE LITTLE GENERAL
1986

LOU HOLTZ GREW UP CATHOLIC IN EAST LIVERPOOL, OHIO, where he rooted for Frank Leahy's powerhouse Notre Dame teams. He and his classmates at St. Aloysius grade school would convene and adjourn each day to the Notre Dame Victory March played on a jukebox. At age 29, while briefly between jobs, Holtz compiled his now famous list of 107 goals he wished to accomplish. They included skydiving, meeting the Pope, scoring a hole in one, and coaching the Fighting Irish.

On November 27, 1985, the day he was presented as the 25th football coach in the history of Notre Dame, Holtz was asked by a sportswriter how it felt.

"Look at me," he said. "I'm five foot ten, I weigh 150 pounds, I talk with a lisp, I look like I have scurvy, I'm not very smart, I graduated 234th in a high school class of 278. What do you think it feels like to be named head coach at Notre Dame?"

This response, which expressed both self-deprecation

and aggression, seemed to sum up the man that Notre Dame had charged with rescuing its program.

In 1956, Holtz escaped the steel mills of East Liverpool and enrolled at Kent State, where he majored in history and lettered at linebacker despite his scrawny frame. He spent the next eight years assistant coaching at five different colleges. At his last and most prestigious stop, Ohio State, Holtz coached defensive backs for Woody Hayes as the Buckeyes won the 1968 national championship.

Holtz began his head coaching career at William & Mary and took the school to its only bowl game before moving up in class to North Carolina State. The previously ailing Wolfpack went to four straight bowl games, which led Holtz to an ill-fated job as head coach of the New York Jets.

Holtz quickly realized he'd made a mistake. He couldn't inspire the Jets, and he got torn up by the city's snarling tabloids. Holtz quit with a 3–10 record, one game left on the schedule, and this candid assessment: "God did not put Lou Holtz on this earth to coach pro football."

Still hyperambitious, Holtz took the head coaching job at Arkansas in 1977. His team went 10–1 in his first season and then faced heavily favored Oklahoma in the Orange Bowl. A few days before the game, Holtz suspended three star players for disciplinary reasons. When Arkansas still won 31–6, his reputation was set. Holtz was a hard-line coach who excelled in big games.

Holtz left the Razorbacks in December 1983 after building a 60–21–2 record. The question was, did he resign or did Arkansas resign him? There were rumblings in Fayetteville that Holtz was preoccupied with his national speaking engagements. Some felt his recruiting had also suffered. In particular, they claimed Holtz was losing too many homegrown prospects to slick-talking Oklahoma coach Barry Switzer.

Holtz had also been criticized for agreeing to endorse Jesse Helms, the conservative senator from North Carolina. Holtz said he didn't agree with all of Helms's politics, but had offered his support because Helms had been friendly and helpful when Holtz was the coach at North Carolina State.

This controversy surfaced shortly before Holtz resigned. Then, at an official press conference, athletic director Frank Broyles described Holtz as "tired and burned out." Only four days later, Holtz was named head coach at Minnesota.

When he arrived in Minneapolis, the pitiful Golden Gophers had lost 17 consecutive Big Ten games. Holtz led them to records of 4–7 and 6–5, including one impressive 13–7 loss to eventual national champion Oklahoma. In December 1985, Holtz took over the Irish at their darkest hour.

Father Joyce, who hired Holtz in conjunction with athletic director Gene Corrigan, explains why Holtz seemed attractive.

FATHER JOYCE: "He had a great won-and-loss record. He had been a college head coach for many years. And he had gotten me interested in him on two previous occasions.

"The first time was in 1977 during the bowl games. While Devine's team annihilated No. 1 Texas in the Cotton Bowl, Holtz's team destroyed No. 2 Oklahoma. Had Oklahoma won, they would have been No. 1. So Holtz actually helped Notre Dame win a national championship.

"Of course, that caught my eye. But what really impressed me is when he stuck by his principles and suspended three of his best players. The fact that he still won the game was icing on the cake.

"He was also at Arkansas when the second thing happened. For one whole year, we both sat on a blue ribbon committee put together by the NCAA. We were studying the problems in college football, and Holtz was the only coach. The rest were college presidents, vice presidents, and ADs. Well, Holtz was very sensible and impressive. I mean, he knew more than all these other guys put together. And he seemed quite at ease with all these important people."

Besides his commanding aura, his 17 years of head coaching experience, his history of repairing tattered programs, and his demand for discipline and control, Holtz was also one of the game's finest technicians. He was the anti-Faust, in other words.

Still, it wouldn't be easy to burn through the gloom created by Faust's 30–26–1 record, the 5–6 finish in 1985, and the 58–7 train wreck at Miami. Holtz's first team would also play a tough schedule, with road trips to Alabama, LSU, and USC, and South Bend clashes with Michigan and Penn State.

In January 1986, his first full month on the job, Holtz wasted no time sending a message. Every morning before classes, he held what he archly described as "agility sessions."

CHUCK LANZA: "Boot camp was more like it. We started working out at six A.M. And this was the dead of winter in South Bend. So we'd be trudging through the snow while it was still dark. Then we'd get to the ACC [Athletic and Convocation Center] and there would be TV crews with all their bright lights on. Your hair would still be screwed up. You hadn't even showered. And you would be cursing Lou Holtz."

NED BOLCAR: "Holtz took over a team with a lot of cancerous niches. Just look at what happened in Miami. Guys were arguing on the sidelines. They were fighting in the airport.

"So what Holtz really wanted to do was bring us together. I think that's what happened at winter workouts. Holtz worked us until we dropped. He took a very splintered team and turned it into a common, working machine that was only gonna get stronger as time went by."

TIM BROWN: "The players weren't on their own program anymore. They were on Lou Holtz's program. The crazy thing was, we enjoyed it. Guys were throwing up and they were happy."

Holtz laughs when he hears his ex-players' comments.

LOU HOLTZ: "Those workouts weren't that hard. I kept telling them how tough they were, and how only a rare person could get through them, and how nobody in the country was working as hard as we were. But it was psychological more than anything. I mean, they might have been harder than last year's winter workouts. But they weren't as hard as they were going to get."

On September 13, the Holtz regime opened at an electrified Notre Dame Stadium. Third-ranked Michigan was expected to play in the Rose Bowl and contend for the national title. The Irish were coming into a season unranked for the first time since Parseghian replaced Hugh Devore in 1964.

Bolcar, the hard-nosed linebacker from New Jersey, recalls what happened during pregame warmups.

NED BOLCAR: "We had this routine we did. We would line up across the 20-yard line and run plays into the endzone. When our warmups ended, we would punt out of the endzone and go into the tunnel. Well, Michigan had to go in through the same tunnel. But instead of running down the sideline, they decided to run right through our drills."

"If Michigan did this to us the year before, we'd have probably just watched them run through our drills. This time, a big offensive lineman named Tom Rheder stuck out his arm and clotheslined a Michigan player named John Kolesar. Then another player grabbed Tom and a little fight broke out.

"Was this our fault? No. Michigan made a decision. They wanted to test us. And we laid down the law: This is our stadium, our field, and nobody comes in here and pushes us around. We're not taking shit from anyone."

This pregame incident, though mostly unreported by the press, foreshadowed a major issue that surfaced two years later: Did Holtz's Notre Dame teams simply stand their ground, or did they provoke their opponents?

In 1986, Michigan won 24–23, but the Irish never punted and gained 455 total yards. Afterward, Steve Beverlein told reporters: "This game could have very easily been a blowout for us." *Sports Illustrated* wrote in its subhead: "As the Lou Holtz era began at Notre Dame, the underrated Irish handled Michigan everywhere but on the scoreboard."

The crowd stood and cheered as Notre Dame left the field, but even this show of support could not console John Carney. With 13 seconds left, Carney had missed a 45-yard field goal attempt.

JOHN CARNEY: "I hit it pure. I thought it would be good when it came off my foot. But it had this awkward rotation, and it landed only five yards beyond the goalpost. So I felt the ball got tipped. But no one from Michigan claimed it being tipped, and Lou just thought I was a flake.

"After it's over, you start putting all the pieces together. Lou Holtz's first game. National coverage. Michigan. Had a chance to be part of history, and blew it. So that next week was hard. You go to class and you hear students whisper."

Three weeks later, in a bitter 10-9 home loss to Pittsburgh, Carney missed another last-second field goal attempt. As Notre Dame's record dropped to 1–4, Holtz's grace period ended. It was time for South Bend to second-guess the new guy.

Meanwhile, Holtz took steps to cut off any doubts in his locker room.

LOU HOLTZ: "I had a talk with the seniors. Now, seniors don't always buy into everything you're doing. They're short-timers. So they might want to ignore a new commander. They might just tread water for three months.

"So I told the seniors, 'There's two ways to quit. One is where you say, 'I quit.' The other is where you quit, but you don't tell anybody. You quit on yourself. Well, we have six football games left. You seniors can start Notre Dame back toward the top.' "

In the next three weeks, the Irish routed Air Force, Navy, and SMU to even their record at 4–4.

CHUCK LANZA: "The Air Force game was important. Because before Gerry Faust, Notre Dame was 11–0 against Air Force. Then Air Force beat Notre Dame four years in a row. So beating them 31–3 was pretty blatant. We finally had the right game plan."

NED BOLCAR: "It's one of the first things Holtz said when he came in there. He said, 'Mark this down. Notre Dame will never lose to a military academy.'"

Actually, his prophecy was wrong. Holtz lost a shocker to Air Force in 1996. But for the first ten years of his tenure, Holtz was 18–0 against military schools.

After winning three straight, Notre Dame lost two heartbreakers: 29–24 to third-ranked Penn State and 21–19 to eighth-ranked LSU. Next came the dramatic finale at 17th-ranked Southern California.

The Irish trailed 37–20 with 12:26 to go, but Tim Brown and Steve Beverlein led a furious comeback. Then, with Notre Dame down 37-35 and 2:15 remaining, Brown went out to return just his second punt all year. Brown broke it for 56 yards to the USC 16. The Irish could not punch it in, so with 0:02 left, Holtz called his final time-out and sent in Carney.

JOHN CARNEY: "Our team had had a meeting the night before. It was in the ballroom of our hotel. Lou talked about every senior who'd be playing in his last game. When Lou came to me he said, 'I hope this game comes down to a John Carney field goal.'

"Well, he got his wish. It was coming down to a field goal, and I was doing all I could to keep my cookies down."

NED BOLCAR: "USC had been killing us at halftime. So Lou was very blunt. He told the seniors, 'You guys are gone. Thank you for everything. But for you underclassmen, your future will depend greatly on the second half of this game . . . and practice starts in two weeks.'

"I remember this feeling of terror went through me. For our lack of intensity, we would pay the price for the next two hundred days.

"We went back out and played a fantastic second half. Then when Carney kicked it down the middle, it was like Notre Dame was reborn. The fans felt it. Lou realized it. And all the younger guys said, 'Whew. Now we have something to build on, and maybe we just escaped some wrath of Lou Holtz.' "

TIM BROWN: "To be down 37–20 and to win 38–37 as time expires? I don't want to call it astronomical . . . but it was pretty huge."

LOU HOLTZ: "We started 1–4 and finished 5–6. So I felt we were making progress. But what meant the most to me was our second-half attitude against USC. We were down 37–20, and our sideline was still intense. That's when we became a football team."

32

❧

WAKING UP THE ECHOES

1 9 8 7 — 1 9 8 8

IN FEBRUARY 1987, AFTER THREE ORDINARY RECRUITING CAM-
paigns, Notre Dame signed the country's top-ranked
freshman class. These blue-chip prospects included Chris
Zorich, Todd Lyght, Ricky Watters, Tony Brooks, Scott
Kowalkowski, Tim Ryan, Mike Heldt, George Williams,
Bob Dahl, Andre Jones and Kent Graham. After leaving
South Bend, all 11 went on to NFL careers.

With this auspicious start, Notre Dame established itself as
one of the nation's premier recruiting machines. From 1987 to
1990, the Irish signed 36 future NFL players, and nine of those
players were drafted in the first round. These numbers reflected two strengths of the Holtz regime: the ability to attract
top college athletes, and also prepare them for NFL careers.

In November 1987, people were calling Lou Holtz a
mastermind. After a 5–6 finish in 1986, the Irish were 8–1
and contending for the national championship. But on a
freezing afternoon at Penn State's Beaver Stadium, Holtz
made what he concedes was a tactical error.

Notre Dame trailed 14–7 just before halftime. With the ball at the Penn State three, Holtz pulled his sophomore quarterback Tony Rice. Freshman back-up Kent Graham, whom Holtz considered to have a stronger arm, came in cold off the bench and threw an interception. Notre Dame went on to lose 21–20.

With their record 8–2, the Irish accepted a bid to the Cotton Bowl and then flew to Miami for their regular season finale against the 11–0 Hurricanes. In the 1985 game, Miami had crushed Notre Dame 58–7 and Jimmy Johnson had run up the score. Revenge would have to wait, though. The Hurricanes won again, 24–0, as their hostile defense contained the Heisman Trophy front-runner Tim Brown.

TIM BROWN: "Miami was Miami. They had words for you after every play. But Jimmy Johnson started talking before we even played them. He said, 'If Tim Brown was on my team, he wouldn't even be starting.'

"That kind of statement you can overlook, but sometimes their players would get a little personal. They'd talk about your mother and all that craziness. Some of their guys were talking about my knees. They said, 'We're gonna blow out your knees, man. You can forget all about the NFL.'

"One guy still wanted a piece of me after the game. That's how brainwashed he was to get Tim Brown. At the time, I was shaking hands with some other players. This guy comes at me, crying. He's crying and he's breathing down my neck. It was actually Michael Irvin who told him to calm down. He said, 'Hey man, look, the game is over.'"

One week after being hounded by Miami, Tim Brown became Notre Dame's first Heisman Trophy winner since John Huarte in 1964. Brown finished his career as the Irish's all-time leader in pass reception yards (2,493), kickoff return yards (1,613), and kicks returned for touch-downs (three punts, three kickoffs). Brown is now an eight-time All-Pro with the Oakland Raiders.

In the 1987 postseason, Miami beat Oklahoma in the Orange Bowl and won their second national champion-ship of the 1980s. Notre Dame ended the year with an-other embarrassment: a 35–10 loss to Texas A&M in the Cotton Bowl.

A season marked by great promise had ended with three straight defeats. Still, the 17th-ranked Irish finished in the Top 20 and played in a major bowl game for the first time since 1980.

In 1988, Notre Dame entered the season ranked No. 13. But the Irish had an interesting mix. Besides all the brilliant young players Holtz had recruited, including tight end Derek Brown, flanker Ricky Watters, split end Rocket Ismail, quarterback Tony Rice, and nose tackle Chris Zorich, there were 17 upperclassmen remaining from the Faust years. Included in this hungry group were four All-Americans and team leaders: offensive tackle Andy Heck, defensive end Frank Stams, and linebackers Ned Bolcar and Wes Pritchett.

Another key performer was junior Pat Terrell. As a sophomore, Terrell started five games at split end and only caught two passes. Holtz then switched him to safety, a position he has played for nine years in the pros.

PAT TERRELL: "In 1988, our motto was never flinch. We heard it over and over from Lou Holtz. I mean, Holtz was a little guy. But he was not a wimp. He wanted his football team to be physical.

"That was our goal, too, especially on defense. We would play by the rules. But we were gonna be hitters. We were going to knock the snot out of your nose.

"That's why Chris Zorich was so important that season. Zorich brought in some nastiness that we needed. Because a lot of teams would not give us respect. They thought Notre Dame was all nice Catholic boys. Zorich showed people that we would kick some tail."

FRANK STAMS: "He was the nicest guy off the field and the biggest maniac on it. Actually, I was kind of scared of Zorich. I just stayed away from him."

DEREK BROWN: "At practice, he always went after Ricky Watters. Ricky always runs his mouth, and he would talk all that stuff during tackling drills. He'd tell Zorich, 'You can't even touch me, man.' And as long as there was open space around, Ricky Watters killed him. Zorich would whiff and miss and start getting pissed.

"But if Zorich and Ricky got into any tight quarters? Ricky would tell him, 'Hey, man! I was just kidding!' Because if Zorich ever took Ricky in his paws, that would be the end. He would crush him with his bare hands."

FRANK STAMS: "In 1988, we opened by beating Michigan 19–17. Zorich was a sophomore. It was his first start. Every time we turned around, somebody from Michigan wanted to fight him."

CHRIS ZORICH: "Obviously, off the field I'm a different person. On the field, I want to rip someone's head off.

"I guess that came from my childhood. I grew up very poor and came from a rough neighborhood. So I would envision the guys who beat me up, or the guys who mugged my mom. Then I would vent my frustrations out on the field."

Zorich grew up amidst drug dealers and winos in a dismal housing project in Chicago. His father ran out on the family before Zorich was born. His mother was robbed on the street repeatedly, and Zorich took several beatings from gang members who wanted him to join them.

Zorich couldn't sleep his freshman year at Notre Dame. It was too quiet, too tranquil. He also says he felt overmatched in the classroom. But Zorich hung in through his struggles and graduated.

On the field, Zorich made ten tackles in his first start against Michigan and went on to rank third on the team with 70. A consensus All-American his next two years, he won the 1990 Lombardi Award as college football's best lineman.

In 1988, after beating Michigan, Notre Dame had a 5–0 record on October 15. That's when they played Miami at South Bend, in one of the biggest games in Notre Dame history. The No. 1-ranked Hurricanes were defending national champs and undefeated in 36 straight regular-season games. They had destroyed the Irish by a combined score of 133–20 in the teams' last four meetings.

Notre Dame came in ranked No. 4, with a chance to beat a top-ranked team in South Bend for the first time since 1968. In the manic pregame atmosphere on campus, some of the fastest-selling tee-shirts read: EVEN GOD HATES MIAMI, CATHOLICS VS. CONVICTS, and YOU CAN'T SPELL SCUM WITHOUT U.M. A banner on one of the dorms said: CAN YOU READ THIS? MIAMI CAN'T.

Finally, Holtz intervened in the form of an open letter to Notre Dame students. "I understand Miami coach Jimmy Johnson has been the recipient of several phone calls and letters from Notre Dame students," Holtz wrote in the campus newspaper *The Observer*. "It seems to me that if we want to display our intelligence, we ought to show a great deal of respect to Miami."

But it was too late for restraint. All the students could think of was 58–7 Miami in 1985, when Jimmy Johnson had his team throwing long passes in the fourth quarter.

FRANK STAMS: "Frankly, there *wasn't* respect between the two schools. When we played USC, it was more of a healthy competition. All the people from both schools really enjoyed it. Whereas when we played Miami, the Holy Cross brothers cringed. Because they never knew what to expect."

WES PRITCHETT: "There was bad blood. There had been for several years. It hit its peak when we had the pregame fight."

When and where has been well documented. After pregame warm-ups, the scuffle began in the northern endzone and spread into the narrow tunnel which leads back inside to both teams' locker rooms.

How the brawl began has always been unclear.

CHRIS ZORICH: "Miami started it. See, their whole reputation was based on intimidation. Then they tried to intimidate us. They got into our face while we were warming up. That's something that we wouldn't take."

WES PRITCHETT: "I honestly don't know who threw the first punch. But I was in there early, and this was an absolute brawl."

NED BOLCAR: "Well . . . I don't want to be known as the guy who started the fight against Miami. But I was right in the middle when it broke out.

"We were lined up in the endzone doing our punting drill. Miami was on their way into the tunnel. But a bunch of their players decided not to go in. They were just gonna stay out there, standing in front of the tunnel, watching Notre Dame do its pregame warmup.

"There were some hard words going back and forth. Then some of their guys started walking into our end-zone. One guy was Leon Searcy, this big offensive line-man. I said, 'Why don't you get the hell out of our endzone?' He started shoving me. We started cursing each other. He said something about my mother. So I jabbed him in the throat.

"Then everything erupted. There was this wave of commotion and all these players went crashing into the tunnel. People were throwing punches. People were grab-bing facemasks. Next thing it got broken up and both teams went straight back to their locker rooms. We were going nuts in there. We were screaming, 'FUCK YOU! WE'LL KILL THOSE GUYS!' "

Junior flanker Pat Eilers, who began his collegiate ca-reer at Yale, transferred to Notre Dame as a walk-on, and then started 18 games, picks up the story from there.

PAT EILERS: "Lou came back to our locker room looking pissed off. He said, 'You guys are here to play a football game. They're trying to take your mind off of what you need to do. If we can focus, *focus* being the key . . . we have an opportunity to win this game.'

"Then he went through some strategy. At the very end, he looked around the room and it was almost silent. He said, 'I want you guys to go out there and play the Miami Hurricanes. But I'll tell you one thing. Save Jimmy Johnson's ass for me.'

"It was beautiful. It was a little stroke of coaching ge-nius. Here's Lou, probably a buck sixty soaking wet. He doesn't look like he could take anyone on. But, you know, 'Save Jimmy Johnson's ass for me.' "

NED BOLCAR: "Most of us believed that Lou would get his ass kicked by Jimmy Johnson. But we all went bananas anyway."

LOU HOLTZ: "I don't know what caused the altercation. But when the Miami players ran through our exercises, it really showed a lack of respect for the Notre Dame players. And the Notre Dame players took offense to that.

"I was upset about it. But I didn't want it becoming a distraction. So I just said, 'There's going to be no fighting, and there's going to be no cheap shots. We're going to play the game the way it should be played. Then, if they want to fight after the game, that's fine and I'll join in.'

"That's about all I recall. I don't recall saying save Jimmy for me. My thing was just this: Play the game the way it's meant to be played. When the game's over, then we'll see what happens."

Tim Layden covered the Notre Dame–Miami game for *Newsday.* Since 1994, he has written about college football for *Sports Illustrated.*

TIM LAYDEN: "When the fight began, I was up in the press box trying to figure out what was going on. And I immediately assumed that Miami had instigated everything. I thought it was Miami just being Miami again, and poor Notre Dame just trying to fight back.

"But I remember as the season went on, and you covered more Notre Dame games, and you were around that team more, and you saw how they played at the Fiesta Bowl, and you got to know some of their defensive players, you were able to look back and realize that Notre Dame surely had as much to do with starting that incident as Miami did.

"I think it was sort of the building to a crescendo of

the toughness that Holtz was trying to build from when he first took the job. I mean, Holtz had been trying to change the mind-set of that whole program. He was a guy who liked to come across as a timid character, but he believed in guys being tough right from the start. And I don't think there's any doubt that Holtz was happy to see his team stand up and fight Miami. He'll never come out and say this. But that particular session with Miami kept Notre Dame from getting pushed around that day or any other day."

In the football game itself, played on a gorgeous South Bend afternoon, fourth-ranked Notre Dame beat top-ranked Miami 31–30. Tony Rice absorbed several huge hits, but still completed eight of 16 passes for a career high of 195 yards. Stams caused two fumbles, recovered a third, and terrorized Miami quarterback Steve Walsh. Pritchett made 15 tackles despite breaking his hand in the first quarter. Terrell returned an interception for a 60-yard touchdown and secured the victory when he batted down Walsh's two-point conversion pass with 45 seconds left.

"This was a win by the Notre Dame spirit," a jubilant Holtz said afterward. "It was a win by the spirit of a group of guys who just refused to fold. They believed, and I congratulate our players for a great football game."

But as Holtz also said to the press, "Maybe this series needs to be cooled down. I don't mean down the road. I mean now."

After this cherished victory over Miami, Notre Dame ended its regular season with an 11–0 record and the nation's No. 1 ranking. Then, on January 1, the Irish met third-ranked West Virginia in the Fiesta Bowl for the national championship.

The 11–0 Mountaineers came in with a celebrated offense averaging 44 points and 482 yards per game. Their star was Major Harris, whose powerful arm and quick feet made him dangerous both as a passer and a scrambler.

NED BOLCAR: "West Virginia came in with a lot of hype. And Holtz kept pumping them up before the game. I mean, he *really* worked the media from West Virginia. Because they felt their football team was God Almighty.

"So Lou just keep feeding and feeding. He'd tell them, 'You're right. How can we stop West Virginia? You folks have the best quarterback in the country. Major Harris makes Tony Rice look like he's standing in cement.'

"Their media ate it up. They would actually ask our players if we thought we could compete against their boys. I remember thinking: How stupid are these people? Do they honestly think we can't beat West Virginia?

"But that was vintage Lou Holtz. He knew how to feed the media machine."

Bolcar is not the first to make this observation. Earlier that year, as the No. 1-ranked Irish prepared to play Rice, Holtz said with a straight face, "I'm scared to death of Rice." When Notre Dame won 54–11, some reporters chided Holtz for being less than forthright.

LOU HOLTZ: "I could care less what people say. I have never tried to fake anything. Now, we never went into a Saturday thinking that we wouldn't win. But I can honestly tell you this: There was never a time on a Sunday or Monday when I didn't think we were quite capable of losing the football game that weekend. I don't care who we played. I coached scared to death. People in the media wanna say that's poor-mouthing? I say it's giving praise, respect, and dignity to the opposition. And that's the first thing you better do. You'd better respect your opponent."

Before the Fiesta Bowl, West Virginia coach Don Neh-
len said, "I'm real confused. Half of America thinks we
shouldn't be here. And Lou talks like we're the best team
since the invention of the jelly bean."

Notre Dame won 34–21, but it was easier than the
score would indicate. The Irish held the Mountaineers to
282 net yards, while racking up 455 themselves. Notre
Dame led at halftime 23–6.

It was a perfect Irish outing, except for the slew of
flags in the game's final minutes. By the time the gun
went off, Notre Dame had its eighth personal foul and
Holtz had run on to the field to scold his defensive players on national television.

FRANK STAMS: "That was a physical game. Pritchett hit
Major Harris so hard a couple times, I really didn't think
he would get up. In fact, I know some people who were
sitting in the stands near Major Harris' mom. They said
she was yelling, 'Take my son out of the game! They're
gonna kill him out there!'

"So it was definitely hard-hitting out there. But I also
thought the refs got carried away. They seemed a little
flag-happy to me."

CHRIS ZORICH: "West Virginia's offensive line was bigger
than some pro teams'. We had an aggressive defense. So
things got heated on both sides. But then our guys started
yelling at the refs. That's when the flags started flying."

LOU HOLTZ: "Going into that game, West Virginia was the
most penalized team in the country. And they had very
few penalties called during the course of the game. I don't
wanna comment on the officiating, but when the game
was over, when we had it won, our personal fouls were

for comments made to the officials. Not for flagrant violations on West Virginia's players.

"Now, is that the best way to handle the situation? No. Not at all. The players should play and the refs should ref. That's what I was telling our defensive players."

NED BOLCAR: "I agreed that we didn't need those personal fouls. At that point in the game, what are we arguing and fighting about? Why are we giving yards on stupid penalties?

"But to be honest with you, I thought Lou was showboating a little. Maybe it wasn't necessary for him to walk out on the field. Maybe he could have waited until the series was over and taken the team on the sideline and grabbed a few facemasks. But this was on TV. He had center stage. And Lou does know how to showboat."

Holtz also knew how to win. Notre Dame entered the 1988 season ranked No. 13. Then it defeated Miami, purged the memory of 58–7, and secured its first national title since 1977. Holtz joined Rockne, Leahy, Parseghian, and Devine by winning a national championship in his third year. In one respect, Holtz surpassed them: No other Irish squad had ever gone 12–0.

33

※

DEFENDING THE CROWN

1 9 8 9

AFTER HIS GLORIOUS ACHIEVEMENT, LOU HOLTZ MET PRESI-
dent Reagan at the White House, authored an article for
Time magazine, and signed his fourth straight class of
highly coveted freshmen. But while Holtz enjoyed the
championship life, he had no illusions about the upcoming year. On his reading list that summer was Sun Tzu's
classic book, *The Art of War*.

Still, the Irish were loaded as they began their quest
for back-to-back titles. Their 15 returning starters included
quarterback Tony Rice, running backs Ricky Watters and
Anthony Johnson, flanker Rocket Ismail, split end Pat
Eilers, tight end Derek Brown, offensive linemen Tim
Grunhard and Tim Ryan, nose tackle Chris Zorich, and
defensive backs Pat Terrell and Todd Lyght. Fifth-year
senior Ned Bolcar also came back after playing behind
Michael Stonebreaker in 1988. In 1987, as a junior, Bolcar
had led Notre Dame with 106 tackles.

The Irish started out ranked No. 2, but after routing

Virginia in the Kickoff Classic, they moved to No. 1 and stayed there through five more wins. Then, on October 21, top-ranked Notre Dame met tenth-ranked USC.

The Irish trailed 17–7 at halftime before rallying to beat the Trojans for the seventh straight year, 28–24. This thrilling home victory gave Notre Dame a 7–0 record, and 19 consecutive wins since its Cotton Bowl loss to Texas A&M.

The bad news was another pregame brawl. Once again it happened near the tunnel. As the Irish finished their warm-ups by punting out of the endzone, the Trojans started running in their direction. That's when the ruckus broke out.

From here the story blurs. According to *Sports Illustrated*'s Doug Looney, the blame belonged entirely to Notre Dame. After all, wrote Looney, "These are nasty, ornery, pit bull Irish, who may be beyond the control of their own coach. Approach at your own peril."

But according to Notre Dame's players, the truth was not so conveniently black and white.

PAT TERRELL: "A handful of USC guys came right through our drills. But then, in fairness to them, how much room did they have to get to the tunnel? So as they were running through, there were some confrontations. And we had a team that wasn't gonna flinch."

DEREK BROWN: "It was a pretty big mêlée. I even remember seeing some assistant coaches throwing blows. But it probably started the same way most football fights do. Someone bumped into someone and all hell broke loose."

PAT EILERS: "I don't think we instigated it. But I also don't think we turned the other cheek."

NED BOLCAR: "I can't help you on this one. I don't know how it started. All I really remember is seeing our third-string quarterback Steve Belles. I happened to look down and Steve was underneath these metal retractable stands. One of the USC guys pushed him down there. I said, 'Attaboy Steve. That was a helluva fight you just put up.' "

CHRIS ZORICH: "I hated the USC guys. They lived in California. They had beautiful swimming pools on campus. They never shoveled snow."

But who started the fight?

CHRIS ZORICH: "They were a bunch of cocky California guys. Of course, they started it. And of course *Sports Illustrated* blamed Notre Dame. Either you hate Notre Dame or you love Notre Dame. And *Sports Illustrated* had no reason to love us."

LOU HOLTZ: "*Sports Illustrated* can write anything they want. I won't even justify that article with a comment. I'll just say this: We were involved in two pregame fights in my entire coaching career. I never had a football player involved in a fight during a game. Now, Southern Cal was involved in five altercations, either pregame or during the game, that year alone. Five altercations.

"Also, their band took over the tunnel where our band was supposed to be. They did this well before game time, and they played the Southern Cal song as loud as they could for two hours. This is our stadium, our tunnel, where our band is supposed to be. And I told our football players before the game: 'This is Southern Cal's way of doing things. And their players have been involved in some stuff this year. And I won't be surprised if they provoke us before the game.'

"But under no circumstances did I want them to retaliate. In fact, I warned them not to. But then it happened anyway. Fortunately, nothing happened during the game."

PAT EILERS: "I remember that *Sports Illustrated* story. That was a piece of garbage. But, in a way, Notre Dame sets itself up for that kind of story. Because sometimes the institution tries to convey this holier-than-thou attitude. Or at least that's how people perceive Notre Dame's attitude.

"But I think there was another factor involved. Notre Dame was on top again. So it was time for the media to rip us back down."

NED BOLCAR: "Just a couple of weeks after USC fought with us, they got into another fight with UCLA. But in between their two fights, we got totally ripped by *Sports Illustrated.*

"We took a lot of heat after that from the general public, and from the Notre Dame administration. Actually, that's wrong. I don't think we ever did hear from the administration. But we heard from Lou Holtz, and I'm sure he was feeling pressure from above. Because he seemed very sensitive about it.

"He kept telling us, 'We're in the fishbowl here. We gotta act properly. Let's not give people a reason to point the finger at us. So if any of our players get caught fighting, if there's any unsportsmanlike conduct, not only will you be pulled out of the game, but you'll be kicked off the team. They can't take away your scholarship, but I can sure kick you off this football team.' "

PAT TERRELL: "Lou said he would resign if we got in any more fights. The first time he said it, we were in a team meeting. So we didn't really believe it. Everyone was saying, 'Give me a break. This man loves the job too much.'

"But then he made the same statement to the press. That's what really scared us. I mean, now it's out there. It's on television and in print. That would make it hard for him to back down."

NED BOLCAR: "He said, 'You can mark it down. If it happens again, I will not be the Notre Dame coach.'

"These comments came out of his mouth every few weeks. I remember thinking: This is ridiculous. What are we supposed to do if another team comes in and tries to intimidate us? Just stand there and take it? Then go out and play football?

"Then that's exactly what happened against Miami."

First there was history to make. While routing SMU 59–6, the 1989 Irish set a new school record with their 22nd consecutive victory (the old mark of 21 had been set by Frank Leahy's fabled postwar teams between 1946 and 1948.) The following Saturday Notre Dame beat Penn State 34–23 to extend its winning streak to 23. That set up the showdown at Miami.

The No. 1-ranked Irish came in 11–0. The 10–1 Hurricanes were only ranked No. 7, but could move back into contention by whipping top-ranked Notre Dame in the regular season finale. The Hurricanes also had payback on their minds. In 1988, their only loss had been to Notre Dame, and it kept them from winning a second straight national title.

A pregame rumble had marred that 31–30 classic in South Bend. Before the rematch at the Orange Bowl, Irish players say, the Hurricanes tried their best to incite another.

TIM RYAN: "It was right before the kickoff. We were on the sideline, and our captains went out for the coin toss. Then

Miami's entire team came marching across the field. They came to start a fight, and we wanted to. But Holtz had just got done giving us a warning. He said, 'Anybody fights, they're not gonna play in this game.' "

PAT TERRELL: "It was the craziest thing you'll ever see. Miami was cursing us out, and Holtz was trying to grab us and keep us on the sidelines."

NED BOLCAR: "Try and picture this. More than one hundred Miami guys lined up across the field about ten yards from us. They're pointing, screaming, heckling Notre Dame. I glance down our sideline and Ricky Watters is trying to mix it up. But then some of our underclassmen are scared to death. They're not afraid of Miami. They're afraid of what Holtz has been saying for two weeks: 'No fights, no matter what. You'll be kicked off the team.' "

DEREK BROWN: "Yes, I think it was a factor in the game. The intimidation factor. We had plenty of guys who were ready to kick their butts, and Holtz pulled back the reins. I'm not gonna say that we condone fighting. But we didn't bring it to them. They brought it to us. They challenged our manhood."

NED BOLCAR: "At the time, I was pissed off. I thought we lost that game before it started, because Lou put us in handcuffs.

"But then, what if he hadn't? That was the drunkest, angriest crowd I've ever seen in my life. If Notre Dame fought Miami, their fans would have broken right though security. There would have been a riot. There's no doubt in my mind. So it was a tough spot for Holtz."

LOU HOLTZ: "The officials should have handled that situation. That should not have been up to me. Since when does your whole team leave the sideline during the coin toss? The officials completely allowed that to get out of hand."

Although Miami won 27–10, the score was tied 10–10 after Bolcar scored a touchdown on a 49-yard interception late in the second quarter. Then Rice threw a key interception just before halftime, which Miami turned into a 17–10 advantage. Once the Hurricanes stretched it to 24–10, the Irish couldn't rely on their powerful running game. "They were like Oklahoma," said Miami safety Charles Pharms afterward. "They look great until they get behind."

DEREK BROWN: "When we got back to South Bend, the lights on top of Grace Hall had been turned off. There was this huge Number One up there, and for twenty-three straight games it stayed lit up. But now the lights were out. That hit us real hard."

After taking final exams and mourning their defeat, the No. 4-ranked Irish returned to Miami to meet No. 1-ranked Colorado in the Orange Bowl. The 10–0 Buffs were the last unbeaten team in college football.

TIM RYAN: "You know what was odd about that game? If we beat Colorado, and Miami won their bowl game, Miami would probably win the national championship. So we had Miami fans cheering for us, whereas the month before they'd been spitting on us."

South Florida got its wish. Notre Dame won 21–6 as Rocket Ismail gained 108 yards and won Orange Bowl MVP. Bolcar made one interception and seven tackles, giving him a team-high 109 for his final season. Rice atoned for his off game at Miami by leading three touchdown drives in the second half.

In the postgame interviews, Holtz and some players laid claim to the national title even though Miami had won in the Sugar Bowl. The Irish said they finished 12–1 to Miami's 11–1, and they did it against tougher competition. Both statements were true, but didn't carry the weight of Miami 27, Notre Dame 10. That decided the matter for most voters, who awarded the Hurricanes the national championship. The Irish finished second.

Yet as the decade ended, Holtz had rebuilt the program even more soundly and swiftly than many expected. Notre Dame turned it around in his second season, captured a national title in his third, and beat its 23rd straight opponent in his fourth. On top of all that, Holtz had a 10–1 record against Top 20 teams.

"If somebody had to mold a Rockne and a Leahy, they couldn't have come up with a better man than Lou Holtz. He *is* Notre Dame," said Irish athletic director Dick Rosenthal.

Coming as it did from Holtz's close friend and ally, that was a little much. But, yes, the road ahead looked dazzling.

PART VI

THE NINETIES

34

THE TURBULENCE BEGINS

1990 – 1991

ON FEBRUARY 5, 1990, AFTER A BRIEF BUT INTENSE NEGOTIA-
tion, Notre Dame and NBC announced a blockbuster deal.
From 1991 through 1995, the network would televise all
Irish home games in exchange for $38 million.

In signing this landmark contract with NBC, Notre
Dame broke away from the College Football Association,
a coalition of 64 major football schools. But Irish road
games would still be part of the CFA package, which
meant ABC and ESPN could broadcast those, too.

This was sensational news for Notre Dame fanatics,
who could feed their habit now on almost every Saturday
in fall. But to critics such as Penn State coach Joe Paterno,
the deal reflected poorly on the school.

"It's been a fun year for all of us," Paterno said. "We
got to see Notre Dame go from an academic institute to
a banking institute."

"I wasn't surprised by this. I was shocked," said Georgia athletic director Vince Dooley. "Surprise, shock, greed

and ultimate greed. That's the reaction I'm getting from people."

Notre Dame countered with its own arguments:

- Of the $38 million from NBC, about $18 million would be paid to the visiting teams who played in Notre Dame Stadium.

- The remaining $20 million would bolster a scholarship fund for general student aid and not for athletic scholarships.

- If the Irish had gone in with the 63 other teams in the CFA, most of their games would have been regional broadcasts, and Notre Dame's following spread from coast to coast.

Three other close observers discuss the NBC deal: Inside linebacker and 1994 captain Justin Goheen, *Sports Illustrated*'s college football writer Tim Layden, and South Bend native and *Atlanta Constitution* columnist Terrence Moore.

JUSTIN GOHEEN: "As a player, I thought it was great. I got to play on national TV every weekend. As for college football becoming big business, that had been true for years. The NBC deal just exemplified it.

"But I can also see where that deal turned people off. Let's say their favorite team is playing a huge game. But they turn on the TV and get Notre Dame–Navy. If the game is on NBC, they also see halftime specials on Ron Powlus. They see Notre Dame guys in United Way commercials. Well, if they hate Notre Dame, they're ready to throw a sledgehammer through the TV.

"But Notre Dame is a funny animal. Even within the school, opinions are divided. On one side of the board, you've got the players and coaches and students and alumni who like football. On the other side, you have some professors and administrators who don't even think Notre Dame should have athletics. But these are the same dumb-asses that are getting $30 million and change from NBC because the football team is bringing in the bucks."

TIM LAYDEN: "My initial thought was, This is an outrage. This is crazy. Selling the rights to one network for all those millions?

"Then you sort of rebound from that. You realize that it makes sense. Notre Dame is the only nationally marketable commodity in college football. So once the opportunity presented itself, they did the smart thing. They would have been crazy not to."

TERRENCE MOORE: "That was a big chunk of money NBC gave them. But I don't think it helps Notre Dame on the football field. In fact, this NBC deal is killing them. Because Notre Dame is now the most well-scouted team in the history of college athletics. Every game's on TV. That's a tremendous advantage for any team that plays them.

"Then you have another factor. The NBC deal makes every other team jealous. So it's good for their motivation. 'Notre Dame has its own network. Let's go kick their ass.' "

Of the three teams that whipped Notre Dame in 1990—Stanford, Penn State, and Colorado in the Orange Bowl—the Stanford defeat was easily the most shocking. The Irish came in 3–0 and ranked No. 1, while the Cardinal was unranked at 1–2. If that wasn't bad enough, this 36–31 upset came in South Bend, where Notre Dame hadn't lost in 19 previous games.

After the season ended and ten Irish players got

drafted, some Notre Dame fans wondered: How could a team with this much pro talent go 9–3?

One factor was Notre Dame's pass defense. Under defensive coordinator Gary Darnell, the Irish allowed a school-worst 267 yards passing per game.

Another factor was selfishness. Notre Dame had key players who cared more about personal stats than team achievements. This became transparent the week before the Orange Bowl, when Ricky Watters complained to the national media that Holtz had not been using him enough, and that he was a better runner than his numbers suggested. As a senior and team captain, Watters should have known better. But Watters was concerned with his NFL prospects.

TIM RYAN: "I'm not pointing to any one player. But something was missing, chemistry-wise, all season. We were loaded with Kodak All-Americans. We had players winning awards. But talent is not the only criteria. You have to have a backbone, and I'm not sure how strong our backbone was. It wasn't the old rah-rah for Notre Dame. It seemed like guys were playing for different reasons."

Irv Smith, a sophomore tight end, played behind All-American Derek Brown in 1990. A prodigious talent himself, Smith probably would have been starting at any other school. But Smith never hurt team harmony by pouting. Later, when Brown graduated, Smith made All-American as a senior.

He comments here on the 1990 team.

IRV SMITH: "It was almost like we had too many stars. Take a look at the running back position. You had Ricky Watters, Tony Brooks, Reggie Brooks, Jerome Bettis, Rodney Culver, Dorsey Levens. I mean, after that year Dorsey

Levens transferred. This guy's an awesome runner. He's balling now for Green Bay. But he couldn't even get on the field for Notre Dame.

"Plus, I haven't even mentioned Rocket Ismail. Rocket ran with the football *and* caught passes. So here you have the Rocket. He's the most lethal weapon in college football. He's on the cover of every magazine. But you also have Ricky Watters. He wants to be The Man, and he has the ability to be The Man. So Ricky just didn't handle it very well. Because he knew if he went somewhere else, he could have been the star."

After the 1990 season ended, there were two important developments at Notre Dame. Recruiting coordinator Vinnie Cerrato took a player personnel job with the San Francisco 49ers, and Rocket Ismail turned pro instead of playing his final year in college.

Ismail's absence would be felt sooner, but Ceratto's was more far-reaching. Young, smart, relentless, and once described in *Sports Illustrated* as "the only guy in South Bend with a tan in February," Ceratto never won over some old-guard Notre Damers. But after arriving with Holtz from Minnesota, he established himself as one of the country's best talent evaluators. From 1986 through 1990, according to a published report quoted by the *New York Times*, Ceratto brought Notre Dame 47 impact players and 20 picks in the first two rounds of the NFL draft.

TIM LAYDEN: "After Ceratto left, recruiting fell off very badly at Notre Dame. They had two or three lousy recruiting years in a row. The low point was clearly 1994, when they went 6–5–1. That was basically the by-product of poor recruiting for a while.

"Part of that may have been simple incompetence. But I would attribute part to the university. As Holtz complained many times, they squeezed him a little on academic standards."

Layden's last statement is seconded by Tim Prister, the veteran editor of *Blue & Gold Illustrated,* the South Bend paper devoted to covering Notre Dame football.

TIM PRISTER: "By 1991, Holtz was going into his sixth year. As he had at other schools, he was beginning to rub people the wrong way. Holtz was a guy who needed to have his way, and there had already been talk about friction between him and the admissions department over Holtz's trying to get in certain kids.

"The result was a tightening of academic standards, which happened near the time Cerrato left. I don't think that was coincidental, either. Later in his career, some Notre Dame people considered Vinnie controversial. Not because he was cheating. I never heard anyone say that. But Vinnie had a craftiness about him that made some Notre Dame people uncomfortable. I mean, Vinnie learned at the knee of Lou Holtz, who's a pretty sly and crafty guy himself.

"So I think it went hand in hand. The administration suggested Cerrato move on, and they tightened up on academics at the same time. All of this had an impact on recruiting."

NED BOLCAR: "Notre Dame, overall, tries bringing in quality people as well as quality athletes. But I think Lou was in a situation his first few years where the school wanted him to get the program back on its feet quickly. So maybe they loosened the guidelines a little bit. And maybe Lou brought in some guys who were great football players, but weren't quite up to Notre Dame's standards in other respects.

"I mean, why do you think Vinnie Cerrato went to the 49ers? I think Notre Dame said, 'Lou, he's a good recruiting coordinator. He's done a great job. But we don't like all the players he's bringing in. He's causing waves. We've heard some negatives. It's time for him to move on.'"

Holtz says there was never any "academic tightening." The only change, he says, was when Notre Dame reversed its policy on Proposition 48 players: players who had to sit out their freshman year while they improved their academic credentials. But Holtz says Notre Dame only took Prop 48 players for one season, so the only two he ever coached were Tony Rice and John Foley.

As for Cerrato, Holtz calls him "honest, talented, and loyal." He says no one from Notre Dame ever told him Cerrato should leave. Holtz does say, however, "I'm sure there were some people uncomfortable with him. That I wouldn't dispute."

On the football field, the 1991 season began with a 49–27 victory over Indiana, a 24–14 loss to Michigan, and a 49–10 shellacking of Michigan State. This last win was overshadowed by the famous Huntley Bakich incident, in which Holtz yanked Bakich from the playing field by his facemask.

Caught by NBC's cameras, the episode brought Holtz a burst of criticism. But not necessarily from his own players.

One of them was defensive back John Covington. Along with safety Jeff Burris, linebacker Pete Bercich, defensive linemen Bryant Young and Jim Flanigan, split end Lake Dawson, quarterback Kevin McDougal, and offensive linemen Tim Ruddy and Aaron Taylor, Covington was in the class of "super sophs," the elite recruiting group that came in during Cerato's final season. All nine would play key roles in 1993, when the Irish made their next true run for a national title.

What set Covington apart was his name, John Shaft Covington, and his family history. Covington grew up in Winter Haven, Florida, where he was one of 20 children. Money was tight and domestic life unstructured, and Covington had some minor brushes with trouble. But he straightened out during high school, received a finance degree from Notre Dame, and became a fifth-round pick of the Indianapolis Colts.

Here he recalls the Bakich controversy.

JOHN COVINGTON: "I thought that story got blown way out of proportion. If the press was at our practices every day, they wouldn't have blinked an eye when Holtz did that. Because Holtz did that to players every day.

"That was part of his routine. At games, normally, he would be very calm. His attitude was not to upset his players. He might pull you for a mistake, but he'd come up and pat you on the back. He'd say, 'Listen, I'm gonna make a change. Just sit down and relax a little while. We'll take care of it at practice.'

"But if you made that same mistake at practice, Holtz would scream and yell and grab your facemask. Maybe to some people that was abusive. I just saw it as football.

"Anyway, that's why none of us blinked when Holtz grabbed Huntley. The only part that was new was Holtz marching onto the field and doing it on national TV."

IRV SMITH: "Some of us felt Huntley had it coming. From the first day he showed up, a majority of our football team disliked him. Because this is how Huntley introduced himself: 'Hi, I'm Huntley Bakich, All-American.'

What he didn't realize is that everyone he met could have said that.

"So that was generally the players' perspective. But to everybody else, it became this big issue. Holtz got a lot of heat from the alumni. He got a lot of heat from the university. Because he had embarrassed this kid and his family, *and* he had embarrassed Notre Dame."

LOU HOLTZ: "Well, I wished I hadn't done it. But, yeah, it was blown out proportion. I mean, Huntley Bakich has come to me since he's graduated with his wife and children. He's thanked me for everything I've done for him, and for helping to make him a man.

"But what happened back then is that Huntley was a talented football player. He was a good person. But he wasn't the most disciplined individual, and he didn't come to us with the greatest work habits.

"Well, Huntley went down on a kickoff, right in front of me, and took a cheap shot at a player from Michigan State. And that bothered me. And any time I want someone's attention, I usually grab him by the facemask to look him in the eye. Not to yank it or pull it or do anything nasty. But just so you can look him in the eye.

"Well, it got blown up like crazy. But then again, when you're at Notre Dame, and you're on national television every week, that's what happens."

At least that's what happened to Holtz, whose actions were sometimes engaging, sometimes excessive, but never conventional. In the aftermath of the Bakich incident, the Irish won six in a row. Then, on November 9 at South Bend, the turbulence started anew with the second shocking home loss of the Holtz years.

With seconds left until halftime, seventh-ranked Notre Dame led 19th-ranked Tennessee 31–7. Then the Irish blew a 24-point lead, which had never happened before in South Bend. The 35–34 loss silenced the sellout crowd, removed Notre Dame from the championship race, and prompted Holtz to call it, "The most difficult loss I've ever been associated with."

JOHN COVINGTON: "That next week of practice was our worst at Notre Dame. It was the first time Holtz ever said we played like girls.

"He also said our players weren't worth coaching. And this was during the time when we heard rumors about Bill Walsh coming to coach at Notre Dame. The media was talking about Bill Walsh, too. So all this was building up inside the team."

PETE BERCICH: "We all heard the rumors about Lou leaving. Then we went to Penn State. On Friday night, we met at our hotel. It was the big team meeting before we went to bed. Then Lou gave us this speech. At first it sounded like a resignation speech. Then, at the end, he just pulled out of his hat that he was staying. He said, 'Nothing's wrong. Everything's okay. I'm more dedicated than I ever was.'

"It was kind of strange. Instead of walking out of there fired up, guys were saying, 'What was that about?' "

JUSTIN GOHEEN: "He brought up the rumors. But he neither confirmed nor denied them. He left it up in the air. It sounded like: 'Hey, I might leave. You guys are just a bunch of sorry asses.' "

JEFF BURRIS: "That meeting was confusing. Coach Holtz said that he had been offered a job, but he had turned it down. He said he was going to stay at Notre Dame and make sure he didn't leave the program in the state it was in.

"Now, maybe he thought it would be a motivation. But I think it hurt us dearly against Penn State. Too many guys were talking about the meeting. The game was secondary."

LOU HOLTZ: "It *was* a very uncharacteristic meeting. And of all the games I've coached at Notre Dame, that was one of the few where we were never really in it. Because almost every game I ever coached—even the ones we lost—I mean we were in that sucker.

"But the players are right. I did have a lot going through my mind at the time. Was I going to leave? Was I going to do this or that? I had indecision in my mind. I just wasn't comfortable with the direction we were going, and a variety of other things. But after that game I made a decision. I was going to stay at Notre Dame."

When asked why he even contemplated leaving, why he then chose not to, and if he had job offers elsewhere, Holtz says he would rather keep that private. Therefore, back to the players.

JOHN COVINGTON: "The morning of the Penn State game, we had another team meeting. Then all the players split up. You had some guys saying, 'Let's go out there and play hard.' You had other guys saying, 'He doesn't seem to care about this game. Let's just wait until next year.' One guy actually told me, 'I'm not gonna bust my ass out there today. I'm gonna wait until Bill Walsh comes in.'"

Of course, Notre Dame got crushed, 35–13. Then, after a tense bye week, the Irish beat Hawaii 48–42 in the regular season finale. But the victory could not obscure the math: Notre Dame's last three opponents, Tennessee, Penn State, and Hawaii, had averaged 39 points per game.

That was the end of the line for Gary Darnell. Though

there was still the Sugar Bowl to play, the defensive coordinator wasn't there. Darnell left Notre Dame with one game left in the season.

Mike McGlinn sat with Darnell on the bus ride back from the Hawaii game to the hotel. McGlinn, an offensive lineman known for his work ethic, never played for Darnell. But McGlinn says they were friendly.

MIKE MCGLINN: "Our offense scored 48 points against Hawaii. But our defense just got blown all over the field. So even though we won, it was a quiet bus ride.

"Then Holtz announced, in front of the team, that all the coaches were meeting when they got back to the hotel. When Holtz did that, it meant he was really pissed. Normally, he would have a little more couth.

"Darnell and I were sitting next to each other. Darnell just kind of paused and said, 'Whew.' I said, 'You guys are having a meeting, huh?' He said yes and I said, 'Well, hang in there.' He said, 'I'm gonna try to.'

"That was the extent of the conversation. But I could tell by the look on his face. At that instant, Darnell knew he was gone."

PETE BERCICH: "He wound up going to Texas before the bowl game. Then the same thing happened again my senior year. This time it was Greg Minter, the guy who replaced Darnell. Minter left before our bowl game, too.

"In Minter's case, he got a better job. He became the head coach at Cincinnati. But when Texas hired Darnell, he went from a coordinator to a position coach. So as players, you notice that. You kind of figure someone told him to go."

TIM PRISTER: "I don't know if he was fired or if he quit. But he wasn't gonna be rehired by Holtz, because their defense under Darnell was a disaster. They were just god-awful. So there was no way Darnell was coming back."

LOU HOLTZ: "When Gary Darnell came into Notre Dame, he brought some film of Florida. That's where Gary was coaching before he came to us. Well, Gary showed our players the Florida defense. He told them that's how they should play. That's not the right way to do things at another school.

"But that was the only thing that ever happened. I think Gary Darnell is a very fine football coach. I have great respect for him. It's just that the football players have to respond, and the whole situation has to come together. And for whatever reason, Gary felt he'd be more comfortable at Texas."

After Darnell departed, Holtz took charge of the defense before the Sugar Bowl matchup against Florida, which in itself was causing wide debate. With 9–3 Notre Dame ranked No. 18, people wondered why it was playing third-ranked, 10–1 Florida in a January 1 bowl game netting each school $3.7 million.

There was printed speculation that the Sugar Bowl deal had been made since the first week of November—before the Irish lost to Tennessee and Penn State. There was also this pregame joke going around: "What's the difference between Cheerios and Notre Dame? Cheerios belong in a bowl."

The Irish came into New Orleans as 18-point underdogs. They not only left with a 39–28 upset, but linebacker Justin Goheen says Holtz outfoxed Florida coach Steve Spurrier.

JUSTIN GOHEEN: "There was no doubt about it. Holtz got the best of Spurrier. In our defensive scheme, no shit, sometimes we dropped *nine* guys into coverage. It was unbelievable: We had two down linemen rushing the passer. So Florida was able to march on us for a while, but every time they got inside the 20, they couldn't complete the damn pass. Because there were so many guys from Notre Dame in coverage, there were no open zones.

"It was insane. Gary Darnell left and Holtz stepped in and did some incredible coaching. That meant a lot to him, too. Holtz really wanted to beat Spurrier. He made these comments about him, like what a great golfer he was. You could just tell he didn't like the guy, and that was very unusual for Holtz. He rarely made our games into something personal.

"Actually, I don't think too many coaches in collegiate football like Spurrier. I mean, he *is* a great golfer. He's a Heisman Trophy winner, and I think his wife's an ex-model. So he's just the guy everyone loves to hate."

LOU HOLTZ: "Number one, I think Steve Spurrier is a great coach. Number two, I didn't outfox anybody. I never won a football game as a coach. The one thing we did was give our players a chance to win. And they won against Florida."

PETE BERCICH: "We didn't just fool Spurrier that game. We fooled the media. We manipulated them the whole month before we played Florida. We kept saying that our defense was gonna blitz and put pressure on Florida's quarterback Shane Matthews. Then we did the total opposite.

"That's just the way it is—in college and in pro. See, we know the inside story. And now that I've been on the inside for a few years, I can see how the media is used as a pawn. So whatever you read in the paper, you can't believe it. I don't care if it's out of the horse's mouth. Because a lot of times that's B.S. too."

35

"KIND OF A LIGHTNING ROD"

1 9 9 2

AFTER ABSORBING SIX LOSSES IN 1990 AND 1991, NOTRE DAME got great news when quarterback Rick Mirer returned for his senior year instead of turning pro. Asked why he stayed in South Bend, Mirer said, "I want to win a national championship."

With their followers demanding nothing less, the No. 3-ranked Irish crushed Northwestern 42–7 in the season opener at Soldier Field. Next came sixth-ranked Michigan in the biggest early game of the college football season.

On a muggy South Bend afternoon, the score was 17–17 when Notre Dame began its last drive at its own 11. With 1:05 and one time-out remaining, the crowd expected Mirer to come out throwing. But Holtz called two handoffs, which used up 35 seconds. After Mirer missed two desperation passes, the game ended in a 17–17 tie.

As the players left the field to scattered booing, NBC's

John Dockery questioned Holtz on his play-calling strategy. Holtz didn't care for Dockery's persistence. The interview got tense and Holtz abruptly walked off.

Holtz and Dockery later made amends. But in the meantime Holtz became grist for sports pages, talk radio, and even CNN, where Holtz made an appearance to explain his thinking.

In short, Holtz said he didn't want to risk punting because Michigan had three time-outs left. He figured the Wolverines would double cover his wideouts, so he felt his fullback Jerome Bettis might be able to break into the secondary for a big gain. As for the second handoff, to Reggie Brooks, Holtz still hoped to get Michigan to abandon its prevent defense. Then, once the Irish started passing, a disastrous interception would be less likely.

Holtz elaborates here on the second-most famous tie in Notre Dame history.

LOU HOLTZ: "They booed us at home that game. That's the only time I think it ever happened. Well, they booed because it looked like I was conservative. But you know what nobody knew about that second draw play? We could have broken that thing out to the 50. That's how deep they were playing. But we had ten men on the field! We ran a different formation, and one of our wideouts came off the field by mistake. So the Michigan guy who was supposed to cover him just walked up and made the tackle.

"Well, I didn't want to come out and say: 'Hey, we had only ten people on the field.' Because I can't stand to have ten people on the field. Or twelve people, for that matter.

"But regardless, it became a very big story. But that comes with Notre Dame. And that comes with winning.

And I'm kind of a lightning rod anyway. Because I say what's on my mind. I don't worry about public relations. I don't worry about anything but being honest."

JOHN COVINGTON: "I thought we'd pass the ball. But that doesn't mean I felt that Holtz was wrong. Holtz is known as one of the greatest college coaches. He's been coaching football as long as I've been living. It wasn't for me to question a guy like that."

JEFF BURRIS: "I didn't fault him at all for playing conservatively. Had we lost, we would have been in serious trouble. With a tie, we could still get hot and win it all."

TIM LAYDEN: "The interview with Dockery I thought Holtz handled badly. But I kind of admired his honesty. I mean, Holtz acted pissed because he *was*.

"As for his strategy, as journalists we always think a guy should air it out. But I've talked to Bobby Bowden about this, too. Bobby has played for wins four or five times in his career. He's been burned almost every time, and regrets every one of them.

"So with a little distance, I can admire Holtz's courage that game. I'm sure he knew his choice would be unpopular. But he had the guts to realize that a tie might be the best thing in a tough situation."

Jeremy Nau, a fiesty sophomore linebacker from Chicago, recalls the Michigan game from his perspective.

JEREMY NAU: "I thought we should have gone for it. It would be different if we needed to score a touchdown. But we had a minute left, and all we needed was a field goal. I don't want to jump ahead to ninety-four yet, but remember when Michigan beat us 26–24? They won it on a last-second field goal. And they basically went the same length of the field, in the same amount of time.

"Holtz told us later why he did it. If we tied, we still had a shot for the national championship. But standing on the sideline with the defense, I couldn't believe he was running up the middle. We busted our ass all summer getting ready for Michigan. Then we let the clock run out with a minute left?"

Three victories later, Notre Dame was ranked No. 7 when it faced 19th-ranked Stanford in South Bend. Two years earlier, the Cardinal had shocked the No. 1-ranked Irish 36–31 at Notre Dame Stadium. This time Stanford fell behind 16–0, then exploded for 33 straight points. Final score: Stanford 33, Notre Dame 16.

It wasn't supposed to happen that way, of course. Notre Dame had nine NFL draft choices on its roster, and Mirer returning for his last blaze of glory. But now that goal was all but impossible. Notre Dame was 3–1–1, and critics asked again for the third straight year: Have the Irish become a team of underachievers?

"Out-played, out-hustled, out-coached," Tim Prister started his next column in *Blue & Gold Illustrated*.

"Last Saturday's 33–16 upset loss to Stanford was the fourth time in the last two years Notre Dame has blown a solid half-time lead and lost a home game with national championship implications," Barry Cronin wrote in that Thursday's *Chicago Sun-Times*.

JEREMY NAU: "After that Stanford loss, we had the shortest postgame meeting I've ever been associated with. Holtz said, 'Practice on Monday. I don't know what we're gonna do after this.' Then he just left.

"I think he was doubly pissed because he lost to Bill Walsh. One season before that, Walsh was announcing our games for NBC. Then he came back the next year to start coaching Stanford. Well, Walsh and Holtz were not real fond of each other. What you had was two big egos on both sides."

MIKE MCGLINN: "Holtz was furious going *into* that game. He didn't appreciate Walsh's arrogance. Because instead of Walsh saying something respectful about Holtz, or about Notre Dame, he came out with some real irresponsible statements. He basically said Notre Dame was a bunch of privileged pansies. And that was coming from Stanford. I mean, isn't that the pot calling the kettle black?"

LOU HOLTZ: "That loss was devastating for a lot of reasons. But Stanford had a good football team that year. Make no mistake about it.

"As for your other question, the players are right. I didn't think Walsh showed us much respect. But then again, that's his decision. You know, I've coached against Paterno an awful lot. And Paterno always had great things to say about you before the game—and nothing good afterward.

"But Paterno is as fine a coach as I've ever competed against. And that's what made it challenging. So you never cared about what another coach said. You cared about how he coached. But I can tell you this much about Stanford: Our football players hung in there. Then Notre Dame went out and won its next seventeen games."

JEFF BURRIS: "Stanford didn't just beat us. They out-toughed us. Lou Holtz couldn't live with that, and neither could we. So there was a lot of hitting our next week of practice. You could hear the popping going on."

JEREMY NAU: "Tempers were very short. There were a lot of fights. Holtz was killing us. But nobody really minded. We needed to get back to Notre Dame football."

What this frequently meant in the Holtz years was controversy. In this case, it occurred against Brigham Young with less than four minutes left in a 42–16 home win on NBC. Linebacker Pete Bercich explains how things got started.

PETE BERCICH: "BYU had the ball. I was blitzing and one of their linemen tackled me. I mean, this guy mugged me. So I got up hollering about being held. Then I looked at the sidelines and Holtz was going postal."

JEREMY NAU: "First he called a time-out. Then he walked on the field and put the ref in a headlock. I think he was trying to show him what happened to Bercich.

"Holtz wound up getting ripped for that one, too. But to the players, a lot of that stuff was comical. We were used to seeing him rant and rave at meetings."

For charging onto the field and draping his arm around Tom Thamert's neck, Holtz earned a 15-yard penalty for unsportsmanlike conduct and this scolding from *Sports Illustrated*: "Holtz's headlock, the latest entry on a lengthening list of questionable behavior by the coach, is an embarrassment to Notre Dame. Has the pressure of coaching in South Bend become too much for Holtz?"

Holtz later apologized and cited frustration. Here he gives his side of the headlock incident.

LOU HOLTZ: "We blitzed a linebacker, Pete Bercich. And honest to gosh, I just felt the center reached out and put a headlock on him, yanked him to the ground, and I saw it, and 50,000 other people saw it. But the guy hired to see it didn't see it.

"By then, we had the game won. So I called time-out. Then Tom Thamert came out. Tom wasn't even involved in the call. But he was the referee in charge of the group. I had him for several games, and I respected him.

"When Tom came over, I put my arm around him. I did not squeeze. I never put any pressure on him. I just said, 'Is this a penalty? Because, Tom, if it isn't, then we have to teach that technique to pick up guys who are blitzing. Because it's a lot better than what we're trying to do.'

"That was the extent of it. And Lord knows, I could not believe how big a story it became."

Two weeks later, as if this season did not have enough big stories, Holtz's detractors accused him of running up the score in a 54–7 rout over Boston College. *Sports Illustrated*'s Tim Layden recalls an interview he did with Holtz a few days before the game.

TIM LAYDEN: "Holtz always seemed beleaguered by his job, but especially during that week. I was still working at *Newsday* at the time, and I remember sitting in his office with Mark Blaudschun from the *Boston Globe*. One of us asked him, 'Lou, has this sort of been an extraordinary year?' Holtz sat back and said, 'Well, let's see. Accused of pushing a referee. I tied Michigan on purpose. Stanford. Bill Walsh. I'd say it's about average.'

"By then he was really into his beleaguered act. He was saying how Boston College was undefeated, and that they had a fresh new coach, and if they beat Notre Dame it's hallelujah, but if we beat Boston College we're still having a tough season. Meanwhile, it was eighty degrees in his office and he had on the usual turtleneck and sweatshirt and windbreaker and pipe. I mean, he looked like a guy who was ready to be pushed right off the edge. Then Notre Dame beat Boston College 54–7."

The Irish led 37–0 in the third quarter when Holtz called for a fake punt on fourth down. After punter Craig Hentrich ran for the first down, even NBC's announcers rebuked Holtz. "Don't think that Tom Coughlin won't remember what happened," said Chris Collinsworth.

Collinsworth was right. The Boston College coach was agitated. But according to several players, it was never Holtz's intention to run up the score.

JOHN COVINGTON: "I know that's what it looked like, but that's not why he did it. We had a big game coming up against Penn State. Holtz wanted them to know that we had the fake punt in our playbook. That way they couldn't rush our punter too hard. And actually, they didn't. If you look at the tapes of our game, Penn State didn't rush us hard. They were always cautious of us faking a punt."

PETE BERCICH: "If you know a team fake punts, it also changes the way you set up your punt returns. You become less concerned with a good return and more concerned with not getting burned on a fake punt."

TIM LAYDEN: "Holtz has said himself that he always ran fake punts to show them to future opponents. Which I have no trouble believing. I mean, it's a sick profession and they do that kind of stuff."

JOHN COVINGTON: "It also goes back to the Holtz/Paterno thing. I don't think they liked each other. Because Holtz would refer to Paterno as 'that guy.' It was never 'Joe Paterno.' It was always 'That guy gets so much credit. And he does get his players ready. But let me tell you something. That guy ain't out-coaching me.'"

But even if we all accept that premise—Holtz had Paterno in mind when he ran that fake punt—it still raises an interesting issue. Was it worth embarrassing Boston College on national television?

JEFF BURRIS: "Well, that's a good question. Because no matter why Coach Holtz did it, it was at the expense of Boston College. And maybe that came back to haunt us one year later."

TIM LAYDEN: "The next time they played Notre Dame, Boston College didn't need any more motivation. Not after losing 54–7.

"But, yes, I would have to agree. From BC's point of view, the fake punt was just another scoop on the pile. Because when you run a fake punt with that big a lead, you're basically making a judgment: Upsetting the other team is not as important to you as making your next opponent prepare for your fake punt.

"But, again, that's the nature of the profession. And if all football coaches leave bodies behind them, then Holtz has left a lot."

LOU HOLTZ: "Absolutely not. We were not trying to run the score up. We were saying, 'Hey, we have a fake punt.' And I wanted every team we played down the line—and particularly Penn State—to feel they better make sure they had that fake punt handled.

"That was the only reason we ran it, and I never looked at it as upsetting Boston College. Because we ran it very early in the third quarter. You've only played about 34 minutes of the game. To me, that means the game is still in doubt."

As Holtz noted earlier, the Irish never stopped winning through all this intrigue and drama. They followed the Stanford defeat with a seven-game winning streak, including a 17–16 thriller over Penn State, a 31–23 victory at USC, and a 28–3 Cotton Bowl drubbing of previously unbeaten Texas A&M.

This improved Notre Dame's record to 10–1–1, and as Holtz told bowl game reporters: "I think we are the best team in the country, and I feel we should be ranked second. To take it one step further, I think we should be ranked first. At the end of the year, we were playing better than any other team I have been around."

Holtz was disappointed the following morning, when both wire services voted Notre Dame fourth behind Alabama, Florida State and Miami. But the first week of January, says Pete Bercich, was simply too late for Holtz to start campaigning.

PETE BERCICH: "Lou always downplayed us during the season. He made the other teams sound great and he made us sound like nothing. And not that his tactic was wrong. Maybe that kept us humble, and kept us from getting complacent.

"But sometimes when you make your bed, you have to lie in it. Because at the end of every season, Lou would always start saying how great we were. But when you have a final poll, and the national championship is decided by people who follow your statements, at some point they're bound to say, 'Hey, listen, pal. You're the one who's been saying all year that your team is terrible. Now we're gonna give you what you've been saying.' "

In 1992, it should be noted, Holtz's gamesmanship did not cost Notre Dame a national title. Losing to Stanford at home, and Alabama's 13–0 record, took care of that.

One year later, however, this issue would resurface with greater ramifications when the voters would have to choose between Notre Dame and Florida State, and also between Lou Holtz and Bobby Bowden.

36

❧

THE UNFORGETTABLE SEASON
1 9 9 3

IN SPRING 1993, LOU HOLTZ DIDN'T SOUND TOO KEEN ON HIS quarterback situation. Rick Mirer was heading northwest to play for the Seattle Seahawks. Ron Powlus was still back east in Berwick, Pennsylvania, wrapping up his senior year of high school. The top two quarterbacks on Notre Dame's spring depth chart, senior Kevin McDougal and junior Paul Fallia, had only one collegiate start between them.

By the end of spring practice McDougal had beaten out Fallia, but apparently not by enough to satisfy Holtz, who referred to them in *Blue & Gold Illustrated* as quarterbacks "No. 1 and No. 1-A." Holtz also told the paper, "We don't have the quarterback situation resolved. . . . We just aren't consistent enough."

Holtz's comments surprised some Irish players, who felt McDougal had turned in a solid spring. McDougal completed 69 percent of his passes, a spring record during the Holtz years, and threw for 230 yards and two touchdowns in the annual Blue-Gold game. Moreover, in his role as Mirer's backup, McDougal had led the offense on 14 drives. Ten had resulted in touchdowns.

So what was the story? Was Holtz really unimpressed by McDougal and Fallia? Was he merely keeping them off-balance, so they would keep working hard in the pre-season? Or by speaking so blandly about his two veteran players, was Holtz clearing the way for his prize fresh-man Powlus?

Certainly Powlus's numbers were impressive. In three seasons at Berwick High School, he threw for 62 touch-downs and a state record of 7,339 yards. In his senior year alone, Powlus threw for 31 TDs and ran for 20 more as the Bulldogs went 15–0 and won the state championship. *USA Today* named him its prep offensive player of the year, further anointing him as the nation's hottest prospect.

When Powlus arrived in South Bend in the summer of 1993, the expectations were clear when he was given the same number 3 worn in the past by Mirer and Montana. According to several players, Powlus also received prefer-ential treatment from Lou Holtz.

JEREMY NAU: "I actually think it started in the spring, with all that No. 1 and No. 1-A stuff. Because Holtz knew he had Powlus coming in, and he knew he was going to make him the No. 1 quarterback. Make no mistake about it. I don't care what anyone says. I don't care what Holtz says. He *knew* he was giving that job to Powlus. And that's the way it happened. Ron had a good fall camp, but McDougal and Fallia never got a fair shot."

JOHN COVINGTON: "Right at the end of camp, Ron moved ahead of McDougal on the depth chart. I never thought he earned it, though. None of the seniors did. We thought

Powlus won the job before he put on cleats, because of all the hype when he came."

TIM LAYDEN: "I did a story on Powlus the following year for *SI*. I talked to Aaron Taylor and Jeff Burris and some other seniors, and they all resented the fact that Powlus was elevated so summarily. They felt that he played well during fall camp, but that he had been put in scrimmage situations where he would succeed, whereas McDougal had been put in scrimmage situations where it was more difficult. McDougal would play against the first-team defense, blitzes, and tough situations, and then Powlus would come in and face the second-team defense. Or if he ever did play against the first-string, he would face a softer look."

JEFF BURRIS: "Yes, we were upset. We wanted Kevin to be our quarterback. We felt he paid his dues. Kevin backed up Rick Mirer for three years. He suddenly lost his job in a two-week span."

KEVIN MCDOUGAL: "I hate to go as far as to say it was orchestrated . . . but it did seem like Coach Holtz wanted Ron to be in there."

LOU HOLTZ: "Kevin McDougal is a beautiful person. He had great confidence and great composure. He's one of the more popular players we've ever had.

"But it isn't true that I wanted Powlus in there. We had our three scrimmages in the fall. I've always done it that way. In our first two scrimmages, neither McDougal nor Fallia were very impressive. Ron Powlus was extraordinary. He picked up the offense, he had a quick release. He was just very sharp.

"And so, as camp went on, there was a chance that Ron Powlus could be our starting quarterback. Then we held our last scrimmage, just before our opening game. Ron got hurt in that last scrimmage. And he was out for the year."

KEVIN MCDOUGAL: "Before our final scrimmage, Holtz pulled me and Paul Fallia off to the side. He said Ron was going to be our starter. That hurt me to death. That was the lowest point. I felt in my heart that *I* was our quarterback. For a guy to come in and get in front of me . . . and the way that it took place . . . I didn't feel he deserved it. Then you know what happened. Ron got injured that same day and I took over from there."

Powlus went down on August 28 with a fractured right clavicle. Seven weeks later the same bone broke again while Powlus was throwing. He ended up red-shirting his freshman season.

This was unexpected, since Powlus was 6 feet 4 inches and 218 pounds and had started a school record of 42 straight games at Berwick. Then again, says Oliver Gibson, high school isn't college.

A 6 foot 3 inch, 275-pound defensive lineman, Gibson was one of the players who crashed into Powlus in that final preseason scrimmage. In 1995, the Pittsburgh Steelers drafted Gibson in the fourth round.

OLIVER GIBSON: "Four of us hit Ron almost at the same time. It was a naked hit, but that's not what hurt him. It was the way that everyone landed on him. Now, we didn't do it on purpose. It was just one of those things, where you're trying to knock the hell out of the quarterback. And I don't think Ron's body was quite acclimated for the collegiate hits yet."

RON POWLUS: "It was hard to deal with. I loved playing quarterback. I loved being at Notre Dame. I felt like I did a good job during the fall, and I thought I had a chance to play a good deal, and possibly be the starter. Suddenly, within seconds, everything ended. So, yeah, I was pretty down. I sat in my room a lot. Probably more than most Notre Dame freshmen do."

TIM LAYDEN: "Everyone seemed to like Powlus. But when he got injured, it actually brought that football team together. Because McDougal was a senior and they loved him. He was a good kid, a great competitor, and he went out and had a fabulous season."

KEVIN MCDOUGAL: "I didn't want it to happen. I had a good relationship with Ron. But once it became a fact, that was my chance to show Lou Holtz and the world that I could do the job."

Still, it was a fragile time for Holtz and Notre Dame. Four days before Powlus snapped his collarbone, Holtz checked into a South Bend hospital with chest pains. Though tests showed no heart defects and Holtz was soon released, the incident shook up some of his players.

OLIVER GIBSON: "It wasn't that we were surprised. Coach Holtz always ran on overtime and empty. He never got much sleep. His diet was terrible. He always drank strawberry milkshakes and Diet Cokes. He'd stay ridiculous hours and watch film, and we had no idea what the hell he was looking for.

"But even when it's not surprising, it's still emotional when your coach is hospitalized. The one good thing is that we knew he'd bounce back. Holtz was always a fighter."

He would have to be. During this same beleaguered period in late August, Holtz was about to be ravaged by Doug Looney and Don Yeager in *Under the Tarnished*

Dome. Among its allegations, the book charged Holtz with condoning steroid abuse, badgering injured players into returning quickly, disdaining Notre Dame's academic standards, and using abusive behavior with players and coaches. The book caused such a buzz upon its September release, Ted Koppel spent one whole episode detailing its charges.

From *Nightline* to the *New York Times* to the *Sporting News,* the book drew wide commentary for the serious questions it raised about Holtz's stormy tenure in South Bend. But the book was so reliant on troubled ex–Notre Dame players with axes to grind, it read more like a diatribe than a reasoned argument.

PETE BERCICH: "Holtz told us about the book before it came out. He tried to turn it around, like this was just another challenge for us. He said, 'This guy is writing a book and he's attacking everything you guys stand for. He's attacking the university you go to. You guys work too hard to let some guy like that try and distract you.'

"But honestly, as players, it really wasn't that much of a rallying point for us. Because number one, it wasn't about us. Number two, we had school and football about to start. So as far as I could tell, none of us read it and none of us really cared."

OLIVER GIBSON: "A couple of ex-players went on *Nightline* and were whining about this and that. But I mean, this is football. It isn't checkers or five-year-old T-ball. Guys who whine in this sport look like punks."

JOHN COVINGTON: "Holtz always stays relatively cool, but you could tell it was on his mind. Because he brought it up almost every time he saw us. We were like: Stop talking about it! If you ain't worried about it, let it drop!"

Holtz would not discuss the book when it was published, repeating again and again at his weekly press conferences, "I have not read the book, I do not plan on reading the book, and I'm not going to answer questions about the book."

LOU HOLTZ: "Haven't read it to this day, and never will read it. Once again, it was the same guy who wrote the Southern Cal fight story. So, you know, you can't control it. But I knew it was coming out, and I told our squad about it when they came back to school. We talked about it and moved on.

"Was it easy? No. Did they try and hype it up with Ted Koppel and everything else? There's no doubt about that. And when it came out, and we went up to Michigan, there were some people ready to bury us. And Notre Dame went out and played great football."

First the seventh-ranked Irish defeated Northwestern 27–12 in the season opener. But since Notre Dame came in as 28-point favorites, it dropped four spots in the polls after a win.

JEREMY NAU: "There's something you don't see every day. They slapped us all the way down to No. 11. Then we played against Michigan at their place. Michigan was good and they were ranked second or third. We were supposed to get killed.

"Then Holtz came right out and said it: 'It's us against the world. They're all trying to bring down Notre Dame. But Notre Dame is bigger than this book. Notre Dame's bigger than anything in this country.'

"That's the way we felt before we played Michigan. I mean, everyone had different feelings about Holtz. But when he turned it on, this guy could get you pumped."

TIM PRISTER: "The book was one controversy Holtz didn't want. But he was definitely at his best during a crisis. I actually feel there were times where he didn't feel comfortable with prosperity."

MIKE MCGLINN: "If our season had one defining moment, it was that second week. The book is coming out. Holtz has been sick with chest pains. We got Michigan next. I recall seeing seniors going up to Holtz and giving him a hug. This is stuff I had never seen before."

KEVIN MCDOUGAL: "The Michigan crowd was huge, but our offense came out smoking. On our very first series, we ran the option. Now, I was never an option quarterback. I hated running the option. You took too many unprotected shots.

"But Coach Holtz liked to run it, and this time the option was perfect. Our fullback Ray Zellars destroyed their linebacker. I came around the corner and went to pitch out, but I saw this big hole. Then I swear I ran faster than I ever have in my life."

After his clutch 43-yard TD run made it 7–0, McDougal completed a 43-yard bomb on Notre Dame's next drive. By halftime he'd thrown for 137 yards, rushed for 72, and sparked the Irish to a 24–10 lead. And the 106,851 fans in Michigan Stadium, the largest crowd of all time for a regular season game?

JOHN COVINGTON: "When the game first started, they were incredibly loud and cocky. We could hear their fans behind our bench, chanting 'TARNISHED DOME, TARNISHED DOME.' A few minutes into the game, those people didn't say jack."

JEREMY NAU: "Had we lost to Michigan, that book might have been a huge event. But after beating them, it was like: Who cares? Screw everyone else."

The Wolverines lost 27–23. Then they all went down the next six weeks: Michigan State, Purdue, Stanford in a revenge game, Pittsburgh, Brigham Young, and USC for the 11th consecutive year. On October 30, before playing at Veterans Stadium against Navy, the Irish were 8–0 and ranked No. 2.

JEREMY NAU: "We ended up winning 58–27, but we were losing at halftime and we played like crap. At our defensive meeting that next Monday, Coach Minter went crazy. He was throwing shit and calling guys prima donnas.

"Then Holtz went off on us when our whole team met. Our next game was Florida State, but Holtz knew we had a bye week. So he did it the Marine way. He crushed us for a week, then built us back up."

KEVIN McDOUGAL: "First he said that Florida State would kill us. As the game got closer, we could probably beat an NFL team."

With two weeks before this certified Big Game—No. 1-ranked Florida State against No. 2-ranked Notre Dame, with each team 9–0 and riding 16-game winning streaks— the major story line was the hallowed tradition of Fighting Irish football and the Seminoles' attempts to demystify it. One Florida State player referred to "the Three Horsemen," and another to "Rock Knutne." Flanker Kevin Knox said, "Mystique? There is no mystique. They should be scared of our mystique." Quarterback Charlie Ward, the Heisman Trophy shoo-in, claimed, "I didn't realize they had their own channel. You know you're big time when you have your own channel."

Meantime in South Bend, Holtz and his players did their humble routine, while privately they seethed. Starting guard Mark Zataveski sets the pregame scene.

MARK ZATAVESKI: "The game was one versus two. So geez, you know, the media went crazy. They were on campus since Monday. And you got the feeling all week that Holtz felt like he had something to prove. Because even though Holtz had won a national title, and Bobby Bowden hadn't, Bowden seemed more well-liked by the media. Now, Holtz didn't say anything bad about Bowden. There was definitely a respect there. But just from his manner, you know how much Holtz wanted to beat Bowden."

PETE BERCICH: "Holtz is different during big games. He's more confident. He's not as worried. If you make a mistake at practice, he doesn't ride your ass like he did the weeks before. What helped us even more is that nobody picked us to win. Florida State was being portrayed as invincible, especially by those clowns on ESPN."

JEREMY NAU: "When Florida State won on the road, they always took home some grass from the other team's stadium. That gave us inspiration, because they started saying how they would do that to us. Holtz said, 'Forget about it. They're not coming in our backyard and pulling grass out of our damn stadium.'

"Holtz was pretty adamant about that. Then he went crazy again when Florida State made fun of Rockne. He said, 'They don't respect Notre Dame. Look at how they talk.' "

TIM LAYDEN: "Holtz had his team ready for the moment, and Bobby Bowden did not. I mean, I don't think Bowden did a bad job. I don't think he failed his team as much as Lou Holtz delivered for his. Holtz was brilliant that day. Notre Dame's attack was diversified, they were incredibly ready, and they were way better than we all realized."

For the millions of Irish fans hanging on NBC's broadcast, there were several clutch performances to cheer. Inside linebackers Bercich and Goheen, whom Holtz had bemoaned as "too slow" during the week, made 13 tackles and several jarring hits. Burris, a consensus All-American at free safety, scored Notre Dame's last two touchdowns when Holtz put him in at tailback near the goal line. Covington intercepted Charlie Ward, the quarterback's first interception in 159 passing attempts. As for Ward's much less celebrated counterpart, McDougal committed no turnovers, directed five scoring drives, completed nine of 18 passes for 108 yards, and, most significantly, maintained his perfect record as a starter.

Notre Dame won 31–24, but as Burris explains, "We were winning 21–7 at halftime and 31–17 late in the fourth quarter. It really wasn't all that close a game."

This victory gave Notre Dame the No. 1 spot in the country. So with one regular-season game left against Boston College, the once-embattled Irish were deep in the hunt for the national championship.

According to a prediction in *Blue & Gold Illustrated*, Notre Dame would stomp Boston College 35–14. This seemed reasonable, since the Irish had their top ranking to protect, they were playing at home, and they had routed the Eagles 54–7 the previous year.

But as *Blue & Gold Illustrated* also noted, there was always the possibility of an ambush. After their monumental win over Florida State, the Irish might be emotionally spent. Moreover, Boston College still recalled that fake punt.

JEREMY NAU: "The week before BC, I remember telling Goheen how dead we looked at practice. The coaches didn't seem too pumped up either. I remember thinking: We can lose this game."

MARK ZATAVESKI: "We had something to fight for that whole year. Michigan was the book. Stanford was revenge. USC was USC. Florida State was the Game of the Century. Suddenly, the week of Boston College, there was no controversy. And for the first time all that year, people were on our side. That gave me an eerie feeling in my stomach. Like we could get slapped in the face here."

LOU HOLTZ: "They had a good team and they were hot. Tom Coughlin was a fine coach. They had Glenn Foley at quarterback. Foley was pretty good when he was in college, and I think he's proven that now in the NFL.

"It was also our last home game, and we never play particularly well then. We get so many tears in our eyes, we can't hardly see who to block and tackle. So, yes, I felt the football game would be tight. But I felt Notre Dame would find a way to win."

KEVIN MCDOUGAL: "You remember in college basketball, when Villanova played out of its head and upset Georgetown? That's how Boston College played against us. Glenn Foley couldn't miss. He could have thrown a BB through a straw. And what did their tight end Pete Mitchell have? Thirteen catches? Ten of them for first downs?"

JEREMY NAU: "Pete Mitchell was unconscious. He and Foley destroyed us."

Boston College led 24–14 at halftime, by which point the scrappy Foley had thrown for three touchdowns and Notre Dame Stadium had fallen deathly silent.

OLIVER GIBSON: "It almost felt surreal. We could not stop them on defense. Holtz was getting more and more frustrated, and the guy feeling that pressure was Rick Minter, our defensive coordinator. Holtz kept looking at Minter like: Okay, it's time to stop them. Can we please stop them now?"

MIKE MCGLINN: "There was a poignant moment during halftime. We were in our locker room, and it was almost like it was sinking in: This is going to happen. We're gonna blow this thing.

"That was very weird. Some of our players seemed a little panicked."

Some, but not McDougal. With Notre Dame trailing 38–17 and 11 minutes left, he led the Irish to 22 straight points. The last dramatic score—a pinpoint touchdown pass on fourth-and-goal at the Boston College four—tied this riveting game at 38–38. The extra point gave the Irish their first lead, 39–38. But a few tense moments later, McDougal and his brilliant comeback became footnotes.

With 1:09 to go and the ball on the Boston 25, Foley missed his first pass. His second pass, over the middle, was nearly intercepted. But linebacker Pete Bercich dropped the ball. Linebackers do that sometimes. This drop was immense, though. If Bercich had held on, he'd be the hero and Notre Dame would likely win.

Foley instead completed four straight passes. Then, with 0:05 left, the Eagles called time-out and David Gordon attempted a 41-yard field goal. The snap was high, but Gordon's holder Foley got it down. The left-footed Gordon kicked a knuckleball, which wobbled through the uprights as time expired, piercing Irish hearts and toppling Notre Dame from its No. 1 ranking.

JOHN COVINGTON: "They won 41–39. To be honest, it's still a sore subject with me."

MARK ZATAVESKI: "We knew exactly what we did. We let it slip through our fingers. I've never seen so many grown men cry."

JEREMY NAU: "Yep. I was crying, too. In 1992, things were more businesslike. In 1993, everybody cared about one another. That was the closest football team I've ever played on.

"You know I still talk to Bercich? I just saw him at Goheen's wedding a month ago. And you asked me what stood out most after that game? When I looked over at Pete and he was bawling his eyes out."

PETE BERCICH: "At first I thought: Good play. You broke it up. Then I thought: Damn, You should have caught it. And then, a few plays later, their guy kicks the longest field goal of his career.

"It was terrible. I mean, it was bad. I broke down for ten or fifteen minutes. Just sat in front of my locker, really hurting.

"Now, it's one of those things that I have to live with. It'll be with me the rest of my years. Because even today, people say it to my face: 'Oh yeah. You're the guy who dropped the ball.' "

What Bercich doesn't mention is what happened after he ran out of tears. Bercich didn't slip out a side door. He faced the media and answered every question. Which takes a bigger man than it takes to catch a football.

One month after this loss, arguably the most crushing in Notre Dame history, the fourth-ranked Irish defeated seventh-ranked Texas A&M 24–21 in the Cotton Bowl.

With the score tied 21–21 in the fourth quarter, Bercich helped win the game with a key interception.

PETE BERCICH: "I knew nobody was going to remember. They'd only remember the black mark. But that play meant a lot to me. Because if it taught me anything, it taught me never to give up. And you can hear that a million times. You can watch a million movies about it. You can tell yourself for a month before a bowl game, 'Things will turn around. You're gonna be okay.'

"But you don't know whether or not you're lying to yourself. Then it happens. You survive."

There was talk before this victory that No. 1 ranked Notre Dame could still finish No. 1 if everything broke just right in the other bowls. Then it seemed to come true. Third-ranked West Virginia lost decisively in the Sugar Bowl. Top-ranked Florida State struggled against second-ranked Nebraska, beating the 17-point underdog Cornhuskers 18–16 on a last-second field goal in the Orange Bowl.

The Seminoles' narrow win left them and Notre Dame with one loss apiece. Since the Irish (11–1) beat Florida State (12–1) in head-to-head competition—and since their 31–24 victory was convincing—didn't they deserve to be national champions? Or at least co-champions?

Not according to voters. Both the coaches (*USA Today*/ CNN) and reporters (AP) put Florida State on top of Notre Dame.

JEREMY NAU: "In 1989, Notre Dame went 12–1 and Miami went 11–1. But they gave Miami the national championship because it beat Notre Dame that season. When the same thing happened in 1993—and we beat Florida State—they gave it to Florida State.

"I think it was politics. I think the voters said, 'Let's give this one to Bobby Bowden. He's never won a ring.'"

JUSTIN GOHEEN: "If that is why they gave it to him, I think that's crap. Just because you've come close a few times, they should give you one? Now you're turning it into a popularity contest?"

OLIVER GIBSON: "Bowden and Florida State were the media darlings. Whereas Holtz consistently harped on the negatives. For ten or eleven weeks, he talked about how much he didn't have. Then he suddenly pleaded his case at the end of the year. Sometimes I used to wonder if that hurt us."

MIKE MCGLINN: "Bobby Bowden played the media like a maestro. Smiling, everything's cool, just a teddy bear. Bowden was the guy you'd want to have a beer with. And that's not to take anything away from Lou Holtz. Because he is a man who should be respected. People who really know him will tell you he's a good guy.

"But Lou Holtz had a routine he would go through with the press. They'd ask him how his team was doing that week, and he'd say the world was crumbling around him. Well, that wasn't the case and everyone knew it. So maybe people got tired of that same old song and dance."

JUSTIN GOHEEN: "That could very well be. But I would hate to believe something like that. How old are college players? From about nineteen to twenty-two? For the most part they're still kids. And for a group of reporters or coaches to get together and take away something really special from one group of kids because they have a grudge or bad vibes against a certain coach is kind of a sad commentary to me."

Holtz again insists that he never poor-mouthed. His pessimism, he says, was genuine. As for the final vote, he calls it "disappointing."

LOU HOLTZ: "How can you justify it one way in eighty-nine, and then do the exact opposite in ninety-three? How can you not give it to one of those Notre Dame teams?

"I'll tell you how. They looked the other way."

KEVIN McDOUGAL: "After we beat Texas A&M, and Florida State barely won, I went to bed thinking: Are they going to give us half or the whole thing?

"Then to wake up and discover you got nothing? Man, I wanted to cry all over again."

37

THE BOSTON COLLEGE HANGOVER
1 9 9 4

ENTERING HIS NINTH YEAR AT NOTRE DAME, HOLTZ HAD COM-
piled a 77–19–1 record. He had won five major bowl
games and one national championship. Since 1988, his
teams had averaged a hefty ten wins per season. If Holtz
could maintain that pace for three more years—the dura-
tion of his contract—his 107 wins would break the school
record (105) held by Knute Rockne.

Yet even with that grand legacy to chase—and with all
that Holtz had already achieved—some players say he
came back a different man in 1994. According to them,
Holtz still couldn't relinquish the 41–39 upset by Boston
College. That stunning home defeat probably cost Holtz
his second national title, and kept him from joining Leahy
(four), Rockne (three), and Parseghian (two) as a multiple
national championship winner.

MIKE MCGLINN: "It's one thing if you never even come
close. But to come that close and not get it, that was
unsavory.

"So there was a lot of criticism in South Bend, and since you can't fire the players, Holtz took most of the brunt. That seemed to change his demeanor in 1994. Holtz was more detached. He started putting some distance between himself and the players."

JUSTIN GOHEEN: "When you're head coach at Notre Dame, you have a tremendous opportunity to be either the hero or goat for probably the largest fan contingency in the United States. Between beating Florida State and losing to Boston College, I think Lou Holtz had the distinct pleasure of being both."

LOU HOLTZ: "Of course, it was hard to let go. But they're all hard. Was that one any harder than the rest? Like I said, they're all hard."

JEREMY NAU: "Boston College devastated him. Holtz may not admit it, but he was hurting. It's obvious when you see a guy every day.

"But you know what the main problem was in my opinion? It was our senior class. Holtz never really liked us. It wasn't that we were bad people. Holtz just thought we weren't very good football players. Holtz just thought he couldn't win with us. And to seniors like me—seniors who busted their ass for four straight years—that was pretty discouraging."

MARK ZATAVESKI: "I guess you could say we felt like the misfit class. Because Holtz really loved the class of ninety-three. He would always call them 'the most gifted in my tenure at Notre Dame.'

"So maybe his feelings toward them—and his feeling toward us—had something to do with his attitude that season. Because if you look at Holtz's early years, he talked about being remembered as one of the greatest coaches in Notre Dame history. He said he wanted to win two national championships. So when the 1993 team didn't win it all, maybe Holtz saw our class as the beginning of his decline at Notre Dame."

JUSTIN GOHEEN: "There were a number of problems with our team, which all came to a head before the Fiesta Bowl. But even before the season ever started, our coaches used the term 'rebuilding year.' With that kind of mentality going in, I was a little shocked when we were ranked No. 3 in the preseason. Because, internally, our coaching staff didn't seem to think we'd be that good."

Even amid outsiders, there were many who were surprised at Notre Dame's high ranking. Ten starters had been drafted from the 1993 team, and another five players had ended up signing pro contracts. But the single biggest loss may have been Kevin McDougal. In 1993, his completion percentage (61.6) was the highest in Notre Dame history. His record as a starter was 10–1, and even in that one loss to Boston College, the Irish scored 38 points.

Replacing McDougal was sophomore Ron Powlus, who had fully recovered from his broken collarbone, but had still never played a down of college football. Powlus would also be throwing behind a green and injury-riddled offensive line, which would result in his being sacked 25 times.

But that was down the road. In Powlus's first college game, he threw for 291 yards and four touchdowns in a nationally televised massacre of Northwestern.

That night, during the telecast on ABC, Brent Musburger started the frenzy by asking, "How many Heismans can this kid win?" The next morning, on ESPN, Beano Cook declared, "Ron Powlus will win the Heisman two times and be the greatest quarterback in the history of Notre Dame." Then there were the trigger-happy headlines: "OVERNIGHT SENSATION. PROMISE IS FULFILLED. HE'S AMONG IMMORTALS."

Two weeks later against Michigan State, Powlus threw four interceptions. That ended the comparisons to Joe Montana. In fact, says one of his teammates, Powlus came home from that game and found several nasty messages on his voice mail. Imagine if Notre Dame hadn't won 21–20.

TIM LAYDEN: "After that first great performance, Powlus had some decent moments and some bad ones. But it wasn't really fair to judge him yet. Powlus was under siege in 1994. Not only was that offensive line young and injured, but Beano Cook and Brent Musburger made those predictions. That wasn't fair to Powlus. All it did was make him a huge target."

JUSTIN GOHEEN: "Holtz didn't do Ron any favors either. After that Michigan State game, Holtz actually started talking about Michigan State's green jerseys, and how they blended in with the artificial turf, and how that made it difficult to see them.

"I remember thinking: Why are we making excuses for this guy? Ron is no longer a little puppy freshman. He's been here for a year now, and everyone's saying he's a big-time player. Well, what about treating him like one and making him responsible for his actions?"

JEREMY NAU: "I thought Holtz snapped when he talked about their green jerseys and the turf. But as the season went on, he protected Ron a lot."

OLIVER GIBSON: "I hate to say it, but Ron Powlus was overrated from the beginning. And Lou Holtz built him up to be Superman."

Holtz doesn't seem to be doing that anymore. Here he makes a concession regarding Powlus and Paul Fallia, the senior quarterback who angrily quit the team before spring practice when Holtz announced that Powlus would be his starter in 1994.

LOU HOLTZ: "That was the biggest mistake I made. Paul Fallia wasn't always pretty, but the guy was a winner. Every time he got a chance, he was productive. Like that game against Southern Cal the year before. McDougal was hurt and Fallia came in and gave us a clutch ball game.

"So that was wrong of me. I should have given Paul Fallia an opportunity. Because I think that really hurt us, and also hurt Ron Powlus in the long run. Maybe it would have helped Powlus if he had more competition. And maybe Paul Fallia was the best quarterback for us."

Still, the Irish were 4–1 and ranked No. 8 going into their game at unranked Boston College. But rather than punish the team that stole its national title, Notre Dame lost 30–11.

After this telling defeat, the Irish lost two of three and saw their record slip to 5–4. That's when most of the finger-pointing started.

MARK ZATAVESKI: "There was tension building. Even Holtz and Joe Moore weren't getting along, and that was unusual. Moore was our offensive line coach, and since Notre Dame always had great offensive lines, Holtz respected Moore and usually left him alone.

"But the offensive line was taking some heat that season. A lot of guys were injured and Powlus kept getting sacked. Then one day at practice, one of our offensive linemen made a mistake. Holtz just threw our whole team out of practice. Holtz did that occasionally, but this time

Moore went nuts. Holtz started walking away and Moore started screaming at him. It was the only time in four years that I ever saw an assistant yell at Holtz."

MIKE MCGLINN: "Once we lost at home to Brigham Young, some of the player factions started showing. It wasn't necessarily vocalized, but you could see it in guys' eyes. You could see it by looking at our sidelines. There was no emotion. Our sidelines were a joke."

JUSTIN GOHEEN: "It was the strangest season I've ever experienced. I can't tell you how many times I thought: What a freaking year to be a captain!"

JEREMY NAU: "We had a lot of guys worried about the NFL. That meant we had guys who were worried about getting injured. 'Hey, man, I gotta get to the league. I gotta get paid.'

"Then we also had players blaming coaches. We had coaches writing off the season and already looking ahead to 1995. We had that big mess before the bowl game."

It began with protests from Fighting Irish haters, as 6–4–1 Notre Dame accepted a Fiesta Bowl bid against 10–1 Colorado. Which only confirmed just how unique Notre Dame was: If it wasn't getting snubbed in the final polls, it was playing in major bowl games it didn't deserve to.

MIKE MCGLINN: "Honestly, I didn't want to go. Notre Dame had a standard, and that standard wasn't maintained during that season. But you figure it out. Notre Dame. TV ratings. Big money. If there was any chance in hell that the Fiesta Bowl people could get away with it, you better believe that Notre Dame would be there."

MARK ZATAVESKI: "It was a little depressing. We were 3–0 in bowl games under Holtz, but we went into this one expecting to lose. It also seemed like we went just for the money. And I thought that stunk, too."

RON POWLUS: "I knew that guys were embarrassed about our record. But I wanted to go. I thought: We're Notre Dame. This is a major bowl game. I don't care who we're playing. We can beat anybody."

JEREMY NAU: "Number one: We just didn't deserve it. Number two: This team had lousy unity. Number three: If we went down to Arizona, I felt it would be the same crap we had all season. Who gives a damn about football as long as we have a good time?"

MIKE MCGLINN: "It was a fiasco. We had several guys who got down there and just didn't care. They were going out late at night, trying to dodge curfew. All that Mickey Mouse stuff that isn't supposed to happen at Notre Dame."

The curfew story was broken by Tim Prister of *Blue & Gold Illustrated*. "Four days before the game," he wrote, "an estimated dozen players—many seniors, several of whom were considered leaders of the team—missed curfew. Sources indicated that one player—a senior—not only missed curfew, but simply failed to show up until sometime the next day."

But even Prister didn't discover what happened a few nights later, when two Irish players nearly got into a brawl. One participant was senior linebacker and captain Justin Goheen.

JUSTIN GOHEEN: "It wasn't something that happened overnight. We had guys on that team all year who just honest to God didn't give a shit. Then we got to the bowl game and a bunch of guys broke curfew.

"Most of them got caught by the coaching staff, but some of them didn't. Then once the coaches found out that there were more players involved, those who didn't get caught had an opportunity to stand up and come forward. Now, there's two schools of thought there. One is 'Hell, I wasn't caught so why should I admit it?' The other is 'Yeah, I was with my teammates. And if I got the balls to go out and break curfew, I should have the balls to be a man. I should step up and take my medicine.'

"These other guys didn't step up. Holtz had their teammates running after practice, doing crab walks, going through all kinds of shit, and these guys just watched it happen. And not only did these guys not stand up, they were bragging about it in the locker room. Bragging about their escapades when they broke curfew.

"So take it from my perspective. Here I am trying to play my last college game. I got nerve damage from my neck down to my arm. A week ago, my arm was literally numb. And I'm gonna try and get out there and play regardless, and I've got these assholes down at their lockers, talking about some girl they picked up the night they broke curfew.

"To me, that epitomized their lack of commitment all season. I mean, do what you want the rest of your life. But you can't be on time before our last football game?

"These guys knew I was pissed. Then it all culminated a few nights before the bowl game. Our entire team went to the Arizona Symphony. That was kind of fun, because they brought us up on stage and played the Fight Song. But then as we started walking outside to our busses, one guy who never came forward made a comment. In his typical way, he didn't make it to me. He made it to his six buddies.

"I was halfway on the bus and I got right back off it. I walked up to him and said, 'What did you say?' He started getting loud in front of his buddies. I ended up pushing him down onto the ground. Then all the guys spilled off the busses and it abruptly ended.

"After the fact, I was really embarrassed about it. Here I am the captain of the team, and I'm wrestling on the ground with one of my teammates."

What struck some players most about this unruly week in Tempe—even more than their football team imploding—was the tolerant reaction of Lou Holtz.

MARK ZATAVESKI: "The players who broke curfew weren't sent home. Their punishment was mostly physical. Running laps, crab walks, that kind of stuff.

"But we all knew what happened in 1988. Holtz sent home Tony Brooks and Ricky Watters for showing up late to a meeting before the USC game. He didn't make them do crab walks. He flat-out sent them home and made an example of them. So some of us were surprised when Holtz didn't come down harder on these guys."

JEREMY NAU: "I would have respected him more if he sent them home. I mean, he didn't even send home the guy who stayed out all night. Holtz actually dressed him for the game. He said it was just for precautionary reasons. In case we needed him."

RON POWLUS: "I put most of the blame on the players' shoulders. Why should a coach even be in that position? Why should he even *think* about sending you home from a bowl game?

"As for how Holtz handled it, maybe he could have

been a little tougher. But I think he found himself in a tough situation. You had eight or ten starters who missed that curfew. They had an obligation to take that game seriously."

When asked about the curfew incident, Holtz's account differs from Powlus's and other players'. He says the wrongdoers were "the nonplayers we brought out." But Holtz does not dispute that he wasn't as staunch as he'd been with Watters and Brooks.

LOU HOLTZ: "When you're coaching at Notre Dame, you're going to be attacked no matter what you do. And after you're under attack for so many things, maybe you become a little more protective. Maybe you try not to be quite as controversial."

At the Fiesta Bowl, on national television, the unranked Irish proved their critics right. They had never been worthy of playing fourth-ranked Colorado, which led 31–3 in the second quarter and went on to an easy 41–24 win.

MARK ZATAVESKI: "I still remember running off the field. The Colorado fans were pointing and yelling at us, 'SIX, FIVE, AND ONE! SIX, FIVE, AND ONE!'

"I happened to be next to Holtz, and he looked really dejected. That was his worst record since his first year at Notre Dame."

38

HOLTZ'S CRYPTIC EXIT
1995 – 1996

FOLLOWING THE TROUBLED COLLAPSE OF 1994, THE IRISH opened at home with what seemed like a guaranteed win. Their lowly opponent Northwestern hadn't whipped Notre Dame since 1962, when Ara Parseghian's surprising Wildcats routed Joe Kuharich's slumping Irish 35–6. Now, 33 years and 14 defeats later, Northwestern was favored to lose by 28 points.

After the 17–15 shocker in South Bend, many of the 59,075 fans who came to celebrate Lou Holtz's 200th career victory sat staring in disbelief at the emptying field. This was supposed to be the year of redemption.

On September 30, a 45–26 loss to powerful Ohio State gave the Irish a 3–2 record and bounced them from national championship contention. But rather than faxing in the rest of the year, as the 1994 team might have done, Notre Dame won its final six regular-season games. The streak wasn't snapped until January 1, when the No. 6-ranked Irish lost a 31–26 thriller to No. 8-ranked Florida State in the Orange Bowl.

The 1995 season also marked the emergence of third-year defensive coordinator Bob Davie as a leading contender to one day succeed Holtz. Davie had come to South Bend from Texas A&M, where he'd spent the past nine seasons as an assistant. Davie was named the Aggies' defensive coordinator in 1989. By 1991, the school's famed Wrecking Crew defense ranked first in the country.

In mid-September 1995, when Holtz entered the Mayo Clinic for spinal surgery, he named Davie acting head coach for that Saturday's Vanderbilt game. After a 41–0 romp, the players carried Davie off the field and the Notre Dame faithful gushed about the new guy. Then, as Holtz recovered from his operation, he spent five games coaching from the pressbox while Davie guided the Irish on the sidelines. During those five victories, it was Davie's calm demeanor, his warm rapport with his players, and his solid standing with Holtz that later contributed to Davie's promotion.

In 1995, Notre Dame finished 9–3 and outside the Top 10 for the second straight season. Still, the team showed character by winning six straight despite Holtz's physical problems and the criticism aroused by the loss to Northwestern. In fact, as this season progressed, that outcome seemed less disturbing. The Wildcats, after all, wound up with a 10–2 record and their first Rose Bowl appearance since 1949.

In December 1995 and February 1996, with only one season remaining on Holtz's contract, he had two significant meetings with executive vice president Rev. E. William Beauchamp and athletic director Mike Wadsworth. Just four months earlier, Wadsworth had replaced Holtz's dear friend Dick Rosenthal. Father Beauchamp had succeeded Father Joyce in 1987, when both Father Joyce and Father Hesburgh retired from their posts after 35 years.

Why were these two meetings consequential? Some associates of Holtz said they left him feeling uncertain about his status at Notre Dame. But Wadsworth describes the meetings as "positive and straightforward."

MIKE WADSWORTH: "Lou had made a comment prior to our meetings. He said, 'I never know where I stand with the administration.' Well, that struck me pretty forcibly. Here's a man who has been here ten years. He ought to know where he stands with the administration.

"Then I also learned that Lou never had any kind of a job description. It had never been laid out exactly what the administration expected from the Notre Dame football coach. So in anticipation of our meeting, I drafted my perception of the responsibilities of the head football coach to Notre Dame. I forwarded it to Lou for his review and suggestions. He sent back a note that it looked fine, and that it was the first time in ten years that he ever had any kind of a job description. The impression I got is that he was basically pleased.

"When we met in February, we used that document as the talking point. One of the main things discussed was our graduation rate, which by then had dropped to about 72 percent. Now, that was for a variety of reasons. Some players, like Jerome Bettis, left because they had an outstanding pro opportunity. But other players left for disciplinary reasons, or academic reasons, or because they transferred. Well, that does become a concern. Because somewhere along the line in our recruiting, we did not get the proper fit for Notre Dame.

"So we talked about this at our meeting. And Lou agreed with us. We knew the numbers were down. In fact, he had already addressed this before we even raised it. Lou had hired a new recruiting coordinator, Bob

Chemiel. And Bob had already been with us for a season, and we had seen the benefits of his work.

"And so the meeting was not at all contentious. We had a frank and factual discussion about where the program had hit some rough spots in terms of recruiting. We felt Lou had already taken positive steps. So we told him in conclusion: 'Now you have a clear understanding of what we expect. From what you've been saying, you buy into it fully. That being the case, you deliver on these things, as you have been delivering for the most part, then you're our head coach for as long as you want to be here.'

"That was the position we took in that February 1996 meeting. And that was the position we took into that fall, when Lou first started talking about resigning. He was still the coach we wanted. And he was delivering on the things we'd discussed."

After that February meeting, there were media reports of Holtz's "lifetime contract" with Notre Dame. According to defensive end Renaldo Wynn, the team's Most Valuable Player in 1996, Holtz made similar statements to his players.

RENALDO WYNN: "He made it clear as day. He said he could be head coach until he decided to leave. He also made it clear that he wanted to keep coaching.

"So at that point, I had no inkling that this would be his last year. I didn't sense any friction between him and the administration. It was just the opposite. He was very enthusiastic about the future."

Still, it seems possible that Holtz felt conflicted. While he loved coaching the Fighting Irish, perhaps he didn't love getting a written job description after ten years at his post. It also seems likely that Holtz, a self-proclaimed dictator, went into those meetings expecting to have his ring kissed. Instead he received a blunt evaluation.

Three veteran journalists give their own perspectives.

TIM LAYDEN: "To understand Holtz and Wadsworth, I think you have to start with Holtz and Dick Rosenthal. Rosenthal was a banker before he became athletic director. He negotiated the NBC deal. He negotiated Notre Dame's initial involvement in the bowl alliance, which was a terrific sweetheart deal that has since been watered down.

"So while Rosenthal ran that end of the athletic program, Holtz ran the football team. And as Holtz ran that team, Rosenthal by and large stayed out of his way. Once Rosenthal left, you could basically start the clock on how long Holtz would be there."

TIM PRISTER: "Rosenthal never functioned as Holtz's boss. It was more like peer to peer. Things were very different with Wadsworth and Holtz. It was very much boss and employee.

"That sounds like Wadsworth was cold about it. I don't think it was like that. But I do think Lou was intimidated by Wadsworth. Because Wadsworth has a strong presence and a very impressive background. He's a graduate of Notre Dame. He played for Ara Parseghian. He was the Canadian ambassador to Ireland. He was a lawyer and a high-level businessman.

"So if there was any division between Lou and Wadsworth, I think Lou created it in his mind. Because as domineering and dominant as Lou is, there's a side of him that's insecure. That's probably why, in Lou's mind, Mike Wadsworth was pushing him out. But I never saw any evidence of that. I felt Wadsworth was just doing his job as athletic director."

TERRENCE MOORE: "I've known Lou Holtz for many years. He's a very good football coach, but he's a very insecure person who constantly has to be stroked. Well, his first athletic director was a stroker. That was Gene Corrigan. A great athletic director, but a stroker.

"Then Corrigan left and Dick Rosenthal came in. Holtz and Rosenthal became good friends. They lived next door to each other. They were golfing buddies. And Rosenthal quickly became one of Lou's favorite people at Notre Dame. Because Lou could do whatever the hell he wanted to.

"So Rosenthal leaves and now you bring in Mike Wadsworth. He has a totally different mind-set from the two guys I just named. He's achieved all these things in his life outside of football. So he's gonna let a football coach tell him what to do? It would be silly for him to have that mind-set.

"So now Lou feels he's lost his support system. He's not going to get it from Father Edward Malloy, the president, and he's not gonna get it from Father Beauchamp. He's not gonna get it from any of the priests. So now Lou is out on this island by himself. And that's eating away at him."

Holtz has declined to elaborate on why he left Notre Dame. This isn't surprising, though. He has been publicly tight-lipped ever since his resignation. Even at his formal press conference, Holtz spoke for 75 minutes but never gave one reason for his departure.

The 1996 season began with Notre Dame ranked No. 6 by the AP. But with 14 starters back from a 9–3 Orange Bowl team, internal expectations soared even higher.

RENALDO WYNN: "We thought we had everything. The talent, the leadership, the experience. So we thought we had a chance to win a national title. We genuinely believed it."

TIM PRISTER: "It wasn't only the team. People all over the country felt Notre Dame was shooting for the national title. But of all eleven seasons Lou Holtz coached, 1996 was probably the most underachieving. That was a 10–1 football team that finished 8–3."

The first defeat came in South Bend, as Ohio State handled the Irish 29–16. But there was no disgrace in losing to the Buckeyes, who ended the season with an 11–1 record and No. 2 ranking, and who then saw their two best players, Orlando Pace and Shawn Springs, become the first and third overall picks in the NFL draft.

The second loss went into the history books. After 18 consecutive wins over military schools—a streak that began in Holtz's first year in South Bend—the Irish lost 20–17 to Air Force.

TIM PRISTER: "That's when it all fell apart. Notre Dame was 4–2. The national championship was impossible. Plus, look at how they lost. They got beat on their own turf. They got beat by Air Force, a team that didn't have nearly as much talent.

"So now you're looking at Holtz and you can't help thinking: This guy has lost the magic."

Two respected seniors recall this crushing home upset: starting tight end and future Detroit Lion Pete Chryplewicz, and walk-on tight end and special teams expert Kevin Carretta.

KEVIN CARRETTA: "I think this was probably the point when Holtz started thinking about his position at Notre Dame. Because he had already been through ninety-three, when

Boston College kept us from winning the title. Then there was the horrible season in ninety-four. Then we had three more losses in ninety-five. Then we lost to Air Force in South Bend.

"So I think Holtz realized that his career hit a plateau. I think he said to himself: 'Maybe I've done all I can at Notre Dame.'"

PETE CHRYPLEWICZ: "Devastated, demoralized, embarrassed. That's how all of us felt. But of course, the head coach is gonna take most of the heat. So a lot of people felt that Air Force was the final straw for him.

"But there's really no telling what happened behind the scenes. It's kind of like JFK. The truth is on file somewhere. But that story is on lock down, and nobody's gonna crack it."

There is no mystery according to Wadsworth. Holtz first mentioned quitting, Wadsworth says, within minutes of the wrenching loss to Air Force.

MIKE WADSWORTH: "Father Beauchamp and I met with Lou in his private locker room. This was typical for us after a game, and particularly when we lost. We would just spend some time and offer support.

"Lou was extremely distressed. He said he thought it was time to make a change. Then he said he was resigning after this reason. And, immediately, without any need to check with one another, Father Beauchamp and I started telling him the same thing: 'Look, that's crazy. We all know how badly you feel about this loss. It's a very emotional time for everyone. This isn't the time to make a decision like this. This is all going to pass. Let's not even consider it at this stage.'"

Wadsworth and Holtz had another talk on Monday. The conversation was similar, Wadsworth says, but this time they met at Holtz's home.

MIKE WADSWORTH: "Lou was still upset. The only difference was that he was more specific. Lou was saying things to the effect of: I think it's time for a change. It would be good for the program. The new stadium. The new locker room. The Rockne record. It's the right time for this. The program needs a fresh start.

"And as he raised each of these issues, I said, 'Lou, these are exactly the reasons for you to be enthusiastic about staying on. Number one, you're only in a position to break Rockne's record because you've earned it. Number two, the expanded stadium and locker room space are both things that you've wanted for a while. Now you're finally getting them. And you should have the advantage of those things. They're going to benefit you.' "

This meeting, Wadsworth says, concluded with Wadsworth suggesting that Holtz not make any fast or emotional decisions. One week later Notre Dame flew to Ireland, where it defeated Navy 54–27 and got some welcome relief from the tempest starting to build back in South Bend.

Marc Edwards, the bruising Notre Dame fullback, recalls this four-day trip to the Emerald Isle, which was only the second time in history that Notre Dame played a game outside the United States. The first was in Tokyo in 1979.

MARC EDWARDS: "That was a great experience. The people were really excited to have Notre Dame there. I mean, we're the Fighting Irish and all that.

"But you know what was funny about it? They didn't know a damn thing about football. They thought it didn't hurt when you got hit. They kept saying, 'Come on. You guys got pads on.' "

KEVIN CARRETTA: "Oh, yeah. They were all over us. How could we be tough if we wore pads? But then they'd start explaining Gaelic football. Which is physical contact, too, but without any pads. So then we understood where they were coming from.

"Then we'd go to a pub at night and sit down with people from Dublin. Have you ever drunk a Guinness? Oh, God. But that's all anyone drinks there. Have you ever seen Willie Wonka and the Chocolate Factory? The chocolate factory is the center of the city, and their whole culture is sort of defined by that?

"That's what the Guinness factory is to Dublin. It defines the whole city. Guinness signs are everywhere, and Guinness is like the elixir that heals everything. The people were telling us stories about when they got sick. Their doctors would tell them, 'Drink a pint of Guinness. That'll fix what ails ya.'"

During the long flight home from Ireland, Wadsworth says, Holtz asked for another meeting. On that Wednesday, Wadsworth says, Holtz resigned for a third time in Father Beauchamp's office.

MIKE WADSWORTH: "Lou said he had no other offers. He wasn't doing this to go someplace else. But he said he had thought it over carefully. And he was settled in his view that he should resign.

"We didn't really know what was motivating him. We felt there might be something else that he was leaving unsaid. But if he wanted to keep that private, that was his right.

"So then we all discussed the issue of timing. If it got into the media now that Lou was resigning, and that we were conducting a search for his replacement, it would be bedlam. So it was our initial request that he make his announcement after the season.

"But Lou was quite specific. He said he would prefer to do it the week of the Rutgers game, which was our last home game. He said it would be best to do it before the end of the season—and to have somebody in place to name at that time—because soon you would be hot into the recruiting season.

"Which is logical enough except for one thing. We really didn't have anyone in the wings. So we would need time to put together a search, and then to interview the candidates. We felt that to do all that, in the full glare of publicity, would be virtually impossible. So we really wanted to expand that time frame.

"But Lou was fixed in his views. He was also saying, 'Besides, this will leak out anyway.' Well, there were only three of us who knew it at the time. And we had hoped that we could keep it quiet.

"But rather than have a disagreement on it, we said we'd start immediately on our search. But we wanted to keep open the timing of this announcement. We wanted to operate, as much as possible, without publicity.

"That's how the meeting concluded. But in the end, it started to leak out. Lou had dropped some hints in the newspapers. I also think he may have had some conversations with some members of the press. In fact, we were told that. But I don't really know. It wasn't something we chased down, because it was immaterial at that point. It was already out. And then, ultimately, it got carried by ESPN. That's when it started to go like wildfire."

TIM PRISTER: "It really happened quickly. Notre Dame beat Boston College the week after Navy. Then Holtz had a press conference that Sunday. And he said something about 'when the new head coach comes in.'

"I was still in Boston at the time. But from what I understand, nobody really followed up on his comment. Then, on the following Tuesday, we started pushing on what he said two days earlier. Lou said he didn't mean anything by it. He denied he was stepping down. Then all that week the story's really racing. It's going national. And Holtz is still denying.

"On November 16, Notre Dame beat Pittsburgh. Holtz denied it again afterward. But then he made that comment: 'Don't ask the monkey, ask the organ grinder. Ask the guy at the end of the chain. He plays the music and I just dance and pass the cup around.'

"Even before that statement, there were all these rumors that he was being forced out. So now Lou makes everyone feel like he *is* being forced out. So now Wadsworth is being painted as the bad guy."

KEVIN CARRETTA: "During that whole Holtz scandal, I felt the athletic department got a pretty bad rap. Especially Mr. Wadsworth and Father Beauchamp. I mean, everyone thought it sounded fishy. But after dealing with Coach Holtz for five years, no one is going to run him out of anywhere. No one will make him do anything he doesn't want to."

PETE CHRYPLEWICZ: "A few days before he resigned, there was all this hearsay in the press. So a lot of guys were bewildered. What the hell is going on?

"The next thing you know, we have this emergency team meeting. Holtz tells us he's staying. He's not leaving Notre Dame. Then a few days go by and we have another meeting. Then he tells us, 'Yeah, I'm gonna retire.'

"It was like a combination from Mike Tyson. Boom, boom—he's in, he's out.

"Personally, I was stunned. Lou Holtz and Notre Dame

football go hand in hand. I was shocked that he was giving up the throne."

MARC EDWARDS: "Holtz told us on Monday, the day before he told the media. But he didn't really say much. He stood up and read us a statement. Then it turned out to be the same statement he read the next day."

On November 19, at a nationally televised press conference jammed with reporters, Holtz made public the worst-kept secret in sports. He was walking away from the only job he ever dreamed of.

"I feel worse than I've felt in a long time," Holtz said. "I do not feel good about this at all. But I do feel it's the right thing to do."

In a calm but rambling 75-minute speech, Holtz repeated that phrase—the right thing to do—again and again, but never revealed why he was departing. Thus the following headlines appeared Wednesday morning.

New York Times: 2 QUESTIONS IN HOLTZ'S WAKE: WHY? WHO STEPS IN?

Chicago Tribune: HOLTZ OFFERS LOTS OF WORDS, NO REASONS.

Los Angeles Times: IT'S TOUGH TO EXPLAIN WHY, BUT HOLTZ LEAVING THE IRISH.

While reading his formal resignation statement, Holtz also invited speculation by expressing his affection for past administrators, including Dick Rosenthal, while never once mentioning Wadsworth. Then, after his farewell speech, Holtz shook hands with sports information director John Heisler, but strode past his two bosses, Wadsworth and Beauchamp, without so much as a nod.

And so the question remained: Was Holtz pressured or did he volunteer?

TIM PRISTER: "In Lou's mind, he probably thinks he was pushed out. But I just don't have any facts that show me that."

TERRENCE MOORE: "One thing about Notre Dame is that history repeats itself. That's why you saw this thing with Lou Holtz coming. Because Lou Holtz is Frank Leahy. Lou Holtz is Knute Rockne. I mean, everything shows that had Rockne not died in that plane crash, he probably would have been fired or eased out. And we all know they basically fired Leahy. Because the overriding theme at Notre Dame is this: We do not want the football program to overshadow the university.

"I think that's what happened to Lou. The priests at Notre Dame felt he was getting a little too big for his britches. Plus, all these controversies kept popping up. Well, that's easier to take when your team is winning. But suddenly Holtz started losing all those home games. I mean, look at some of the most agonizing losses in Notre Dame history. Many came under Holtz, and all of those were at home since 1990. Stanford, Tennessee, Stanford, Boston College, Northwestern, Air Force. Every year, they were having these unbelievably shocking losses. Until it became routine. It wasn't even a shock anymore.

"Now, I don't think he left because of those losses. But I do think it made it easier for them to make a change. And while I wouldn't say that he was flat-out fired, I do believe that he was sort of shoved. I think he wanted assurances from them. I think he wanted to be stroked. When that didn't happen, Lou said, 'Well, then I'll resign.' Notre Dame said, 'Well, go right ahead.' "

KEVIN CARRETTA: "No. I don't think there was a conflict between Notre Dame and Lou Holtz. The conflict was in Lou Holtz. He loved Notre Dame and didn't want to leave. But he realized it was time to make a change. I think that was the conflict people saw. And they perceived it as being between him and the administration.

"But I did think he was right. It was time for him to go. Lou Holtz was one of those coaches who did a lot of yelling. But the kids playing college football are different now. They don't always listen when their coach yells. They would prefer to be spoon-fed. So maybe his style of coaching was getting stale."

MIKE McGLINN: "In the end, I think it was mutual. Lou Holtz and Mike Wadsworth weren't on the same page. They both saw the writing on the wall. So they decided to end it sooner than later."

There are additional theories: Notre Dame didn't want Holtz to break Knute Rockne's school record of 105 victories. Too many Holtz recruits had incidents off the field. Holtz irritated Wadsworth by wanting to sign Randy Moss, the hugely talented but troubled high school prospect.

Wadsworth responds by saying: Holtz had earned the right to become Notre Dame's all-time winningest coach. Any player transgressions took place before Wadsworth arrived, and his only focus was Notre Dame's present and future. After Randy Moss was turned down by the admissions office—based strictly on the quality of his application—Holtz never pressed the issue.

As for the notion that Holtz had eclipsed Notre Dame, Wadsworth refers to it as a "gross distortion."

MIKE WADSWORTH: "I would agree with the principle that no athletic coach should ever become more important than the university itself. But I would disagree that it ever happened, or that Notre Dame felt threatened that it could. I also don't think Lou aspired to something like that. I think he was just proud to be part of the family."

Then why does Wadsworth think Holtz left the nest?

MIKE WADSWORTH: "I think Lou was tired. He went through eleven years of high demands. He coached during an era of intense media scrutiny. He was riding an emotional roller coaster.

"So, again, I think he was tired. But I don't think Lou wanted to say that publicly, because people might get the impression that he was finished with coaching. And I don't know if that's an impression he wanted out there. Because I think he wanted to leave open the opportunity of coaching again.

"Now, he never said that to us. But Lou did make several comments about how a new Notre Dame coach would bring in a new level of excitement. He said a new coach would have the wind at his back. And I just remember thinking when he said it: I wonder if he's talking about himself. Maybe if he went somewhere else, he'd get that wind at his back once again."

On November 23, in Holtz's final game at Notre Dame Stadium, the Irish slaughtered Rutgers 62–0. This gave Holtz his 100th victory, leaving him only five behind the fabled Rockne.

TIM PRISTER: "After they beat Rutgers, Lou stayed out on the field and spoke to the crowd. He was obviously happy at that moment. He had this peaceful smile on his face.

"Then we went into the tent for the press conference. Lou talked and got very emotional at the end. When he left the tent I followed him. Then I gave him my press pass and asked him to sign it for me. Lou signed it, but never looked up. He just said thank you and handed it back to me.

"I didn't realize why until I saw the *South Bend Tribune* the next day. They had shot a picture of him a few seconds before that. He was flat-out crying."

On the following morning, Bob Davie was named as the 26th football coach at Notre Dame. Davie, 42, had spent the last three seasons as Holtz's most trusted assistant. He had 20 years overall in college football, including eight as a defensive coordinator. Davie was well-respected by players and fellow coaches, and considered to be an excellent recruiter. His pep talk before the 1996 Texas game, several players say, was so electrifying that Holtz put aside his own speech and told the players, "Just go."

Still, Davie was taking over the most visible coaching job in America. And with only one game (Vanderbilt) of head-coaching experience, he was not exactly a big name.

Wadsworth explains why Notre Dame stayed in-house and promoted an assistant.

MIKE WADSWORTH: "Of course, we considered that Bob was not a head coach. But if you cancel a candidate for that reason only, that only lets you off the hook. Because it doesn't really answer the question. Does he have what it takes to succeed at Notre Dame?

"So we tried to identify several key areas: The way our coach would represent the university. His ability to deliver results on the football field. The model that he would be for the student-athletes here. Would he come in here and try and change Notre Dame, or would he embrace its values and traditions?

"In each of these respects, we felt Bob would make an excellent fit. We felt he possessed the strength of character, the leadership potential, and the football intelligence to be a great head coach at Notre Dame."

Six days after Davie's hiring, Holtz was still the coach when the Irish played USC in the regular-season finale. A victory for Notre Dame (8–2) would almost certainly clinch an $8.3 million Fiesta Bowl berth. A victory for the Trojans (5–6) would possibly save head coach John Robinson's job.

On a chilly Los Angeles evening, the Irish led 14–6 with 11:40 remaining. Then the bottom fell out. Notre Dame lost one fumble at USC's one, lost another at their own 12, and missed a crucial extra point with a 20–12 lead. With the Los Angeles Coliseum now rocking, the Trojans scored eight quick points and sent the game into overtime tied 20–20.

Notre Dame won the toss and Holtz gave the Trojans the ball. After the Irish allowed a touchdown pass, they couldn't score themselves as Powlus continued to struggle with his passing. USC won 27–20, ending its 13-game winless streak against Notre Dame, and leaving Holtz 9–1–1 against the Trojans.

PETE CHRYPLEWICZ: "That was Lou Holtz's last game. It was my last game in college. And it ended in Los Angeles, of all places.

"So there were a lot of emotions as we walked off that field. But the strongest emotion I had is that we broke the streak. We were the ones who lost to USC."

With their record still a decent 8–3, why had the Irish's season just ended? Because they later declined two bids from minor bowl games, the Independence and Copper.

As Notre Dame sat out the postseason for the first time in ten years, school officials were criticized for their "arrogance." Actually, they made a good decision. Holtz, their lame-duck coach, had already cleared out his office and gone home to Orlando. Beforehand, Wadsworth says, Holtz had said no thanks to coaching a second-tier bowl game. That left it up to Davie, who felt it more essential to concentrate on recruiting and getting his staff in place. When most players agreed to skip a smaller bowl, administrators chose to end this turbulent year and start anew in 1997.

As for the legacy of Lou Holtz, he came into a program devalued by Gerry Faust. Then Holtz made Notre Dame football big-time again. After his national championship in 1988, NBC paid millions to join the Fighting Irish bandwagon. Holtz never had a losing season in South Bend, and he took his teams to nine straight New Year's Day bowl games. He finished with a record of 100–32–2, including winning streaks of 23 and 17 games.

Still, Notre Dame underachieved in 1990 and 1991, losing six games despite having 18 pro draft picks. In 1994, the Irish fell from elite status after losing to Boston College the previous November. Since that haunting home defeat, Holtz's last three teams went 23–11–1 and never again contended for No. 1.

Holtz, in sum, was an excellent football coach. But in his 11 years at Notre Dame, did the second part of his tenure fulfill the great promise of the first?

No. No, it did not. Holtz, in the end, may be best remembered for two things: waking up the echoes, and never winning a second national title.

39

NEW MORNING IN SOUTH BEND

1 9 9 7

HOW STRANGE A YEAR IN SPORTS WAS 1997? TIGER WOODS, a 21-year-old, won the Masters golf tournament by an astonishing 12 strokes. Mike Tyson bit off a chunk of Evander Hollyfield's ear during their heavyweight championship bout. Latrell Sprewell attacked and threatened to kill his coach P.J. Carlesimo. Marv Albert got fired by NBC after he pleaded guilty to assault and battery.

By comparison, life at Notre Dame seemed tranquil. But there were still some oddities in South Bend.

In expanding Notre Dame Stadium from 59,075 seats to 80,225, the university spent $50 million. Then, in the season opener, one of the revamped stadium's water mains broke and flooded the concourse level. The 11th-ranked Irish nearly washed out, too, squeaking past unranked Georgia Tech 17–13.

If that put a crimp in Bob Davie's honeymoon, the line between love and hate got even thinner when Notre Dame lost to Purdue for the first time since 1986 and to

Michigan State for the first time since 1985. Then, for the first time since *1936*, Notre Dame entered Michigan Stadium unranked. The 1–2 Irish played without six injured starters, before a crowd of 106,508, against a powerful Wolverine team that would end up 12–0 and ranked No. 1 by the AP. Yet Notre Dame scared Michigan in a 21–14 loss.

After playing their heartiest game of the season, the Irish got waxed by Stanford 33–15. Even worse, the Cardinal rammed their running game down Notre Dame's throat. Which was how the Fighting Irish had once won football games.

But not during this unusual season. Under Davie and his offensive coordinator Jim Colletto, Notre Dame had switched to a more pro-style offense that emphasized passing. This would showcase the talents of Ron Powlus, who some felt had been stifled by Lou Holtz's ground-oriented attack.

That was the plan anyway. In reality, Notre Dame dropped to 1–4 after losing to Stanford and Davie's detractors compared him to Gerry Faust. That's when Davie returned to the power running game and salvaged his rookie season.

The turnaround started at Pittsburgh, where the Irish rushed the ball 52 times for a season-high 317 yards in a 45–21 romp. Then the "first time since" syndrome returned for one more week. As some Irish fans booed, USC beat Notre Dame in South Bend for the first time in 16 years. Afterward, one embattled coach came to the aide of another.

"Bob Davie will win a hundred games at Notre Dame," USC's John Robinson said. "I'll bet my ass on that." Robinson was fired two months later.

On November 1, Notre Dame improved to 4–5 with a

21–17 victory over Navy. But on the game's final play, in the stadium overlooked by Touchdown Jesus, the Midshipmen nearly won on a last-second Hail Mary pass. This blasphemy was averted when a hustling Allen Rossum pushed Navy's Pat McGrew out of bounds at the Irish one.

The next Saturday unranked Notre Dame faced 11th-ranked LSU in Baton Rouge, where the Tigers had already beaten No. 1-ranked Florida. Not only did the Irish win 24–6, they didn't commit any turnovers or penalties. This was unprecedented in the 110-year history of the program.

On November 29, Notre Dame beat lowly Hawaii 23–22 on a field goal with five seconds on the clock. Yet fans and alumni cheered because it pushed Notre Dame into the postseason.

Even that became controversial, though. In 1996, the Irish were 8–3 when they turned down the Independence Bowl. This year Notre Dame was 7–5, with those three near-upsets by Georgia Tech, Navy, and Hawaii. But the Irish accepted a bid to the same Independence Bowl it had snubbed the previous winter.

Actually, says Wadsworth, the situations were different. The Davie regime had been in place for one year. Notre Dame was unranked and could possibly move into the Top 25 with a second victory against No. 15-ranked LSU. And after climbing from 1–4 to 7–5, many of Notre Dame's players were eager to play in even a minor bowl game.

First, on December 14, came the most astonishing story of the season. The University of Southern California, while shopping for John Robinson's successor, had reportedly offered the job to Lou Holtz. "Absolutely not," Holtz told the *Los Angeles Times*. "Nothing could be further from the truth."

Still, the rumors created a buzz throughout Los Angeles. Trojan receiver Billy Miller said, "You play at USC, you learn to hate that guy. Now, he's going to be your coach?" The *Los Angeles Times*'s Mike Downey ripped the USC administration for offering the position to "Lou Holtz, the former coach of Notre bleepin' Dame." Another *Times* columnist Bill Plaschke wrote, "If the Trojans can avoid choking on their pride, they would realize that Holtz would be a good choice."

The Holtz rumors died abruptly when USC hired Paul Hackett. Holtz held on to his job at CBS, where he was a first-year studio analyst.

On a cold and rainy December 29, at the Independence Bowl in Shreveport, Louisiana, Notre Dame's curious season ended with a 29–6 loss to revenge-minded LSU. This gave the Irish a record of 7–6, and proved emphatically that Notre Dame fans should not look for miracles yet.

Of course, they will anyway. Because they know the legends and the lore. Because they know the truth.

At the University of Notre Dame—home of Rockne, the Gipper, Four Horsemen, seven Heismans, 11 consensus national championships, the Golden Dome, and Touchdown Jesus—miracles do happen. Breathes there an Irish fan who doesn't believe that?